# BIBLICAL FAITH AND NATURAL THEOLOGY

# Biblical Faith
# and Natural Theology

*The Gifford Lectures for 1991
Delivered in the
University of Edinburgh*

JAMES BARR

CLARENDON PRESS · OXFORD

Oxford University Press, Walton Street, Oxford OX2 6DP

Oxford New York

Athens Auckland Bangkok Bombay Calcutta Cape Town
Dar es Salaam Delhi Florence Hong Kong Istanbul Karachi
Kuala Lumpur Madras Madrid Melbourne Mexico City Nairobi
Paris Singapore Taipei Tokyo Toronto
and associated companies in
Berlin Ibadan

Oxford is a trade mark of Oxford University Press

Published in the United States by
Oxford University Press Inc., New York

British Library Cataloguing in Publication Data
Data available

Library of Congress Cataloging in Publication Data
Biblical faith and natural theology: the Gifford lectures for
1991, delivered in the University of Edinburgh/James Barr.
(The Gifford lectures for 1991)
Includes bibliographical references.
1. Natural theology.  2. Bible—Theology.  3. Barth, Karl
1886–1968.  I. Title.  II. Series: Gifford lectures; 1991.
BL182.B34  1993      231'.042—dc20
ISBN 0–19–826205–1
ISBN 0–19–826376–7 (Pbk)

1  3  5  7  9  10  8  6  4  2

Printed in Great Britain on acid-free paper by
Bookcraft (Bath) Ltd., Midsomer Norton, Avon

*For*
*Catherine, Allan, and Stephen*

# Preface

It goes without saying that it was a great honour to be invited by the University of Edinburgh to deliver the Gifford Lectures. I am deeply grateful to the University for that honour, and also for the kindness and generous hospitality with which my wife and I were received and entertained. But beyond that my sense is of the intense pleasure that it was for me to be back in Edinburgh for the period of the lectures. I was an Edinburgh boy (though, admittedly, born in Glasgow!) and all my education was in Edinburgh. The year in which I was Gifford Lecturer, 1991, was a significant one for me, for it was exactly fifty years earlier, in 1941, that I entered the University as a student in classics. I left again, after one year, for wartime service, but that was meaningful also, for when I returned in 1945 I was to be in the same second year of classics as Jane, who is my beloved wife. I was never a student elsewhere: I did indeed some studies in other places, but was never a registered student except in Edinburgh. So all that I know I learned there, or else invented it myself later on, out of a native Scottish ingenuity that had been fostered there. One other anniversary: it was in 1961, just thirty years earlier, that my first book, *The Semantics of Biblical Language*, was published, at the end of my six years as professor in Edinburgh.

Our friendships in Edinburgh are so numerous and deep that it is difficult to make adequate acknowledgement. It was a special pleasure, at the first lecture and others, to see Professor Norman Porteous, who had been my first teacher in Hebrew and whose colleague I was later to become. I was delighted by the attendance at the lectures of many from a large variety of academic fields—from medicine, the sciences, social studies, philosophy, and classics, among others—just the situation, of course, that the Gifford Lectures exist to promote. The members of the Gifford Committee of the University were particularly kind. As visitors, we were kindly looked after by Professor and Mrs John O'Neill, and I benefited greatly from contacts and conversations at New College, the Faculty of Divinity. The lectures as published show the valuable influence of discussions with Dr Peter Hayman, Professor J. C. L.

Gibson, and Dr David Mealand, and some of these are acknowledged at particular places.

The relation between biblical study and natural theology has always interested me, and I always had vague ideas of working over the ground and perhaps writing something; but very likely nothing would have come of this but for the invitation to deliver the Giffords. Having done it, I feel I owe a great deal to this opportunity. Knowing that the preparation of the Giffords lay before me, I made a variety of soundings, experimental lectures, and researches which gathered information and helped me to form my mind on the questions involved. I approached various portions of the subject in lectures delivered in Oxford, in Norway, Sweden, and Finland, in France, and in South Africa, and gained much from the responses and reactions of colleagues there. The Cole Lectures, a series of three, which I delivered in Vanderbilt University in 1988, when a visiting professor there, were an important stage in the process. Going further back, the studies which I carried out while at the Rockefeller Research Institute at Bellaggio, Italy, in 1984 provided valuable knowledge which I was able to incorporate. And I was greatly assisted by the resources of the Divinity Library in Vanderbilt University, and by the helpfulness of its librarians.

The lectures are published more or less as delivered, except that they have been expanded, especially with footnotes: or, more correctly, they had to be reduced in length in order to fit with the lecture format, and then re-expanded afterwards. The bibliography, touching on many very wide areas, makes no attempt at completeness, and I list mainly either books that have been specially helpful to me, or books that are recent or are otherwise likely to offer fresh ideas to the reader. If I had to name the two writers to whom I owe the most, the names would be those of Christof Gestrich and Christian Link. Both of these, however, approach the subject from the side of systematic theology, while my own approach is from the side of the Bible itself. Biblical quotations are from a variety of versions, mostly the Revised Standard, and sometimes the translation is my own. Chapter and verse numbers follow the numbering of the English Bible, with the Hebrew numbers added when they differ.

J.B.

*Nashville*
*November 1991*

# Contents

*Abbreviations*                                                                    xi

1.  Natural Theology in This Century: Concepts and
    Approaches                                                                      1

2.  Paul on the Areopagus                                                          21

3.  St Paul and the Hebrew Background                                              39

4.  Natural Theology in the Jewish Tradition                                       58

5.  Within the Old Testament                                                       81

6.  A Return to the Modern Discussion                                             102

7.  Religion, Tradition, and Natural Theology                                     138

8.  The Image of God and Natural Theology                                         156

9.  Science; Language; Parable; Scripture                                         174

10. Natural Theology and the Future of Biblical Theology                          199

*Bibliography*                                                                     223
*Indexes*                                                                          237

# Abbreviations

| | |
|---|---|
| AV | Authorized (King James) Version |
| BDB | F. Brown, S. R. Driver, and C. A. Briggs, *A Hebrew and English Lexicon of the Old Testament* (Oxford: Clarendon Press, 1907) |
| BJRL | *Bulletin of the John Rylands Library* |
| BJRUL | *Bulletin of the John Rylands University Library* |
| BSOAS | *Bulletin of the School of Oriental and African Studies* (London) |
| BWANT | Beiträge zur Wissenschaft vom Alten und Neuen Testament |
| BZAW | Beihefte zur Zeitschrift für die alttestamentliche Wissenschaft |
| CD | Karl Barth, *Church Dogmatics* (13 vols., Edinburgh: T. & T. Clark, 1956–70) |
| DC | Deutsche Christen (German Christians) |
| ET | English translation |
| Ev. Th. | *Evangelische Theologie* |
| Exp. T. | *Expository Times* |
| FS | Festschrift |
| HBNT | Handbuch zum Neuen Testament |
| HTR | *Harvard Theological Review* |
| ICC | International Critical Commentary |
| IDB | *The Interpreter's Dictionary of the Bible* (Nashville: Abingdon, 4 vols., 1962, and Supplementary Volume, 1976) |
| JAAR | *Journal of the American Academy of Religion* |
| JJS | *Journal of Jewish Studies* |
| JSNT | *Journal for the Study of the New Testament* |
| JSOT | *Journal for the Study of the Old Testament* |
| JSS | *Journal of Semitic Studies* |
| JTS | *Journal of Theological Studies* |
| KBRS | *Kirchenblatt für die reformierte Schweiz* |
| KD | Karl Barth, *Kirchliche Dogmatik* (14 vols., Zurich: Evangelischer Verlag, 1947–70) |

| | |
|---|---|
| *K. u. D.* | *Kerygma und Dogma* |
| LSJ | H. G. Liddell and R. Scott, *A Greek–English Lexicon*, new edn. rev. and aug. H. S. Jones (Oxford: Clarendon Press, 1940) |
| MT | Masoretic Text |
| NEB | New English Bible |
| *NTS* | *New Testament Studies* |
| *NZST* | *Neue Zeitschrift für systematische Theologie* |
| REB | Revised English Bible |
| *RS* | *Religious Studies* |
| RSV | Revised Standard Version |
| *SEÅ* | *Svensk Exegetisk Årsbok* |
| *SJT* | *Scottish Journal of Theology* |
| *St. Th.* | *Studia theologica* |
| *TGUOS* | *Transactions of the Glasgow University Oriental Society* |
| *Th. Ex. H.* | *Theologische Existenz Heute* |
| *VTS* | *Vetus Testamentum Supplements* |
| *ZATW* | *Zeitschrift für die alttestamentliche Wissenschaft* |
| *Z. d. Z.* | *Zwischen den Zeiten* |
| *Z. Th. K.* | *Zeitschrift für Theologie und Kirche* |

# Natural Theology in This Century: Concepts and Approaches

I propose to begin with a fairly wide, doubtless somewhat vague, but at any rate comprehensive, notion of natural theology, and one which, I think, follows much accepted tradition of usage.

Traditionally 'natural theology' has commonly meant something like this: that 'by nature', that is, just by being human beings, men and women have a certain degree of knowledge of God and awareness of him, or at least a capacity for such an awareness; and this knowledge or awareness exists anterior to the special revelation of God made through Jesus Christ, through the Church, through the Bible. Indeed, according to many traditional formulations of the matter, it is this pre-existing natural knowledge of God that makes it possible for humanity to receive the additional 'special' revelation. The two fit snugly together. People can understand Christ and his message, can feel themselves sinful and in need of salvation, because they already have this appreciation, dim as it may be, of God and of morality. The 'natural' knowledge of God, however dim, is an awareness of the true God, and provides a point of contact without which the special revelation would never be able to penetrate to people. Note that natural theology, thus understood, does not necessarily *deny* special revelation: it may, rather, make that special revelation correlative with a 'general' or 'natural' revelation that is available, or has been granted, to all humanity. But it does, in its commoner forms, imply that valid talk about God without any appeal whatever to special revelation is possible and indeed highly significant and important. The avoidance of any such appeal to special revelation was a condition insisted upon by Lord Gifford in his founding of this present series.

There are several reasons for using this wide definition of our subject. We may illuminate these by considering some alternatives.

One alternative is to define natural theology as that which may be known of God by *pure reason*, apart from any other force or influence, and this is also an important traditional understanding. But this definition is of comparatively little use for the discussion of my chosen theme, 'biblical faith and natural theology', for it is not probable that we shall find in the Bible much that depends on *pure* reason in that sense. The Bible may, however, give evidence of an anterior knowledge of God which human beings have in advance of special revelation, and that knowledge of God, however ill defined, may form the basis upon which the pure reason may build; but it is not something known by pure reason alone.

Again, some have found it convenient to describe natural theology as the attempt to *prove the existence* of God. Thus the eminent philosopher of religion Alvin Plantinga offers us a clear and simple suggestion in one sentence: 'Suppose we think of Natural Theology as the attempt to prove or demonstrate the existence of God.'[1] And unquestionably the project of demonstrating, by reason alone (Plantinga does not specify this, but it is commonly included at this point), the fact of God's existence has been one of the major features and one of the obvious preoccupations of most natural theology. Nevertheless there are important reasons why we should not accept Plantinga's formula as definitive for our purpose. Several of the terms of his sentence may well be questioned. We may question whether all natural theology seeks to 'prove': it may, on the contrary, merely *indicate*, merely register, what people *think* about God. Secondly, it may work not by *reason* only, or even primarily: on the contrary, it may work from what is thought to be known, what is accepted in society, what is felt, what is the culturally inherited semantic content of words; and it may do all this without claiming to have the exact and absolute authority of pure reason. And, thirdly, it may be concerned not purely with the *existence* of God but much more with our picture of what God is like. A natural theology, if we have one, may very well assign limits to our idea of the sort of being God may be. Indeed, this is one of the reasons why natural theology is distrusted by many religious people: by laying down some sort of guidelines for what God may be like, they feel, it may make it more difficult for people to accept him as he in fact is. To sum up this point, then, natural theology as it has traditionally been

---

[1] In his 'The Reformed Objection to Natural Theology', *Proceedings of the American Catholic Philosophical Association*, 54 (1980), 49.

has included much more than the proof by reason of the existence of God.

And a third reason why we should define natural theology more loosely, as we have done, is that this approach fits with one of the great classic debates of the theology of this century. The disagreement between Karl Barth and Emil Brunner, which set the stage for so much modern theology, and about which we shall have much to say, took this form: is there any human knowledge of God antecedent to his self-revelation in Jesus Christ? We conclude, then, that we are on solid ground in proceeding in this way.

Something more has to be said to define our theme in relation to two concepts, firstly the philosophy of religion, and secondly theism. The philosophy of religion is not necessarily or absolutely linked with natural theology: for example, one might pursue a philosophical approach to religion while denying natural theology altogether. Nevertheless it seems that there is a common tendency in the opposite direction: traditional natural theology has provided much interesting matter for the philosophy of religion, for example the traditional arguments for the existence of God. And conversely the denial of natural theology has commonly gone along with a strong emphasis on revelation, and this in turn has been taken to mean that there are no adequate human resources for a philosophical understanding of God. In extreme cases, the emphasis on revelation has been taken to mean that philosophical discussions of God and of religion have no relevance for Christian faith whatever. The 'God' of philosophers, according to this view, is a mere postulate of the human mind, an idolatrous reflection of sinful human self-understanding, a theoretical being quite unrelated to the God of Abraham, Isaac, and Jacob.

Theism, on the other hand, we might define as a particular universal religious view which asserts the existence of a personal, active, supramundane, God.[2] Theism has qualities of universality and abstraction. Christian theism would then be theism with some of the special characteristics of Christian faith added in, as it were. Theism may not necessarily require natural theology as its support, but natural theology appears often to support a theism to which the special content of Christian faith is added by special revelation. Seen in this way, Christianity is a special case within the general

[2] I adapt this from the words of Heinrich Beck, *Natürliche Theologie: Grundriß philosophischer Gotteserkenntnis* (Munich: Pustet, 1986), 33.

category of theism, which would include other theistic religions also. Those who deny natural theology commonly deny also the belonging of Christianity to any general category of theism, and deny the relevance of theistic arguments to Christianity.[3] If theism seems to validate a variety of theistic religions, and if only one of these religions is true, its adherents will obviously be likely to dislike theistic talk, because it associates their religion with others which they consider erroneous or at least defective.

In connection with Christianity, or indeed with any other religion, the function of natural theology can be perceived in two different directions. The first is an *apologetic* function. Apologetics, traditionally, is the discipline, or portion of a discipline, which maintains and refines the defence of faith against those who doubt and question it. If people say, 'we can't believe in some of the miracles', or 'we can't believe that the world was created by a transcendent God', apologetics assembles and clarifies the arguments that support or justify faith: in the stronger case they endeavour to show that faith is right, in the weaker case they endeavour, if not to prove that faith is right, at least to show that faith is reasonable, that it makes some sort of sense, that it is not a purely chaotic bundle of irrational and self-contradictory notions. Not all apologetics depends purely on natural theology, in the sense of that which humanity, by pure natural reason, can know about God: in modern times an increasing amount of apologetics has related to the fields of science or of history, seeking to show, let us say, that scientific accounts of the world still leave room for divine creation and providence, or that historical investigation does not make the resurrection incredible. Apologetic argument, in these senses, is a familiar element in religious discussion, and we shall have to say more about it later. But at this moment all we have to register is that, while apologetics of this kind is not identical with natural theology, there is a considerable overlap of interest and of scope. Like natural theology, apologetics presupposes, or is commonly taken to presuppose, that there is some fulcrum outside faith, some ground other than faith itself upon which one may stand in order to argue for truths affirmed by faith.

But, if this is so, there may be a contrary influence: argument of the apologetic type, if it is allowed at all, may not only support faith but may also exercise upon it a *critical* function: it may say, well, yes, we believe, and faith is justifiable, but it will be more easily

[3] On this aspect, see again below, Ch. 7.

justifiable if we keep it within certain bounds. We can demonstrate the reality of God, but only if our faith in God remains fairly close to the sort of God whose reality we can demonstrate. Science may leave room for divine creation, but not if we insist that divine creation took place in one week in 4004 BC and in the exact sequence described by Genesis. Historical study may leave room for divine action in history, but only if that divine action is seen in a less crude and more sophisticated way than a literal understanding of some biblical passages would seem to suggest. Thus the apologetic functions which include natural theology do not only support faith but they also tend to act critically upon faith, to correct it, to guide it into certain channels. Because it works in this double direction, I will later use the term 'the apologetic axis' to indicate both directions at once. And it cannot be doubted that it is the *critical* direction, which is the other end of the apologetic axis, that has caused some theologies to repudiate apologetics altogether, and natural theology along with it. According to this point of view, faith should never stand on any kind of support outside special and direct divine revelation: if it tries to do so, it only distorts the reality of God into the idolatrous image which humanity makes of him.

Another aspect that comes close to natural theology is what we may call interreligiosity or interculturality. Special revelation, as usually understood, belongs to a limited circle: let us say, Judaism and Christianity; maybe Islam counts as part of the same limited area. But once we begin to speak of ideas of God that are more widely spread, that are known to, let us say, ancient Greek thinkers, or Hindu thinkers, or modern philosophers who have no personal religious commitment at all, then we come much closer to talking in terms of natural theology. By this criterion, anything in the Bible that shares conceptuality or attitudes with religions or philosophies outside the accepted circle of revelation will suggest natural theology. We will see that numerous cases of this will be relevant.

One last concept may be mentioned briefly: that of 'natural religion'. Those who believed in a special revelation, in which God was known within a limited circle, had to admit that religion existed outside that circle, indeed that religion appears to be a 'natural' characteristic of humanity or at least of much of it. It is factually there. But is it a good thing? Those who dislike ideas of a special revelation may well think that 'natural religion', being somehow intrinsic to humanity, is about the best that religion can be. Those who believe in special revelation, on the other hand, will tend to regard 'natural religion' as something rather disgraceful, as a manifestation of the human tendency to elevate its own culture, experience, and ideals to the level of the divine. This problem also will recur occasionally during our discussions.

With the above as a very simple preliminary conceptual map, we may turn to some aspects of the modern discussion of the matter. During the twentieth century natural theology has been one of the great crisis points of theological discussion; or at least so it was said, and said with some vehemence. The matter was brought vividly to the attention of theologians through the conflict between Emil Brunner and Karl Barth in two pamphlets published in 1934: the English version was called *Natural Theology* and was edited by the leading Edinburgh theologian John Baillie (1946), with an introduction of his own. Within the English-speaking world these two Swiss theologians had, up to that time, been generally regarded as two birds of the same kind of feathers; and people were surprised by the vehemence of the disagreement that now broke out. Brunner in a short pamphlet entitled 'Nature and Grace' had suggested that now was the time to start looking for a new natural theology, and that this was a major task of the moment. Barth's answer was entitled 'Nein' and opened with an 'Angry Introduction'. Brunner, he said, was a man of 'determined will-power', an expression which he might well have extended to include himself.[4] According to Barth, there was no place at all for any natural theology; it must be totally rejected. There must be no sort of theological system that depended on, or built upon, something that was previous to, or separate from, or supplementary to, the revelation of God in Jesus Christ. There was no 'point of contact' on the human side: 'point of contact' (*Anknüpfungspunkt*) was one of the keywords of this mighty conflict. The revelation of God did not fit into a point of contact that was already there: it made its own new contact, quite independently of any such previously existing contact point. Even if there was one, revelation did not use it. The ensuing conflict and estrangement between Barth and Brunner was bitter and far-reaching.

Karl Barth's position is a good point of entry for our present discussion, because he was invited, quite early in his career, to deliver the Gifford Lectures, and he did so, at Aberdeen University in 1937 and 1938. The lectures were based on the Scots Confession of

[4] *Natural Theology* (London: Bles, 1946), 67.

1560 (doubtless in deliberate contrast to the Westminster Confession which later became the dominant doctrinal standard of the Scottish Church) and were published under the title *The Knowledge of God and the Service of God.*[5] It was paradoxical, no doubt, that he was invited to lecture in a series explicitly defined as devoted to natural theology, and doubtless he had some difficulty in making up his mind to accept. From the start his approach to his subject was bound to be a peculiar one, since his central conviction in the whole matter was that no such subject as natural theology existed at all. When he did use the words 'natural theology' he put them in quotation marks, as if to indicate that this was a beast like the unicorn: the word existed, but no such thing existed; or, maybe, it was an expression internally contradictory, like 'hot ice' or 'black milk'. Now, you might have thought that Barth could reasonably interpret the invitation as an invitation to talk about natural theology in the sense of developing his arguments against it, showing why it was wrong. By no means: what he did was to refuse to talk about natural theology at all. How could one give a series of lectures about a non-existing subject? What he in fact did was to give a series of lectures on revealed theology, of a Calvinist Reformed kind, a series which largely ignored even the question of natural theology.

Moreover, in doing this Barth developed an unusual piece of casuistry. He did not dispute that Lord Gifford had meant what he said: natural theology, in Barth's words 'a knowledge of which man as man is the master', was the topic; but no such subject existed to be discussed. There was nothing to say about it at all. This is what Barth thought. But he did not state this as his own personal opinion. He ascribed it to his being a theologian of the Reformed Church. 'As a Reformed theologian I am subject to an ordinance which would keep me away from "Natural Theology", even if my personal opinions inclined me to it.' To be a Reformed theologian entailed in itself that there was no such thing as natural theology.

Now it is true, said Barth, pursuing this remarkable argument, there have been people who have thought that this strange beast, natural theology, existed, at least as a subject that might be theoretically discussed. In particular, Roman Catholics think so, and, according to Barth, the traditions of 'Modern Protestantism' imply

---

[5] The preference of the Scots Confession over the Westminster was of strategic importance, for a study based upon the Westminster would have had to recognize the very substantial part played by natural theology in the latter.

the same: both these traditions, he said, are based on compromises with 'natural theology'. But, he went on, 'the Reformation and the teaching of the Reformation churches stand in an antithesis to "Natural Theology" which is at once clear and instructive for both'. Reformed theology thus ignores 'natural theology', while natural theology exists, in so far as it exists at all, solely by virtue of opposition to Reformed theology—somewhat as, he might have said, darkness exists only through the absence of light. Thus in his Gifford Lectures, after the first page or two, Barth seldom bothers even to mention natural theology at all, and, amazingly, provides no attempt at a critique of it. All he does is to lay down what he considers to be Reformed doctrine, implying at the most that the differences from natural theology will somehow emerge (which in fact they do not).[6]

But even on the basis of the Reformation Barth had to make some substantial admissions. The major Reformers, he admits, did make use to some extent of that non-existent animal natural theology. Sometimes they made a guarded and conditional use of it, as Calvin did in the first chapter of his *Institutes*; and occasionally they made an unguarded and unconditional use of it, as did both Luther and Calvin in their teaching on the law. But, he goes on, we today after the developments of the last four centuries can see more clearly than they could then do. In other words, the history of theology and experience of the Church since the Reformation have shown that any concession to supposed 'natural theology' is disastrous and is totally opposed to the principles of the Reformation.

In this sense therefore Barth appeals to the principle of the Reformation rather than to its execution, to a theoretical Reformation rather than the one that actually took place, to what the Reformed Churches *ought to have done* rather than to what they did in fact do. The principle, he says, is that the Church and salvation are founded on the Word of God alone, on God's revelation in Jesus Christ, as it is attested in the scriptures; and this is the clear opposite of any form

---

[6] All this was no passing aberration on Barth's part: he meant it seriously and said it repeatedly in different words. Thus: '"Natural theology" does not exist as an entity capable of becoming a separate subject within what I consider to be real theology—not even for the sake of being rejected ... Really to reject natural theology means to refuse to admit it as a separate problem ... If you really reject natural theology you do not stare at the serpent, with the result that it stares back at you, hypnotizes you, and is ultimately certain to bite you, but you hit it and kill it as soon as you see it!' All this in *Natural Theology*, 75 f.

of teaching that declares that man himself possesses the power and capacity to inform himself about God, about the world, and indeed about humanity itself.

Now Barth's argument in all this, surely, is simply preposterous. It is his opinion, whether well founded or not, that there is no room for natural theology. He then sovereignly declares that his opinion is the opinion of 'Reformed theology', although he admits that Reformed theology, even in the persons of both Luther and Calvin themselves, has not shared this opinion. Nor does he even mention, or even hint at, the very large part that natural theology, of one kind or another, has had in the Reformed tradition (previous to 'Modern Protestantism') in the centuries after the original Reformers. And, although admitting that Reformed theology even in Luther and Calvin had owed some debt to natural theology, he then says that he cannot even converse with natural theology or talk about it, not because he himself is against it, but because as a Reformed theologian he is forbidden to do so. All this is double talk.

To this another aspect has to be added. Barth noted, and correctly, the important role that natural theology has played within traditional Roman Catholic theology; but when he went on to say that the same applied to 'Modern Protestantism' he was slanting the facts in a very tendentious way. He was seeking, of course, to make the impression that much Barthianism at that early stage strove to make: namely the impression that it was equally aligned against Catholicism on the one side, against liberal or modern Protestantism or whatever we call it on the other.[7] But this way of putting it concealed the strong position of natural theology within the *conservative* currents of Protestant theology, for example in Dutch Calvinism or in important currents of Anglo-Saxon evangelicalism.[8] In particular, however hardly we may judge 'Modern Protestantism', we may question whether it was in fact based upon a 'compromise with natural theology', as Barth insinuated, and, since he would not discuss the matter, and gave no examples, he failed to justify it. I mention this at this point only because I shall come back

[7] Since Barthianism has often been regarded as an extreme position, it is important to understand that Barthians did not see themselves in this way. As seen from within, Barthianism occupied the middle ground. It arrogated centrality to itself, and supposed that it walked the narrow line of central theological truth, avoiding the chasms of error that lay on both sides.

[8] On this see further below, Ch. 6.

to it later, and will then suggest that the relation of 'Modern Protestantism' to these ideas was a very different one.

We have to go further, however, in order to place in context Barth's extreme opposition to natural theology. His earlier work had not made this so clear or brought it to so sharp a profile. He had indeed emphasized the strangeness of God, his otherness, his distance from the world, and it was for this that his name was then best known; but he had not so expressly singled out natural theology as the danger which must at all costs be avoided. For example, in his commentary on Romans, which in some ways is Barth's most characteristic work, he had to deal with that famous passage Romans 1[20 f.], about 'that which may be known of God' and how his 'everlasting power and divinity' can be perceived 'through the things that are made'; and, while his comments are typically paradoxical and perhaps negative, few readers could have known from that commentary that a total assault on all natural theology was soon to emerge. Thus it would be understandable if Brunner, who belonged to the same general trend of theology, came to the point of calling for a new natural theology without—apparently—having any expectation of the violent storm that was soon to break over his head.[9]

The factor that brought the question of natural theology into the centre seems to have been political.[10] As we all know, Barth was strongly opposed to the rising Nazi movement in Germany. Reacting to its impact, he diagnosed the disastrous developments in Europe as the natural culmination of a long process of the history of ideas, especially theological ones. Start along the line of natural theology, he thought, and sooner or later you will end up with something like the 'German Christian' (DC) movement. The DC ideas that nation or race or culture were in-built structures of humanity and that religion must accommodate itself to them were,

---

[9] This is how it appears from the familiar published works, and hence my word 'apparently'. I am informed, however, that there had been a considerable debate in correspondence between Barth and Brunner over several preceding years, in which these issues were already canvassed. I have not seen this material.

[10] I agree with C. Link, *Die Welt als Gleichnis* (Munich: Kaiser, 1976), 130, that it is wrong to suppose that Barth's polemic against natural theology was conditioned *purely* by the political controversies. I am sure this is not so. All I suggest is that these political circumstances acted as catalyst for the theological disagreement which soon broke out. In fact, as I indicate below, it seems more likely that it was precisely Barth's own theological requirements that led him to diagnose the German developments as constituting a case of natural theology.

as Barth saw it, the logical result of the long compromise with natural theology. And thus from the beginning he taunted Brunner with having given comfort to the DC and having had favourable reviews in the Nazi press. Brunner was playing into the hands of Hitler.

In saying this, we do not necessarily accept that Barth's perception of contemporary political experience was correct. One can look at this in two ways. One can say, and this is perhaps the traditional version, that the perception of Nazi ideology made clear the fateful inheritance of natural theology. One might also take the opposite line, and say that it was the internal theological development in Barth's mind that caused him to *perceive* the German situation in terms generated by his own theology, and therefore to see it as a final manifestation of natural theology. I believe that the latter may have more truth in it.[11]

In any case, it was thus the rise of German totalitarianism, whether rightly interpreted or not, that brought the issue of natural theology into an absolutely central position. It was not surprising, therefore, that the Barmen Declaration, which expressed the dissent of the Confessing Church, was framed in terms entirely Barthian: for it the issue, as there expressed, was whether there was, or was not, any form of revelation or authority, other than the revelation of Jesus Christ, that could have authority or influence in the Church.[12] To those who thought in this way it seems to have been simply obvious that those who accepted natural theology would be sympathizers with the Nazi movement, while those Christians who seriously opposed Nazism would manifestly deny the legitimacy of all natural theology.

In other words, the conceptuality of Barthian theology was resolutely clamped upon the picture of the political conflict in Germany. There was no attempt to analyse the various possibilities of natural theology in order to see whether some varieties of it might point in a different direction. Not a moment's consideration was given to the idea that natural theology, if properly understood, might itself be a useful force of resistance to Nazism—this even though the Catholic population, whose Church fully accepted natural theology, was arguably stronger than the Protestant popu-

---

[11] I return to this question in Ch. 6 below.
[12] See for example passages like *KD* ii/1. 194ff.; *CD* ii/1. 172ff.

lation in its reluctance to do what the government wanted.[13] Moreover, there was an element of contradiction or embarrassment on the world scene, since foreign Church opinion, outside Germany, was almost total in its opposition to the Church policy of the German government, but actually supported some natural theology of creation and was against the total rejection of the same by the Confessing Church.[14] Barth was entirely aware of this aspect, but discounted it. 'No one outside', he later argued, 'really had the right to cast a stone at Germany', because the only difference was that Germany had carried out with logical thoroughness what had already been implicitly granted or implied by all forms of natural theology.[15] There was thus no difference between different forms of natural theology: all of them alike, if properly understood, led directly or indirectly to what was done in Germany. Or, to put it in another way, all theologies which did not completely reject natural theology—i.e. all non-Barthian theologies—shared alike in responsibility for the fearful evils of National Socialism.

Now for the present we shall not follow this line further. Let it suffice that we have done something to describe the position of one who, within the Gifford Lecture series, put forward the most drastic opposition to natural theology that there could be—or at least apparently so. One of the consequences of this was a further split in the dialectical theology. This powerful movement, no doubt the most powerful of all the theological movements of this century, split more than once. One such split was that between Barth and Bultmann, over a whole series of issues; another, between Barth and Brunner, was, as we have said, more striking, in that Barth and Brunner had been seen as so close to one another, and indeed many 'Barthians' of the older times were often Brunnerians except where they perceived a conflict between the two great thinkers.[16] And in fact

---

[13] As has been shown, at least for certain parts of Germany, by the work of Ian Kershaw, *Popular Opinion and Political Dissent in the Third Reich* (Oxford: Clarendon Press, 1983), which shows, from internal Nazi documentation itself, how administrators confessed themselves unable to do anything with the Catholic population because of the strength of their religious convictions, while suggesting that the Protestant population was much more favourable to the Nazi movement.

[14] See the comments of the Swiss ecumenist Adolf Keller as quoted by Klaus Scholder, *The Churches and the Third Reich* (2 vols., Philadelphia: Fortress, 1988-), ii. 235 and nn. 160ff. on 349.

[15] See *KD* ii/1. 196; *CD* ii/1. 174.

[16] On this cf. S. W. Sykes in his *Karl Barth: Studies of his Theological Methods* (Oxford: Clarendon Press, 1979), 7 ff.

they were not exactly parallel to one another in their opposition: Brunner was not so much for natural theology as Barth was against it. And, though many people liked Brunner more, for what was thought to be his moderation and his good presentation of ideas, it was Barth who seemed to win the day in the end: it was he who came to be esteemed as the great theologian of the century, the one who found his way into university syllabuses along with Thomas Aquinas and Schleiermacher, he who was more and more studied.

The sequel, curiously, was that the issue of natural theology became less of an issue, came to be less talked about. One heard less of it, as if it was no more a question—this although a great many people had not been convinced that Barth's absolute opposition to it was right. Many people doubted it, but did not summon up the force for an outright counter-attack against him. And at the end of the day, in fact, the reverse happened: Barthianism itself became more positively interested in natural theology. In the 1960s Barth himself can be found to say: 'Later I brought natural theology back in by way of Christology. Today my criticism would be: all you have to do is to say it differently, and that means Christologically.'[17] Thus people who were very much in the Barthian line of thought began to talk as if some kind of natural theology, or something a little like it, might after all be acceptable and even necessary—but all this without dismantling the earlier basic structures of Barthian theology which had, beyond all doubt, taken the absolute denial of natural theology as a central and non-negotiable position.[18] There was no talk of a revision, still less of an abandonment, of the violent earlier attacks on natural theology.[19] The new position, one might say, was that only through the death of all sorts of the older natural theology could one come to the resurrection of a new natural

[17] I quote from A. Szekeres, 'Karl Barth und die natürliche Theologie', *Ev. Th.* 24 (1964), 229-42; citation from 229.

[18] For an example, see T. F. Torrance, 'The Problem of Natural Theology in the Thought of Karl Barth', *RS* 6 (1970), 121-35.

[19] In view of later suggestions that Barth might have accepted some kind of natural theology if it had been of a different kind from what Brunner had in mind, one must reiterate the absoluteness of Barth's rejection at that time. Thus in *Natural Theology*, 71, Barth rejects all 'true' natural theology in the same breath as all 'false' such theology. The fact is, the debate in these pamphlets is of pretty low intellectual standard. Little was done to get behind the surface disagreement, to define terms, to consider new possibilities, to overcome misunderstandings. Barth sometimes got credit for having analysed the 'presuppositions' of natural theology but this was undeserved. He did nothing of the sort. This is easily understandable in view of his refusal to consider natural theology as a subject at all.

theology. Since this is so, we are justified in taking the position of complete denial of natural theology, Barth's position in his Gifford Lectures, in his controversy with Brunner, and in the earlier volumes of the *Church Dogmatics*, as the classic Barthian position.

But these more advanced and modern lines of thought must be left aside for the present. We are still back at the beginnings of the modern discussion. And there were, of course, plenty who thoroughly disagreed with Barth's approach to the matter. As a good example from among the Gifford Lecturers we may take Canon Charles Raven, who was quite well known as a speaker in Scotland and who delivered the lectures here in Edinburgh in 1951, under the title 'Natural Religion and Christian Theology'. Raven was an enthusiast for natural theology, though for him this meant less the philosophical proofs of God's existence, and more the integration of nature, as known through scientific investigation, and of evolutionary process, with divine purpose and incarnation. Raven had no sympathy or liking for Barth.[20] Indeed his degree of understanding of Barth was just as low as Barth's would have been of Raven, if he had ever heard of him, which is unlikely. Following a remark of Dean Sperry of Harvard,[21] which, he said, fitted in with his own views, Raven said that Barth's 'condemnation of nature and the natural man would have been much modified if he had spent the First World War in the trenches instead of in neutral Switzerland'.[22]

---

[20] On Raven see F. W. Dillistone, *Charles Raven* (London: Hodder & Stoughton, 1975); also A. R. Peacocke, *Creation and the World of Science* (Oxford: Clarendon Press, 1979), 14 and elsewhere.

[21] In his *Jesus then and now* (New York: Harper, 1949), 207.

[22] C. E. Raven, *Natural Religion and Christian Theology* (2 vols., Cambridge: Cambridge University Press, 1953), ii. 46 n. Note that Raven describes this as a belief 'which I have also held', which suggests that by the time of his Gifford Lectures Raven had somewhat softened his judgement. This would fit in with his Note ix 'On the recent reaction in theology', ibid. i. 212–15, described by Peacocke, *Creation*, 14 n., as a 'mild version' of Raven's commonly 'trenchant' or even 'acrid' opposition. Even so, Raven's statement was sharper and carried a more hostile nuance than Sperry himself may have intended. First, the utterance was not Sperry's own, but was part of a lengthy quotation from the memoir of Harnack by his daughter (Agnes von Zahn-Harnack, *Adolf von Harnack* (Berlin: Bott, 1936), 529ff.). Though Sperry clearly sympathized with the passage as a whole, we cannot be sure that he would have uttered this as his own judgement. The voice was really Harnack's. Secondly, the actual statement is more an attempted explanation and less a suggestion of personal blame than Raven's formulation of it. The relevant section read: 'The war had given the original impetus to this development [the dialectical theology]. It was no mere accident that of the three leaders of the new movement—Barth, Thurneysen and Gogarten—two had spent the war years as neutrals in Switzerland, and so had stood

Such a remark, though not untypical of the ethos of the time, was thoroughly misguided as well as being uncharitable. For it is probable that Barth's theology bears more traces of the experience of the trenches than Raven's does. On the whole, that experience did not do much to strengthen natural theology. A whiff of poison gas does little to encourage the belief that God has revealed himself through the goodness and beauty of the created world—a point to which we shall have to return.

According to Raven, the Bible was full of the love of nature. The world is God's world. In the Bible nature is not illusory or unreal, but at the same time it is never treated as perfect nor is it identified with deity. This argument is interesting, for it shows that Raven was aware of, and was guarding himself against, an argument that could very likely have arisen from the Barthian side. It was at just about this time, and in parallel with much of Barth's influence, that the 'Biblical Theology Movement' was tending to depict all natural theology as dependent on Greek philosophy and to suggest that it therefore disparaged the natural world through comparison with the eternal and abstract ideas. By contrast, according to this viewpoint, the Jewish idea, which was essentially revelational, had a warm appreciation for nature.

Raven, however, did not fall for this argument, or rather he turned it around the other way. The Jewish background, he thought, only strengthened his case. It was the Jewish heritage that strengthened the argument for natural theology, and it was neglect of that heritage that had brought about the strong and violent contrasts which he so deplored in Barth's position. It was 'failure [on the part of "Protestant theologians under the influence of the new orthodoxy"] to appreciate his Jewish heritage', Raven argued, that 'has been mainly responsible for the perversion of St Paul's teaching and for the assigning of a scriptural authority to doctrines of the total depravity of the world and the radical antithesis of nature and grace'.[23]

In Raven's view, by contrast, things work together, transitions are gradual, there is development and evolution. The Jewish spirit and the Greek, starting from very different origins, come to work

on the side line from which war's horrors, its sinfulness and its rage of destruction were alone evident, but from which they missed the exultation that thrills through a people ready to sacrifice life itself for its brothers.'

[23] Raven, *Natural Religion*, i. 21 f.

together. 'The result of the fusion is to maintain and enrich the Old Testament insistence upon the worth of the natural order, both in itself and as the symbol and instrument of the divine.'[24] Thus, as Raven sees it, Jesus himself is something of a natural theologian. He 'breaks away from the general tendency of religion at His time and, instead of concentrating upon the abnormal or clothing His message in the language of the demonic and supernatural, bases His teaching upon the ordinary and commonplace'. He teaches 'by bidding men consider the lilies and the birds, by setting a child in the midst, by telling stories of sowers and fishermen, of women baking bread and merchants seeking pearls. The background of His discourse is nature not supernature and He aims not at turning our eyes and minds away from the natural order but at enabling us to discover in it and through it the manifestation of deity.'[25]

And so it goes on. Nature and grace dovetail smoothly into one another. The incarnation of the divine is in keeping with the whole character of the physical world, since God loved it. This fitting together of opposites completes and fulfils something that goes back not only behind the New Testament but behind the Old and into the total world of human religion.

Well, that is a fairly extreme case on the other side. I was about to say that we can hardly expect to reconcile Barth with Raven, not in this world. Yet Raven's spirit may have smiled a sardonic smile on finding that, in the end, Barth admitted that under certain circumstances there might be 'certain true words alongside the one Word of God',[26] that this was said in connection with the parables of Jesus, and that some offshoots of Barthian tradition ended up depending on natural science and appealing to it just as much as he, Raven, had done. These results were reached, of course, by a different path; indeed so. 'Of course', Raven would doubtless have said, 'they had to say that'.

Nevertheless, as I say, if we look back at the theological currents of our century, now near its end, it looks as if Barth was the successful one.[27] For most twentieth-century theologians, at least within

---

[24] Raven, *Natural Religion*, i. 30.    [25] Ibid. i. 31 f.    [26] *KD* iv/3. 126; *CD* iv/3. 113.

[27] Thus—a good instance—Hugo Meynell, no Barthian partisan, begins his book *Grace versus Nature* (London: Sheed and Ward, 1965) with the sentence 'Barth is the greatest living Christian theologian'. Whether this success was deserved, of course, is another matter, on which opinions naturally vary. For recent studies of the reception of Barth, especially in the English-speaking world, see S. W. Sykes in Sykes (ed.), *Karl Barth: Studies of his Theological Methods*, and R. H. Roberts, 'The Reception of

Protestantism, natural theology fell into the background.[28] Lecturing on the subject up and down, I have met people who have had a full theological education in the latter part of this century and had never heard of natural theology, knew nothing of such a concept, had never even heard the expression. Particularly in biblical studies has this been the case. Dictionaries and encyclopaedias of biblical studies produced in modern times contain no article entitled 'Natural Theology'.[29] Works in biblical theology, for the most part, proceed as if they had never heard of any such thing. Commentaries on individual books of the Bible mostly do not even raise the question whether some affinity with natural theology is to be found in them. In spite of the widespread preference of Brunner over Barth in the English-speaking world, it was Barth who came to

the Theology of Karl Barth in the Anglo-Saxon World', in S. W. Sykes (ed.), *Karl Barth: Centenary Essays* (Cambridge: Cambridge University Press, 1989). In the Scottish context of the Gifford Lectures it is proper to mention the judgement of the impressive theologian Paul Lehmann. Lehmann thought that in Scotland Barthianism had been disastrous to the life of the Church, and the only place where he thought it had been creative was in Japan (!). He wrote in 1970: 'In Scotland a virulent "Barthian scholasticism" obstructs the freedom of God in his revelation to be God for man in the world, and enervates the faith and life of the churches. Only in Japan, it seems, does the dynamic and liberating creativity of Barth's thought function as a life option'—so 'Karl Barth and the Future of Theology', *RS* 6 (1970), 105 f. This is all the more striking in that Lehmann was one of the most creative of those under strong Barthian influence; he was described by Roberts, 'Reception of the Theology of Karl Barth', 145, as one 'powerfully influenced by Barth whose fidelity remains steadfast despite the changes and pluralistic diversity of his environment'.

[28] Cf. H. J. Birkner, 'Natürliche Theologie und Offenbarungstheologie: ein theologiegeschichtlicher Überblick', *NZST* 3 (1961), 279, first paragraph. To paraphrase his eloquent statement, the beginner in theology knows nothing about natural theology and the graduate in it knows only one thing about natural theology, namely that there is nothing in it. Modern theology is emphatically revelational theology, and the ignoring of natural theology is the agreed and conventional wisdom.

[29] Thus there is no such article in familiar works such as *The Interpreter's Dictionary of the Bible* or *Harper's Bible Dictionary* (San Francisco: Harper & Row, 1985), or in the excellent *Dictionary of Biblical Interpretation*, ed. R. J. Coggins and J. L. Houlden (London: SCM, 1990). The absence of such an article does not necessarily mean that the good editors are hostile to natural theology. They may be quite positively inclined towards it, but they seem to indicate that it is not material for inclusion in a *biblical* dictionary. The revised *Hastings' Dictionary of the Bible*, rev. F. C. Grant and H. H. Rowley (Edinburgh: T. & T. Clark, 1963) contains (pp. 690 f.) brief articles on 'natural' and 'nature', but these seem mainly concerned to minimize the role of these terms in biblical thought and neither of them has anything about possible connections with natural theology. The lengthy article on 'Paul's Theology' in the same work (G. B. Caird, 731–42) appears to contain no mention whatever of the possibility of natural theology. Examples can be multiplied indefinitely.

be recognized in the end as the greater theologian, and not much was ever heard of the new natural theology for which Brunner had called. The plaintive pleas for some kind of new natural theology that are uttered from time to time by other people seem seldom to lead to anything much. One reason for this, no doubt, is the failure to show how any natural theology, old or new, meshes with the material of the Bible itself.

A revival of interest in natural theology has certainly taken place, let us say in the last twenty years. One might, perhaps, distinguish several distinct streams in which something akin to natural theology has been pursued: (1) works continuing the older idealist natural theology and virtually ignoring Barth and the main theological development of this century, well exemplified by Cleobury; (2) works seeking a new approach through something like Process Theology, well illustrated by John Cobb; (3) works that are distinctly 'post-Barthian' and seek to incorporate the basic Barthian insights while re-examining the issues of natural theology: notably Jüngel and Link; (4) the striking revival of interest in philosophical theism; (5) works concerned to build a 'theology of nature' in view of the ecological problems of the present day—too many to mention examples here, but note Link's concerns in this area; (6) an approach that seeks to base itself less on absolute philosophical or dogmatic concerns and more on our normal daily or 'natural' life (Wisnefske). But this renewed thinking about natural theology has been somewhat quietly pursued by various people in their various corners and has as yet made rather little impact on the theological and religious public.

Yet, paradoxically, the fact is that, if we look at the middle ground, at the large number of people who were considerably influenced by Barth and had at least some sympathy for what he was saying, I think we would have to say: there seem to be few who are convinced that he was right on this particular problem. If he is remembered and revered, it is more for other things than this. Even among those who recognize him as the greatest theologian of the period, few today feel that his rejection of natural theology was his masterstroke, few accept that it was right to make this into the central and pivotal issue. There was something in it, no doubt, people think. Thus some agree that Roman Catholic theology had depended too much on natural theology and that it benefited from the impulse of these discussions, which enabled it to move towards a more biblical type of utterance. But the absoluteness and the rigidity displayed in the conflict with Brunner were ridiculous. Nor was it ever proved by Barth, nor did he even attempt to prove, that all Roman Catholic theology, and all 'Modern Protestantism', that is, more or less all theologies other than his own, were compromises of some kind with natural theology. The developments in which later Barthianism, even including Barth himself, came round to some sort of natural theology, even if carefully differentiated from the older natural theology, themselves testified against his classic position. Even if there was something in it, most people felt they could leave the subject shrouded in a mist of mild uncertainty, and that other things could move ahead apart from it.[30] It certainly has not remained the storm centre of theology, even in the heritage of the dialectical theology, as it seemed to be some decades ago. Lack of lively interest has been a major reason why the very consciousness of the subject has come to be dimmed.

But the absence of conflict is not always a sign that all things are well. One area upon which the matter touches is the nature of the Bible and the mode of its interpretation. Any negation of natural theology appears to throw more emphasis upon the Bible, the Bible being one of the main accepted channels of special revelation. In Barth's theology the Word of God existed in three forms: Jesus Christ as the living, personal, Word; the Bible as the written Word, which testifies of him; and the preaching of the Church, in so far as it speaks of him and in accordance with the testimony of Holy Scripture. The Bible therefore belongs very definitely and distinctly to the movement of divine revelation from God to humanity. This is a well-known and in some ways a useful and creative mode of stating the situation.

But what if scripture itself sanctions, permits, evidences, or in some other way depends upon natural theology or something like it? In the passage already quoted we saw Barth insisting that 'church and salvation are founded on the Word of God alone, on God's revelation in Jesus Christ, as it is attested in the Scriptures', and taking it as obvious that this implied the denial of all natural

---

[30] Thus, to give only one example, the two volumes of essays edited by Sykes include no essay on the question of natural theology, and mention the matter very little.

theology.[31] But if the Bible accepted or implied natural theology this argument falls to pieces: the Word of God, as attested in the scriptures, must then *include* natural theology as part of revelation, or as the background to it, or as an implication of it or mode through which it is communicated. And this is, after all, what had been supposed by the earlier theological trends, including Luther and Calvin: they all supposed that there was in the Bible some authorization for natural theology. Barth, for his part, strongly insisted on the Bible as criterion for his theology. It was not open to him to say that the Bible had simply misunderstood the matter, had just got it wrong at this crucial point. In the building of his theology the Bible was one pillar, and the rejection of natural theology was another. How did he get around this difficulty? The answer is simple: he thought he could argue that the biblical passages which have been taken to support natural theology did not support it at all. In other words, he thought that he could exegetically overcome or evade all the arguments that seemed to support natural theology on scriptural grounds. Or else he, or his followers, simply soft-pedalled these passages and gave much more emphasis to others.

But the essential thing is this: the denial of natural theology was the prior decision—logically if not chronologically. Not at the start of his career, but at a certain stage in it, Barth came to diagnose natural theology as the source of theological sickness, on dogmatic grounds and on grounds of the problems of historical theology and contemporary thought; when he came to look again at the biblical evidence he was already committed in his mind to this. His doctrine of scripture was formulated in a way that did not have room for the possibility that it might affirm or include natural theology. His exegesis was similarly predetermined.

With this as introduction, we shall in the next chapter look at one of the most important of the biblical passages concerned, the speech of St Paul on the Areopagus in Acts 17.

---

[31] Barth's assumption that the authority of scripture implies the denial of natural theology is obvious in many places, e.g. *Natural Theology*, 82, 87, 107, etc. He repeatedly (and absurdly) attacks Brunner for denying the supreme authority of scripture, as well as for upsetting the principles of *sola gratia* and *sola fides*. In *Natural Theology* there is no attempt on Barth's side to consider as a real question whether scripture might sanction or imply natural theology.

# 2

# Paul on the Areopagus

In Chapter 1 we gave a brief preliminary survey of the idea of natural theology and related concepts, and some remarks about the controversy surrounding natural theology in modern discussion. I talked particularly about Karl Barth, as the person best known for his complete rejection of all natural theology, and we noted how the denial of natural theology went along with a strong emphasis on the Bible as one of the forms of the Word of God. Seen in this way, the Bible naturally belonged to revelational theology and was a principal channel of divine revelation to humanity. But what if the Bible itself sanctioned, or depended on, or implied, natural theology, or at least something that had an affinity with natural theology? Our next step therefore is to consider some of the biblical passages that were always, traditionally, supposed to have this character, and see what we find. We shall begin with the magnificent passage of Paul's speech on the Areopagus, Acts 17[16 ff.].[1]

Paul was waiting in Athens, and his spirit was provoked by the fact that the city was κατείδωλος, idolatrous or full of idols. So he argued in the agora with Jews and god-fearers, and with anyone he met. Among these were philosophers of the Stoic and Epicurean schools. People were curious about Paul's ideas and speculated about him. Some said: He seems to be a preacher of foreign divinities (for he preached Jesus and the resurrection). So they took him to the Areopagus, which was a sort of court or official assembly, and wanted to know what this new teaching was; for the Athenians, and

---

[1] The importance of the Areopagus speech for traditional natural theology is too obvious to require exemplification. To mention an example from a modern work that continues that tradition, A. R. Peacocke, in the Coda which concludes his *Creation and the World of Science* (Oxford: Clarendon Press, 1979), writes (p. 358): 'To believe in God as Creator, is simply to acknowledge that we live and move and have our being in One who is not far from any of us'—exactly the language of the speech. He goes on to say that in our being and acting creatively and responsively we are manifesting *ipso facto* the very creativity of God himself.

even the foreigners who lived there, were very curious and always longed to hear something that had novelty.

Paul began his speech with the remark that the Athenians, as he perceived, were very religious (δεισιδαιμονέστεροι), more than usually respectful of deity. For as he passed by and looked around their shrines he had seen an altar with the inscription 'To the Unknown God' ('Αγνώστῳ Θεῷ). 'What therefore you unknowingly (ἀγνοοῦντες) revere, this I declare to you' (v. 23). So what is the content of the declaration that follows?

It begins with the fact of *temples*, in relation to the one creator God. God who made the world and is Lord of all things does not live in temples made by human hands nor does he receive care from humanity as if he was in need of anything. On the contrary, he created human life and gives all that it needs to live. He made out of one (it is not clear whether 'from one man', or 'from one stock' (so REB: γένος no doubt being the word implied); AV 'of one blood' derives from a different text) every nation of the world and determined the times and boundaries of their habitation: that they should seek God, in the hope that (εἰ ἄρα γε) they might feel, grope,[2] after him and find him. Yet in fact he is not far from each one of us. 'In him we live and move and have our being', as even certain of the Greek poets have said, 'For we are indeed his offspring' (τοῦ γὰρ καὶ γένος ἐσμέν).

But the thought of being offspring of God brings us back to the thought of idolatry, which was the starting-point of Paul's impressions in this city. Being offspring of God, we should not think that deity is like gold or silver, idols made by people. The past times of ignorance—he means, presumably, ignorance in this respect, i.e. the ignorance involved in idolatry—God has overlooked, but now he commands all everywhere to repent. He has fixed a day in which he will judge the world in righteousness by a man whom he has appointed, and of this he has given assurance to all by raising this man from the dead. At the mention of the resurrection some mocked, others said they would like to hear more on another occasion. Some became believers, including Dionysius the Areopagite and a woman called Damaris, and some others.

---

[2] The word 'grope', ψηλαφάω, is significant, for it would doubtless correspond to a Hebrew שׁשׁ or related form and would have its best parallel in the Zadokite Document I[9] where that (Jewish) sect in its earliest days 'groped' after the truth: 'they were like the blind and like them that grope their way (מגששים דרך) for twenty years.'

Now, how did the Barthian position deal with this famous and prominent passage? What was always done, in my experience, was that Barthian theologians selected and quoted with great emphasis those few phrases within Acts 17 that seemed to conform with their own kind of revelatory theology: thus that Paul 'preached Jesus and the resurrection' (v. 18), and similarly the conclusion of the speech, with the judgement of the world and the assurance given by the raising of a man from the dead. According to this point of view, everything said within the main text of the speech was to be seen as governed by these two sayings, one of which was not within the speech at all, the other of which brought it to a premature end. Likewise v. 23, in AV 'whom therefore you *ignorantly* worship, him *declare* I unto you', was lovingly cited, with a stress on the *declare* because it is or sounds a kerygmatic sort of word, and a stress on the *ignorantly* as if it meant that the Athenians had no real knowledge at all.[3] These particular points, which appeared to agree with an interpretation as purely revelatory theology, were much emphasized.[4] 'Schlechterdings Alles, was Paulus den Athenern zu sagen hat, ist hier offenbar als sein christlich-apostolisches Wissen um sie an sie heran und in sie hinein getragen.'[5] Any knowledge of God that one of the Athenians had in hearing the speech was totally new knowledge and unconnected with previous supposed knowledge except in so far as he now knew that he had previously been totally ignorant of God. In essence, Barth is here trying to get rid of the difficulty to his position by just defining it away: since Paul was a Christian apostle, it followed that his argument could not have been based on anything but knowledge gained uniquely through Jesus Christ.[6] The argument assumes what it seeks to prove: it assumes that a Christian apostle's knowledge contained no element

---

[3] REB, I notice, has gone this way also with its 'What you worship but do not know—this is what I now proclaim.' RSV with its 'What therefore you worship as unknown, this I proclaim to you' offers a very different understanding.

[4] Cf. recently for example T. F. Torrance, 'Phusikos kai theologikos logos: St Paul and Athenagoras at Athens', *SJT* 41 (1988), 11–26, and in particular 13.

[5] *KD* ii/1. 136; *CD* ii/1. 123.

[6] Barth, *KD* ii/1. 136; *CD* ii/1. 123. Cf. also *KD* i/2. 333, *CD* i/2. 304 ff., where Barth in his paradoxical way tells us: 'That they come to know this is something quite new. And to us also it is quite new that we also come to know this, that they did already know it'. According to Barth, Paul is saying: 'You did indeed know of this God, this God from being a known God has become to you an unknown God . . . I speak to you out of my knowledge of Christ as your own knowledge in and in spite of your complete lack of knowledge.' See H. Berkhof and H.-J. Kraus, *Karl Barths Lichterlehre* (Theologische Studien 123; Zurich: Theologischer Verlag, 1978), 35.

of natural theology: being a Christian apostle, Paul agreed with Barth.

But these arguments are entirely invalid, because they do not constitute *exegesis* of the Areopagus speech at all: they pick out the few aspects that can appear to favour the Barthian dogmatic position, and they simply ignore the tenor of the total argument and its content. For instance, there is no question that Paul in Athens was 'preaching Jesus and the resurrection'; the question was the way in which he was doing it, the mode in which he approached it, the logic with which he developed his argument. Paul's approach as reported in Acts is entirely contrary to what any Barthian approach could have been. In his argument he says nothing about the Old Testament or the people of Israel, nothing about the patriarchs or the prophets, nothing about the law given through Moses. There is thus a substantial shift of emphasis as against the general approach taken in most of his letters and in most of his other speeches within Acts. The emphasis is entirely universal. God, being creator of the whole world, does not live in temples made by human activity. He has no needs for which he is dependent on humanity.[7] He has given life and breath to all human beings, in the hope or chance that they might feel after him and find him. This hope or chance is not a completely remote or impossible fancy: for he, though transcendent, is not far from each one of us. This is so, because we live and move and have our being 'in' him: 'in him we exist' (REB). God is the all-encompassing medium, it seems, which surrounds and envelops us all. We live with God around us, and, moreover, it is from God that we come. Throughout the passage 'we' includes Greeks and others, all humanity is together in this. And to confirm that we all come from God, that we are his offspring, Paul cites a verse from a Greek poet. So that, at this point, if there is any 'scriptural' evidence to support the argument, any confirmation from an ancient written source, it comes not from a Hebrew prophet but from a Greek poet, one of the very few places where a definite quotation from a Greek poet or writer is made in the New Testament. The fact that the god of whom that poet was writing was—almost certainly—Zeus only makes more striking the use of the quotation by Paul.[8]

---

[7] A point already made in Ps. 50[8 ff.], but there in respect of God's having no need to be nourished through sacrifices—a theme also of the satire in Bel and the Dragon.

[8] I am indebted to Dr Eugene Lemcio for suggestions in this regard.

Where then does this lead? Back to the transcendence of God. God is not a physical substance like gold or stone, least of all is he like any image made by man. In the past he overlooked human ignorance in this respect (Paul's expression here is surely the source of the later Muslim concept of the *jāhiliyya* or 'time of ignorance' before Islam), but he now commands all people everywhere to repent. And here he comes back to the more customary themes of Christian preaching: God has fixed a day in which he will judge the world in righteousness by a man whom he has designated, and of this he has given assurance to all by raising him from the dead.

Now it is not to be pretended that this passage is typical of the normal New Testament approach: it is not. There are many highly peculiar features:[9] the complete absence of support adduced from the history, the law, and the experience of Israel; the strong universalism, with God seen as determining alike the bounds and times for *all* human peoples; the clear prospect that any of these might feel after him and find him; the conjunction of the high transcendence of the deity and his close presence and immanence; especially the idea that we live and move and have our being within him, the nearest approach, no doubt, to pantheism in the Bible, coupled with the idea that we, i.e. all humans, are his offspring; also the idea that, though repentance is now demanded, faults of earlier times are to be overlooked. The passage, then, is highly individual. But there can be no doubt that it depends on, supports, and involves some sort of natural theology.[10] Its shape and construction, the course and strategy of the argument, cannot possibly be provided with an explanation along the accepted Barthian lines. And there is no better evidence of this

[9] H. Conzelmann, *Acts* (Hermeneia; Philadelphia: Fortress, 1987), 145, comments that 'Both the understanding of God and [that] of humanity in this passage are unique in the New Testament.' Contrast Barth, who maintains that, as Luke sees it, 'Paul proclaims on the Areopagus the crucified Christ in what is basically the same manner as he proclaimed him always and everywhere' (*KD* ii/1. 135; *CD* ii/1. 122)—of which one can only say: rubbish! Or—if we press the phrase 'as Luke sees it'—this can only mean that Luke thought the natural theology of the Areopagus speech underlay all the other speeches of Paul in which it is less evident.

[10] Thus P. Vielhauer, 'On the "Paulinism" of Acts', in L. E. Keck and J. L. Martyn, *Studies in Luke-Acts* (London: SPCK, 1968), 34 ff., takes it as manifest that the speech is a manifestation of natural theology, and considers this to be an aspect of Luke's own theology and one contrasting with that of Paul himself. Equally, or even more, Conzelmann, *Acts*, 217 ff: cf. for instance his sentence on 221: 'By tacit implication the claim is made: you, too, had in truth always but one God, the only real one.' On another aspect of Conzelmann's judgement, see below, Ch. 6.

than the following fact: although Karl Barth wrote an immense amount of biblical exegesis, especially in the small-print sections of his *Church Dogmatics*, nowhere, so far as I can discover, did he provide a full-length exegesis of Acts 17.[11] For a man who could write about fifteen pages of small print on the sacrifice of two birds plus various goats in Leviticus,[12] and about thirty on details in the story of Saul and David,[13] this cannot but be significant. One can only interpret what one likes. Barth liked stories that told about election, the topic under which he expounded these Old Testament materials. He did not like stories that led towards natural theology. This is what I myself remember from the older Barthian days: apart from the feeble arguments cited above from Barth, which carried little conviction, what was generally done was to ignore the passage. Acts 17 cannot be fully expounded without opening the gate towards some sort of natural theology. If you are as completely against all natural theology as Barth was, the only honest thing to do is to say that Paul, as represented by Luke in this chapter of Acts, was *wrong*, and wrong in one of the most essential elements dominating the structure of Christian theology. And, somewhat later, we shall have to look at the consequences if that view is taken.

There are two possible ways of escape from our argument, and we now have to look at these. First of all, it may be said that Luke, in the writing of Acts, misunderstood or misrepresented Paul. Paul never thought and never said all these things we have been discussing. The very peculiarity of the thoughts and arguments, their difference from what is normal elsewhere in the New Testament, could be used as an argument to this effect. Where there are similarities, one could continue on this line of argument, these are a sign that Paul had said a few things of this kind, but that Luke, misunderstanding him, had built up a quite different structure of the whole. Historically this might be quite possible. Thus, to quote one modern and well-reasoned opinion,

---

[11] His main discussion of Acts 17 lies in *KD* ii/1. 134ff.; *CD* ii/1. 121ff. Other passages which refer to the speech say very much the same thing. Cf. the *Register* volume to *KD*, p. 139.

[12] *KD* ii/2. 393ff.; *CD* ii/2. 357ff. It is interesting that this passage, plus the following one on Saul and David, is quoted by David Ford, 'Barth's Interpretation of the Bible', in S. W. Sykes (ed.), *Karl Barth: Studies of His Theological Methods* (Oxford: Clarendon Press, 1979), 65, along with one other, as 'remarkable pieces of exegesis' showing the relation of all Old Testament history to Christ.

[13] *KD* ii/2. 404ff.; *CD* ii/2. 366ff.

John Ziesler in his *Pauline Christianity* points to many substantial differences between Paul and Acts and writes:[14]

The 'natural theology' of Paul's Areopagus speech is akin to the attempts of people like Justin Martyr in the second century to discover a preparation for Christ in pagan philosophy and religion, and this too suggests a post-Pauline date. Was Acts therefore written by a contemporary who did not understand him (Paul), or by a later person who was inadequately informed?

But theologically, if we follow that path, we are left with a divided witness within the central portions of the New Testament and about a central issue: a conflict between a Luke who was something of a natural theologian and a Paul who was not. And there are people, very likely, who accept quite happily that this is the situation and throw in their lot either with Luke or with Paul. But if the situation is truly thus divided, it may mean that natural theology has substantial but not universal support within the relevant parts of the New Testament; or else it may mean that we rate Luke well above Paul, or Paul well above Luke, as not a few would do: 'ich hasse Lukas', after all, is said to be an exclamation of a distinguished New Testament scholar. Luke, according to this viewpoint, misunderstood and ruined every distinctive insight that Paul had made clear. If we should deny natural theology on the ground that Paul, the historical Paul, did not support it, even if Luke depicts him as supporting it, then we are consciously moving to the *sectional* authority of Paul rather than the total authority of scripture. Such a position is a possible one, and some theologians probably adopt it, but it is not one that Karl Barth himself would have accepted. For him, the entire scripture gave a unitary theological witness in all essential points, and this was certainly an essential one. On the question whether Luke's picture of Paul is a good historical picture or not we shall have something to say at a later point; and the answer depends, in good measure, on the background and content of ideas which we consider to have been involved.

On this aspect it is worth while to contrast a conservative evangelical approach as represented by one of the great Scottish scholars of our time, my late colleague and friend F. F. Bruce. For Bruce the central issue is not natural theology, but the historical reliability or

[14] John Ziesler, *Pauline Christianity* (Oxford: Oxford University Press, 1983), 130. Cf. also J. C. O'Neill, *The Theology of Acts in Its Historical Setting* (London: SPCK, 1970).

accuracy of Acts. If Acts is in these terms 'reliable', Paul must indeed have made very much the speech which Acts reports. In order to demonstrate this, Bruce uses arguments which, without exactly saying so, maximize the kinship of the speech with natural theology. Paul 'adapts himself to the Athenian atmosphere' (p. 332).[15] 'Paul's speech before the Areopagus is just such a speech as we might expect from so versatile a preacher in attempting to influence his philosophic Athenian audience' (p. 334). 'Here [at Acts 17[25]] are combined the Epicurean doctrine that God needs nothing from men and cannot be served by them, and the Stoic belief that He is the source of all life. Paul consistently endeavours to have as much common ground as possible with his audience.' On 17[28]: 'The Zeus of these Stoic poets is of course the λόγος or world-principle which animates all things. Their language, however, is largely adaptable to the God of revelation. By presenting God as Creator and Judge, Paul emphasizes His Personality in contrast to the materialistic pantheism of the Stoics' (pp. 338 f.). Again, 'Paul was, moreover, much more likely than Luke to know the tenets of Stoics and Epicureans so as to make such delicately suited allusions to them'[16] —an argument intended to show that the speech much more probably came from Paul himself than from Luke's creative imagination. Finally, on the similar events at Lystra, 'This is the first recorded Christian address to a pagan audience. The appeal is made to such knowledge of God as they might reasonably have, i.e., by "natural revelation" '—and here Bruce compares the first two chapters of Romans, and the Areopagus speech.[17] The historically conservative arguments are apologetic in character, which may imply a kinship with natural theology; exegetically, they support the case for natural theology in the passage; and they rank the question of historicity as higher in theological importance than the issue of natural theology.

A second alternative approach is what we may call the Failure

---

[15] All quotations are taken from his commentary on Acts (London: Tyndale Press, 1951); later editions sometimes altered the wording somewhat, but the 1951 edition provides a good and clear example of this line of interpretation.

[16] This is actually a quotation made by Bruce from J. H. Moulton and W. F. Howard, *Grammar of New Testament Greek*, ii (Edinburgh: T. & T. Clark, 1929), 8 n. 3: Bruce, *Acts*, 339. They add that Luke's knowledge of Greek literature, apart from medical writers, was too limited for him to have known this sort of thing—thus making it more probable that the speech is really by Paul, who did have this kind of knowledge.

[17] Bruce, *Acts*, 283.

Theory.[18] The approach described in Acts 17 was indeed carried out by St Paul but was a momentary lapse or mistake on his part. Here in Athens, a relative newcomer to mainland Greece and a total new-comer to its intellectual capital, he made the attempt to argue from natural theology; but the attempt failed, and afterwards Paul aban-doned it. After leaving Athens he reverted to a purely revelational approach, and stuck to it thereafter. Evidences of this have been seen in certain remarks in 1 Corinthians, and remember that when Paul left Athens it was straight to Corinth that he went. Thus 1 Corinth-ians 2[1 f.]: 'When I came to you, brethren, I did not come proclaiming to you the testimony of God in lofty words or wisdom. For I decided to know nothing among you except Jesus Christ and him crucified ... my speech and my message were not in plausible words of wis-dom ... that your faith should not rest in the wisdom of men but in the power of God' (RSV). And likewise especially 1 Corinthians 1[21 ff.]:

For since, in the wisdom of God, the world did not know God through wisdom, it pleased God through the folly of what we preach to save those who believe. For Jews demand signs and Greeks seek wisdom, but we preach Christ crucified, a stumbling block to Jews and folly to Gentiles, but to those who are called, both Jews and Greeks, Christ the power of God and the wisdom of God. For the foolishness of God is wiser than men, and the weakness of God is stronger than men. (RSV)

So there is evidence that *could* be used to argue that all this grew out of the unhappy experience of Paul's experiment with natural theology a short time before.

And purely historically such a course of events might be quite possible. Paul could have tried an approach which he later regret-ted. Perhaps he did make a mistake, and learned from it never to commit it again. But this argument is no solution to our question. For chapter 17 of Acts still remains as our text, and for Luke, as that chapter shows, the attempt was not at all a failure. The entire

---

[18] Barth himself also uses this terminology: 'ein offenkundiger Mißerfolg', an obvious failure, *KD* ii/2. 135 top; *CD* ii/2. 122. He uses this of both the Areopagus speech and the Lystra incident. But he does not mean the same thing as the Failure Theory we are now discussing. He does not mean that Paul tried an approach through natural theology, found that it failed, and thereafter abandoned that approach. He means that *if* it is understood as a use of natural theology, *if* it had been an attempt to 'make contact' through that which they already knew, it was an obvious failure; but, since it had nothing to do with natural theology or 'making contact', the question of failure does not arise. There was no failure, no change of approach on Paul's part, and no inconsistency of any kind.

description in Acts in no way depicts it as a failure, nor does Acts contain a single word that indicates a change of mind on Paul's part. He makes Paul deliver a magnificent oration, and several people believed and attached themselves to Paul, including Dionysius the Areopagite, who, even if he was not the great theologian he was later reputed to have become, was at least an important person. He was one of the most distinguished of those to have been converted by Paul's preaching according to Acts, and all the more strikingly so because he must in all probability have been a genuine Athenian citizen and not a 'god-fearer' or one already loosely attached to the synagogue and partially trained in Judaism. Along with him there was a woman called Damaris, and some 'others'. Even in numbers this was no 'failure'. If it was only 'some' who believed, it was only 'some' again who 'mocked',[19] and 'others', perhaps about the same proportion, who wanted to hear more.

Paul's preaching seems to have been thought to have a very variable response, even where there was no question of natural theology. In Thessalonica, in the very same chapter, where Paul had very definitely preached the sufferings and resurrection of Christ, and this on the basis of the scriptures, it was again only 'some' of the Jews who believed and attached themselves to him (Acts 17[4]), but a πλῆθος πολύ, a substantial number, of the Greek god-fearers and 'not a few' (οὐκ ὀλίγαι) of the leading women; at Beroea soon afterwards, apparently after a similar approach, 'many' of the Jews believed, and again a similar group of women. Acts does not seem to be interested in correlating any particular 'approach' with success or failure. And we shall shortly consider the experience of the apostles

---

[19] It is an interesting further question why these hearers mocked. The occasion was, of course, the mention of the resurrection of 'a man' whom God had appointed. But why did this cause them to mock? Many discussions leave the impression that it was because the idea of a resurrection from the dead would seem incredible. As Acts itself makes clear, the philosophers had an easy, familiar, and ready diagnosis for such talk: it belonged to the cults of 'foreign gods' (17[18]). Why would such a claim have caused mockery? Not so much, perhaps, because resurrection was remote from a Greek mind, but because it belonged to the familiar category of foreign cults of which they had already heard enough. Might it be, on the contrary, that Paul's approach, as far as we can tell from Luke's presentation of it, gave no adequate linkage between the natural theology of the main part of the speech and the part played by this 'man'? For the resurrection of 'a man' has no great theological meaning until we know a good deal more about the background and nature of this person. One might consider speaking about a 'failure' in this regard, but the failure would not be because of the natural theology of the speech, but because of the abrupt bringing in of this quite different element without adequate preparation or explanation. In any case, as has been emphasized, the passage gives no indication that the mockers were the majority.

at Lystra, where an approach markedly analogous to that of Paul
on the Areopagus produced a sensation and led to an established
Church.

One cannot say, then, that the reception on the Areopagus was an
overwhelmingly negative one. To anyone who reads the text as a
whole, there can be no doubt that for Luke the incident was not a
momentary error or a failure but a high point on the total progress
of the gospel from Jerusalem to Rome, through the great cities of
the world. Athens, indeed, did not become one of the major centres
of early Christianity, as did (say) Antioch and Ephesus, and even
Corinth in some measure, and this fact only increases the reader's
conviction that for St Luke the Athenian incident was of major
symbolic importance. The story is told in great detail by Luke: it is
there not because of the later history of Athens within Christianity,
but because of the symbolic significance of the city. The Acts narrated the movement of the gospel from Jerusalem, the religious
centre of the world, to Rome, the centre of administrative and military power, and, half-way between them, the visit to Athens, the
intellectual centre, could not but be significant. Paul's Areopagus
speech was, in St Luke's conception, a major and controlling statement of what Christian faith was all about, and, above all, a key
statement of how the Christian faith must sound when stated for
reception by an audience totally, or almost totally, Gentile, who
had no background whatever in Hebrew scriptures, or in Judaism,
or in the synagogue. For remember that the speech at Athens is much
the most important among the speeches of Acts to have been delivered to an audience without background in Judaism of some
kind. As Gärtner well expresses it: 'Whether Pauline or not, the
Areopagus speech can legitimately be considered a typical ex-
emplar of the first Christian sermons to the Gentiles.'[20]

Or put it this way: historically it is quite conceivable that Paul
committed a momentary lapse at Athens; but as a solution this only
apparently papers over the cracks, and what comes out of it is much
the same as the previous suggestion, namely that Luke was just
wrong about Paul. For the text that Luke wrote was one that took
this incident on the Areopagus as a glorious moment, and Luke
commemorated it with one of the finest of his many fine speeches.
It stands in line with the Good Samaritan, the Prodigal Son, the

---

[20] Bertil Gärtner, *The Areopagus Speech and Natural Revelation* (Uppsala:
Gleerup, 1955), 71.

Speech of Stephen, and Paul's speeches before Jewish authorities and before Agrippa. And that in turn is a reason why it is not easy to reduce the authority of Luke to a secondary level. Even if Luke somewhat mixed up the words that were historically spoken, and produced something of his own theology rather than exactly what was said at the time, from the point of view of the authority of scripture the effects on Christianity, if Luke's depictions are to be taken lightly, would be enormous.

We retain, therefore, the view that the speech on the Areopagus must count as an extremely important and authoritative piece of scripture, and its qualities in those respects are not affected by the possibilities either that Luke misunderstood Paul or that the whole episode was regarded as a failure. But now we must go on to examine some aspects of its content.

First, the philosophers. Although there were Stoic and Epicurean philosophers whom Paul had met in the market-place, in his speech before the Areopagus itself Paul pays little or no attention to their respective philosophies. He certainly uses terminology that would be known in Greek philosophy, and mainly from the Stoic side. This preference for the Stoic side would not be surprising, for it was shared by much of ancient (and indeed of early modern) Christianity, while Epicureanism was seen as a godless and meaningless set of ideas incompatible with any worthwhile religion. Thus Hebrew adopted, and perhaps by this time had already adopted, the word *apikoros* to mean any person of totally carnal and unprincipled character. Nevertheless, whatever he had said in his conversations in the agora, in his speech on the Areopagus Paul does not expressly discuss either of the two schools; he does not compare them, nor does he attack them. Nor, more important still, does he do anything to attack Greek philosophy as a whole or its modes of thinking.[21] Nor does he try, as he might have done, to exploit the deep opposition between Stoic and Epicurean as a means to drive a wedge between these two parties—a rhetorical technique that Paul was to use on other occasions, within Judaism, as between Sadducees and Pharisees (Acts 23[6 ff.])—or to suggest the ultimate failure of Greek philosophy as a whole. Far from using these and other like divisions as a means to introduce Christianity as a third

---

[21] Contrast Barth, *KD* ii/2. 136; *CD* ii/2. 123, who avers that the purport of Paul's speech is that 'Stoic and Epicurean philosophy and all other philosophy is at an end'. If so, why did Paul say nothing to that effect?

force of totally different character which will transcend existing conflicts, Paul's speech is distinctly friendly to Greek thought and displays no polemic in principle against it. He moves unembarrassedly within its language, terms, and categories—just as other Jewish thinkers of Greek speech did.

What Paul does focus on, as an aspect of Greek culture, is something else: namely, the presence of idolatry. This was the first thing that he saw in Athens, that the city was κατείδωλος, full of idols, and this made him furious. In the Areopagus speech he comes back to this: God, he says, does not live in temples made by human beings, he is not like gold or silver or images that they have fashioned. In making this attack on idolatry, Paul does not quote the Law of Moses which prohibited it. And I think there is a reason for this. Two different things were involved: idols, and temples. The first were statues or pictures of a deity; the second were buildings in which gods might be supposed to be housed or to dwell. The speech mingles these two things, and not surprisingly, for Paul, arriving in Athens, certainly saw plenty of temples, and maybe even more temples than idols in the sense of statues of gods. Why should this make a difference?

The difference is this: that idols are clearly and severely forbidden by the Law of Moses, and pretty well throughout the Hebrew Bible. But temples are not. There are indeed certain occasional indications that seem to favour a worship without a temple: in Mosaic times there was a portable tent, and occasionally there are suggestions that the religion could carry on well enough without a permanent temple, as indeed it was forced to do for a time; and the Lord himself, when David first proposed the building of a temple, notoriously refused, indicating that he had never expressed any desire for such a thing. But the main emphasis goes the other way: a temple was in fact built, and the Hebrew Bible celebrated it, described it in detail, considered it the centre of the world, and, most serious of all, seemed to affirm that it *was* the abode of God, his dwelling-place.

Thus Paul could not easily use the Old Testament for his argument that God 'does not live in temples made by human beings', for the Old Testament said very clearly that he did that very thing:

> I have built thee an exalted house,
> a place for thee to dwell in for ever

said Solomon at the dedication of the temple he had built (1 Kgs. 8[13]), and similarly David swore not to sleep

> until I find a place for the Lord
> a dwelling-place for the Mighty One of Jacob. (Ps. 132[5])

Thus for anyone who knew the Old Testament the evidence for the dwelling of the God of Israel within a building made by human hands was very obvious. How could one on biblical grounds blame the Greeks for building temples when David and Solomon had done the same, and even Moses if we count the tabernacle? Now of course one can say: biblical people knew quite well that God was not confined within a particular building. Indeed there were a few occasional statements that pointed this out. But this is exactly the line of argument that leads up to Paul's speech. God may have a dwelling-place, an actual temple made by human hands, but that does not mean that he is physically inside the building like a dog in a basket or a stone in a box. He is, after all, the creator of the world: he is transcendent and universal. All such thoughts feed into the Areopagus speech of Acts. The Old Testament terminology of God's 'dwelling' within a building is understood to be partly figurative. But this line of thinking, which was very natural for Jews, and was forced upon them particularly by their contact with Greek culture, was something that was very obvious to Greek thinkers also. They did not for a moment suppose that Athena was a divine lady somehow boxed up within the Parthenon. Paul was thus using a line of very natural Jewish interpretation of older Hebrew materials, which as it happened was very close to a significant line of Greek understanding of the same subject. Paul's thinking is close to a commonplace of Hellenistic Judaism. It was the Jewish argument itself, and not only the Greek point of view, that was basic to Paul's thinking: God did not locally 'dwell' within any building. The contrary position, namely that God was entirely transcendent, but also, for certain purposes, universally immanent, arose from the Jewish understanding, but agreed also with the common Greek view of the same problems.

*Idolatry* was a different matter. To speak about God's 'dwelling' in a temple was acceptable as a way of speaking, even if it could not be taken literally; but to represent a god by an idol of stone or wood or metal was not acceptable at all, even if explained figuratively. In many places in the Old Testament, but especially in Second Isaiah, idolatry was satirized and mocked: how absurd it is that one should take a piece of wood, cut it in two, use one piece as firewood to cook one's dinner, but shape and mould the other half, set it up in the house, and then fall down before it, saying to it, 'Deliver me, for thou art my god' (e.g. Isa. 44$^{9\,\mathrm{ff.}}$)! The prophets went on at great length with this sort of polemic, and it was still lively in later times: see a good piece in Wisdom 13$^{10\,\mathrm{ff.}}$. This kind of satire showed no real understanding of the pagan, idolatrous culture: *of course* those who used idols did not think that the idol *was* the deity, of course they had fairly sophisticated viewpoints which went far beyond the simple stupidities that the iconoclasts attributed to them, but most Israelite polemic did not know of this more sophisticated view, or chose to ignore it, and depicted the idolater as one who regarded the image as *being physically* the deity.[22] But to say that a stone, or a chiselled piece of wood, was an actual deity, to bow down and prostrate oneself before such an object, to ask it to guide one on a journey when it itself could not walk, invited scorn, satire, and mockery. Could a piece of stone create the universe? Could it bring salvation? Could it tell what is going to happen in the future? Of course it could not.

But this is essentially rational argument: it uses the enormous qualitative difference between the piece of wood or stone and the transcendental deity, creator of the world, to mock and discredit idolatrous worship. But—and this is the sequel—Greek thinkers did just the same with the statues and idols of their own culture. The Areopagites, Stoics, and Epicureans of Paul's time in Athens did not for a moment suppose that a statue of wood or metal *was* an actual deity to be worshipped. Thus the Paul of Acts, starting out from a traditional topos of Hebraic origin, was uttering and claiming something that his Athenian audience would be very likely to accept as reasonable. Far from having a hard task to persuade them, he could probably assume considerable agreement, perhaps much more than he himself understood. Of course the Athenians, even if they saw his

[22] Similarly Protestant polemic long afterwards, building upon the Old Testament viewpoint, evaluated the statues of Mary and the saints in Roman Catholic churches as 'idols', and the Mass as idolatry, ignoring the actual attitudes with which worshippers used them. These attitudes have had an important influence on the meaning of the term *idolatry*. Anyone who had or used or revered an image in worship was, through the suggestions of this term, regarded as one who actually worshipped the image as being itself divine. We would do better to make a distinction in terms, and speak of persons who 'possess, use, or respect' sacred images, reserving the term 'idolater' for those who actually worship them or regard them as divine in substance.

point, were not going to do anything about it: they were not going to go out and destroy all statues and images of the divine in their city. But then Paul was not asking them to do that: his actual proposal, his message, was something else in any case.

Thus it is not particularly necessary, and in my opinion not valid, to argue that Paul in his speech to the Areopagus was simply adapting Stoic or other Greek philosophy to his needs. It is more likely that his arguments came from Jewish tradition and were familiar from a long time back in the Jewish self-statement as against the Greek world. Their background in Jewish tradition and in the Jewish cultural situation did not alter the argument's implication of a kind of natural theology. For it was simply a fact that this aspect of Jewish and biblical tradition, when it came to be presented to and within the Gentile world, fitted in rather closely with the natural theology of that world. The adoption of terms and ideas from Greek philosophy thus came very naturally as a response to the needs of the Jewish heritage itself. Natural theology, as we shall see, thus has its roots just as much within the Jewish and Old Testament background of Christianity as within the Greek environment of the New Testament and the early Church. As for the Areopagus speech, the chief question is not whether it implied natural theology, but what kind of natural theology it implied. That we are not yet in a position to say.

That this interpretation of Acts 17 is correct is confirmed by another passage in the same book. Earlier on, in Acts 14[8 ff.], Paul and Barnabas come to Lystra in Lycaonia and perform a healing. When the crowds see what has happened, they cry out in their own language, 'The gods have come down to us in the likeness of men!' The local priest of Zeus brought along oxen and garlands and wanted to make sacrifice to them. Paul and Barnabas were of course horrified. 'We are human beings', they cried, 'subject to the same forces as you are; we call on you to turn from these vain things to the living God, who made heavens, earth, sea and all that is in them. *In past generations* [exactly the same argument as in the Areopagus speech] he allowed all nations to walk in their own ways, but he did not leave himself without witness, for he did good and gave rain and fruitful seasons, food and gladness.' Once again, in shorter space and in a more primitive form, the essentials of the argument of the Areopagus speech: *nothing* about Israel, the patriarchs, or the Law of Moses, and all statements universal: God made himself known through the created world; he will overlook past idolatry. Here once again we have the apostolic response to a situation of direct contact with Anatolian paganism, separate from all contact with Jews and the Jewish background. And there is no suggestion of a 'failure theory' here. The apostles certainly caused a sensation. We are not told how many became believers; but it seems that Paul and Barnabas were not very long there before they had to leave, and afterwards (14²¹) they returned to strengthen the Church, so that a Christian community must certainly have been established.

I will mention only briefly at this point the theme of *creation*. In both the speeches of which we have spoken Paul takes the creator God as a starting-point, and this is of course done in good Jewish style: the one God who made the heavens and provides the seasons and the rains. But though this is genuine Old Testament material, it is again material which would not have seemed strange to Greek audiences. That the world had come from God in some way was not unintelligible, and if it had it made more sense to have one God— the essential Jewish point—behind it than a whole lot of different gods. And in the Areopagus speech the insistence on the creator God, which is clearly enough made, becomes very much more attuned to Greek ears by what follows, when the audience hear that this God is not far from each one of us, that we live and move and exist in him, and that we are his offspring. The Hebrew material is selected, combined, and expressed in a way that establishes communication on a plane similar to that of natural theology.

Finally, a word about the inscription 'To the Unknown God'. How much was meant by this word 'unknown', and how much by the ἀγνοοῦντες, 'not knowing, ignorant', that qualifies the veneration of this deity by the Athenians? Does it mean, to take it at its most extreme and stressful, that it really was the unknown God and that the Athenians really knew *nothing*, nothing at all, so that all that Paul was to tell them was absolutely new? Needless to say, that extreme position would be welcome to those who wish to deny natural theology absolutely. But such a position fails to make sense of what is said in the rest of the speech, and notably the almost pantheistic expressions and the citation from the Greek poet. In saying that the Athenians worshipped 'ignorantly', Paul was not going so far. The fact that the altar to the Unknown God was there at all was a sign that someone knew something, someone knew at least that there was an unknown God. Likewise, the δεισιδαιμονέστεροι was not necessarily ironic or contemptuous: I think it was rather a mild compliment, suitably attached at the beginning of such a speech. The Athenians had some aspect of real insight in their religion. 'Ignorantly', said of them in their worship, was a proper acknowledgement of what they themselves admitted by calling this deity the Unknown God. None of this diction, then, means that Paul supposed his audience to be devoid of all knowledge relevant to the knowledge of the true God. If he had thought there was absolutely no knowledge there, he would no doubt have taken a quite other line, going through the patriarchs and Moses, the kings and prophets, as much modern theology would have liked him to do. But Paul, if he did not think there was total darkness there, did not necessarily think that there was a great deal of light either. He does not offer an evaluation of Greek culture. But he does imply that within it there are significant signs of knowledge of the ultimate: the altar was one such sign, the lines of the poet were another, his own whole ability to phrase the Christian message in this way is another.

To return to Barth's own handling of the passage, one has to register its complete failure to convince. Even if one approaches the text with a deep scepticism towards natural theology, and even if one has an open ear for the legitimate concerns that animate his opposition to it, one's final verdict must be: no! What he offers has not the slightest likeness to a serious exegesis of the text. On the contrary, it is a travesty of exegesis, indeed a denial of exegesis: for it makes no attempt to follow out the content of the passage, and is a transparent endeavour to force his own modern dogmatic position upon the text. In its operation it is more like pulpit rhetoric than scholarly exegesis: Barth is shouting down every contrary opinion, defying anyone to think or say anything other than what he thinks and says, inventing specious forms of words to bring the text into conformity with his views. But even as pulpit rhetoric it is bad rhetoric, for it is preaching *against*, not *with*, the whole trend and shape of the passage, and all that Barth demonstrates is his own complete lack of empathy with it.

To sum up this far, therefore, the argumentation of the Areopagus speech shows a clear affinity with principles that would normally be counted as belonging to natural theology. But what sort of natural theology, and how it fits in with other things, we have not yet started to consider; and the next step must be to look at some of the other great biblical passages, beginning with Paul's utterances in the Letter to the Romans.

# 3

## St Paul and the
## Hebrew Background

We began with the Areopagus speech, and not with the Letter to the Romans, not because the speech is more important—for many would consider Romans to be more important—but because it seems to be a very clear example of something like natural theology. In the case of Romans, on the other hand, there is more difficulty and doubt, and some considerable difference of opinion among experts. To Romans we must therefore now turn.

I will summarize the texts. In Romans 1[18] Paul says that the anger of God is revealed from heaven against all the impiety and injustice of men who hold the truth in unrighteousness, because that which can be known of God (τὸ γνωστὸν τοῦ Θεοῦ) is manifest (φανερόν) in them or among them, for God revealed it (ἐφανέρωσεν) to them. So, he continues in v. 20, from the creation of the world onwards, the invisible reality of God (τὰ ἀόρατα αὐτοῦ) is plainly discerned, being known by the things that he has made, and this means his eternal power and divine nature (δύναμις καὶ θειότης), so that they are without excuse. Following this, Paul goes on to talk about the corruptions to which human beings had become liable, or, as he put it, to which God had given them up: idolatry led on to lust, and this to 'unnatural' vice (i.e. vice that contradicts the φυσικὴ χρῆσις or 'natural' sexual relations, 1[26,27]), and this meant that God had handed them over to all sorts of wickedness, which are listed in detail.

This leads on to the great summing up: 'therefore you are without excuse (ἀναπολόγητος), every one who judges' (2[1]). You who judge are doing the same things as those whom you judge. But God will render to everyone according to their works, and this is the same for Jews and for Greeks. God will recompense trouble and pain to every one who does evil, the Jew first and also the Greek, but glory and honour and peace for every one who does good, the Jew first and also the Greek ($2^9$). For, he explains, there is no respect of persons with God: everyone is taken on the same basis. Those who have sinned without law (ἀνόμως) will also perish without law, and those who have sinned under law (ἐν νόμῳ) will be judged by the law. It is not the hearers of the law that are just before God, but the doers of the law will be counted just.

And this brings us to the second expression which has seemed to imply a kind of natural theology: Romans $2^{14}$. When the Gentiles who do not have the law do by nature (φύσει)—note the word 'nature', which suggests a certain pointer towards 'natural' theology—the things of the law, they, not having the law, are a law unto themselves. They show the work of the law written in their hearts, their conscience (συνείδησις) also giving witness together, and their thoughts or cogitations (λογισμοί) reciprocally accusing or defending—all, he concludes, in the day when God judges the hidden things of humanity according to my gospel through Jesus Christ. The Gentiles, then, not having the special revelation of God, lacking the law, are a law to themselves or operate as such a law, their own thoughts and consciences somehow taking a part in this.

Now is there natural theology, or a sanction for natural theology, or a basis which might by extension imply a ground for natural theology, in all this? Here we have to be careful, for New Testament specialists themselves appear not to agree, and some of them explicitly deny that there is anything like natural theology in Romans. Moreover, as a survey of recent writing makes clear, the problem is tied up with questions of the audience to which the letter is addressed, its purpose and function and the like, all questions which I would not feel competent to address on a professional level. One might summarize a large variety of positions somewhat like this:

1. There is no sort of natural theology anywhere in Romans, and nothing like it.
2. There is something rather like natural theology but it is quite marginal and insignificant: this can be combined, perhaps, with the further opinion that, though there is plenty of natural theology in Acts, there is effectively none in Paul, and this carries with it the implication that the passages of Acts which we have discussed do not properly represent Paul.
3. There is indeed something of a natural theology in Romans but it

does not come from Paul and is not part of his real message, indeed (in one version) he did not write this portion of the book at all.

We will look swiftly at some of these options. The first of these, of course, is the nearest to the Barthian viewpoint, and for it we can cite the two distinguished British exegetes Barrett and Cranfield. Thus Barrett in his commentary tells us that: 'It is not Paul's intention in this and the following verses to establish a natural theology; nor does he create one unintentionally. He is concerned with the moral principles of God's judgement.'[1] And again, a little later: 'Paul does not teach that there exist rational means of proving from creation that God exists. A mechanistic or fortuitous account of the universe never occurs to him.' And Cranfield,[2] adding that 'Barrett is surely correct over against a great many interpretations', expresses a similar judgement: 'The result of God's self-manifestation in his creation is not a natural knowledge of God on men's part independent of God's self-revelation in his Word, a valid though limited knowledge, but simply the excuselessness of men in their ignorance.'

Now before we go further we can make some comments on the position taken by these two influential exegetes. First, it may indeed be argued, as it is especially by Cranfield, that there is 'no natural knowledge' here 'independent of God's self-revelation in his Word'. If something is known, it is God who 'has revealed it to them' (Rom. 1[19]). If, then, there is some sort of revelation in creation, it is real self-revelation by God, and in that sense it appears at first sight not to belong to natural theology as traditionally defined. But this, if so, does not solve as much as might seem to be the case. For it might mean only that the definition of natural theology has to be widened or adjusted. For, if this knowledge of God through creation is accessible and available to *everybody*, indeed in some degree attained or possessed by everybody, Jew or Gentile, it seems to come to the same thing as natural theology in effect. They all know it, or know some trace of it. If they all know this trace of it, why can one not build some theology upon this fact? If there is a divine revelation in the natural or created world, and if this is available to everyone, why can we not argue from it, which is what St Paul appears to be

[1] C. K. Barrett, *A Commentary on the Epistle to the Romans* (New York: Harper & Row, 1957), 35.
[2] C. B. Cranfield, *Romans* (ICC; Edinburgh: T. & T. Clark, 1975), 116.

doing, and that in the line of much Hellenistic Judaism before him? If there is some kind of revelation to which all human beings have been given access, it means that, even if it comes by revelation of God, it can operate in the mode by which natural theology, or some kinds of it, traditionally operated. It may mean something like a kind of revealed natural theology: in other words it may suggest that the traditional boundaries between revealed and natural theology cannot be sustained or must be reconsidered, and that is a possibility to which we shall have to return.

Secondly, it is commonly said in the Reformational tradition, and we see it in Cranfield's remarks just quoted, that the only effect of God's manifestation in creation is that people are without excuse. The word *only* (or likewise 'simply'), however, is exegetically unjustified here.[3] People are without excuse, yes, but there is no basis for insisting on the *only* at this point. The effect, and no doubt the purpose, of that *only* is to diminish the positive importance of the self-manifestation in the created world. But it is more probable that the manifestation of God in creation is intended by Paul as a highly powerful factor of a *positive* kind, and not one mentioned *only* because it leaves people without excuse.

That this is so may be observed from the fact that Paul in Romans *twice* observes that people are ἀναπολόγητοι, without excuse: the first time in connection with God's revelation of what is knowable of himself in creation, $1^{20}$, and the second at $2^1$, where he writes, 'Therefore you are without excuse, every man who *judges*.' Thus, if humans are without excuse, this is not the total and only result of having a chance to know God through his creation, it is the result of other specific human acts, in particular the result of judging. The inexcusability of human beings is *not* mentioned purely as a consequence of their having failed to recognize the deity in his created works. By the same token it is likely that the whole matter of divine self-revelation in the created world has more in the way of positive consequence than 'only' that humanity is without excuse. There is no exegetical basis for this *only*, which is no more than a reiteration of certain dogmatic traditions.

Thus the statements quoted from Barrett and Cranfield are sub-

[3] Even for Calvin himself, much as he liked the theme of human inexcusability, he did not think that this was the 'only' effect: there was the other effect on which he dwelt very heavily, the impossibility of atheism, central to the first chapters of the *Institutes*. This belief in its turn has great implications for the presentation of the gospel.

ject to two criticisms: first, they give the impression of confessional assertions rather than exegetically backed interpretations, and secondly, even taken as exegetical interpretations, they are logically inadequate, in that they do not exclude natural theology but only certain limited and partial forms of it or interpretations of it.

On the first of these points, both Barrett and Cranfield give the impression that they are uttering expressions of loyalty to a basically Barthian viewpoint, rather than providing close exegetical evidence for their conclusion. Barrett, for example, in his preface wrote: 'If in those days, and since, I remained and have continued to be a Christian, I owe the fact in large measure to that book [Barth's *Romans*].'[4] Cranfield's exposition creates something of the same impression.

And, on the second aspect, both scholars slip into their comments additional attributes which might indeed apply to some conceptions of natural theology but do not necessarily apply to all. Thus when Cranfield says: 'God's being manifest in his creation is the result of his own deliberate self-disclosure and not something in any way *independent* of his will',[5] this does not really close the door against natural theology: even the most natural of all natural theologies did not suppose that the knowledge accessible through natural theology was *independent of the will of God*. All natural theology assumed that that which was 'naturally' known was known because God had willed it to be naturally known. Again, of course, as Barrett argues, Paul does not teach that 'there is a rational means of proving' from creation that God exists. But that leaves open the possibility that there is some other kind of natural theology than one that furnishes rational proof of the existence of God. When Barrett adds that Paul had no idea of a 'mechanistic or fortuitous account of the universe', no one ever supposed that he had. Natural theology does not advocate a theory of the universe as mechanistic or fortuitous; quite the contrary, one of its chief errors down the centuries, one might say, is that it has assumed too readily a universe carefully and rationally planned. All these remarks are obvious misrepresentations of natural theology and introduce irrelevant considerations which obscure the reality of the decisive issues concerning the latter. What Romans does appear to imply is that there is something 'known of God', which is revealed through his created works, which is accessible to all human beings through their being

[4] Barrett, *Romans*, p. vi.     [5] Cranfield, *Romans*, 114.

human, and which, as constituted through the law 'written in the heart', forms a resource through which moral decisions may be taken.

These last remarks are directed mainly at the first portion of the Romans text, and before we go further we have to add some consideration of the phrases about the Gentiles being 'a law unto themselves' ($2^{14\,ff.}$). This famous sentence is of a somewhat different scope and character, and yet it is equally relevant, though in a different way, to the question of natural theology. It does not say directly anything about whether Gentiles have or do not have a knowledge of God. And it is clear that they do not have the 'special' law of God, manifestly the Jewish law delivered through Moses. But they may nevertheless 'by nature'—and as we saw, this terminological link with the concept of 'natural' theology makes the passage specially distinguished for our purpose ('by nature' seems to mean, by means of resources that these Gentiles have as human people, as distinct from the resources that might be gained from the law specially given by God through Moses)—do things that belong to the functions of that law.

And the passage seems to imply that it is quite possible that Gentiles might achieve this: it is not expressed as if this was a totally theoretical discussion, so that no Gentile ever 'by nature' actually did anything good. On the contrary, it is expressed as if it was accepted experience, 'when' ($\H{o}\tau\alpha\nu$) the Gentiles do this, which obviously they sometimes do, they function as if they were to themselves a law. Moreover Paul seems to know how this works, and tells us something about the machinery of the matter: the work of the law written in the heart, assisted by the operations of conscience and the mutual accusations and defences of their own reckonings. It is as if he has seen it working. Gentiles doing what the law requires are a realistic possibility. Precisely for this reason he has to come back to the question in $3^1$, 'What then is the advantage of the Jew?'—exactly because one can do what the law requires without having the law, and one can have the law but not fulfil its requirements. If Paul thought that no Gentile 'by nature', and in spite of the resources indicated by this term, had ever done anything of this work of the law, the argument of $3^1$ would have been unnecessary. So, though the passage at this point does not speak in terms of a natural 'knowledge' or 'awareness' of God, it does speak of a resource, available 'by nature', just by being human, which can at least in principle perform the sort of moral requirement that the revealed divine law can perform (or can fail to perform). Whether or not there is a natural 'knowledge' of God, there is a 'natural' resource which can do the same work as the revealed resource can do. The existence of such a 'natural' resource would seem, even if nothing more is said explicitly, to give some support to the idea of a 'natural' awareness of God upon which some kind of 'natural theology' might be built.

In respect of this passage, we should mention also that it includes a term such as συνείδησις, 'conscience', which is said to have a distinctly Stoic ring about it, and also that the use of νόμος in 'being a law to themselves' is strikingly different from the typical usage relating to the Mosaic Law.[6] If some connection may be suggested with Jewish traditions that some divine laws had originally been given to the Gentiles, the actual wording comes closer to Aristotle's phrases to the effect that the refined and well-bred man (χαρίεις καὶ ἐλευθέριος) is 'as it were a law to himself' (οὕτως ἔξει, οἷον νόμος ὢν ἑαυτῷ—*Nic. Eth.* 1128ᵃ31), or that 'there can be no law dealing with such men [men of outstanding virtue] for they are themselves a law' (*Politics*, 1284ᵃ14). Following these lines, the connection of *nature* with the divine law, whether written or unwritten, was a well-established theme of Jewish argument. For the moment, however, we shall not attempt to evaluate these facts, until we have explored more widely the ramifications of the material. We shall want, in a moment, to make a comparison of this material with the speech of Paul on the Areopagus as reported in Luke, and we shall want to consider its background in earlier Jewish sources.

As always in such matters, a variety of exegetical opinions remains possible. On Romans we may quote three more, in addition to those of Barrett and Cranfield which have already been discussed. First, we may mention the argument of Bo Reicke, which comes perhaps the nearest to a possible interpretation compatible with the Barthian view of natural theology.[7] In Paul, says Reicke, as generally in the Bible, the knowledge of God rests upon revelation; this is so even in the Areopagus speech (p. 155). The world by reason cannot know God (1 Cor. 1²¹). Nevertheless, through a universal divine revelation people ought to be able to know God. This, Reicke

---

[6] Cf. here also the use of νόμος in places like Rom. 7²¹ ᶠᶠ·

[7] B. Reicke, 'Natürliche Theologie bei Paulus', *SEÅ* 22–3 (1957–8), 154–67. Reicke's exposition follows that of Barth himself, and, earlier, that of Augustine.

says, is unmistakable in Romans 1[18 ff.]. In a certain sense, therefore (p. 159), Paul grants the *possibility* of a natural theology. The truth is accessible to humanity. But one cannot go on to say that Paul accepts the *actuality* of a natural theology. All this potential knowledge is turned into lies, idolatry, insults against God, who replies by letting loose his wrath from heaven. It is thus (p. 165) only through the gospel that a certain 'point of contact' (*Anknüpfungspunkt*) is created. This fits with the words about the 'works of the law' which the Gentiles may do without having the law. According to Reicke, these works of the law which are done in the hearts of Gentiles correspond to the work which according to Paul took place in the heart of Jews, in the missionary situation of their conversion to Christian faith. In other words, Paul is not referring to good works which Gentiles do in their natural, pagan state, but to an operation through which they may become Christians, just as Jews may.

I must say that I find this an unconvincing intrusion of a position of Barthian type on a text that looks very different. As Christian Link, one of the most profound recent writers on these matters and himself very much in the Barthian tradition, rightly remarks,[8] Reicke's explanation is an easy way of getting rid of the problems of natural theology by intruding the modern contrast of reason and revelation into the Pauline text. From the beginning Reicke imposes a Barthian dogmatic framework when he says: 'As in the Bible in general (*überhaupt*), so in Paul one finds the conception that the knowledge of God rests upon a revelation of God.'[9] But it is by no means clear that this fits for the Old Testament, where there is no general indication that there is no knowledge of God except through a revelation of God; and if the situation in the Old Testament is different from what Reicke claims, then it is all the more likely that Paul's opinion was different too. And, in detail, I find it quite implausible that when Gentiles 'do the work of the law', with their conscience and thoughts acting upon them, this refers to the process of their becoming Christians. I mention it in order to illustrate how a position of Barthian type has been maintained, rather than because it has high intrinsic merits.

Much the most powerful exposition among the commentaries I have consulted comes from Käsemann.[10] Käsemann fully recognizes

[8] C. Link, *Die Welt als Gleichnis* (Munich: Kaiser, 1976), 87 and note.
[9] Reicke, 'Natürliche Theologie bei Paulus', 155.
[10] See his Rom. commentary, *An die Römer* (4th edn., Tübingen: Mohr, 1980), esp. 32 ff. on Rom. 1[18 ff.], 57–64 on Rom. 2[12 ff.].

the many similarities between our New Testament passages and Hellenistic sources, especially Jewish sources in Greek. But he distinguishes Paul from Acts, in which, he thinks, there is certainly natural theology.[11] For Paul it is significant just what he accepts, and the extreme restrictiveness he exercises in what he accepts. Thus in the genuine Pauline letters creation is not an 'independent doctrinal theme' (*kein selbständiges Lehrstück*), and thus Paul has no theoretical or isolated interest in the beginnings of the world. Rather, his view is eschatological. Reality before the Fall cannot be reconstructed, not even as something to think of as an ideal state for life as it is. Even of God Paul speaks only in his relation to humanity and the world after the Fall: he says nothing about his attributes and his essence, or about the διοίκησις or τάξις of the cosmos as a basis on which to found the knowledge of God. Metaphysical questions do not interest him. The rhetoric of Romans 1 is one of accusation and curse (pp. 37 f.)—he does not enlighten, prove, defend, or 'establish contact' (*anknüpft*—again an allusion to the term of Brunner's argument against Barth). On the contrary he accuses, he reduces the Greek motifs to the extreme, characterizes God's deity as a power that confronts, and sees human guilt not in ignorance but in revolt against the Lord who is known. Thus the tendency observed in Philo is much more strongly 'radicalized' in Paul. 'Radicalization' is extremely prominent as a value marker in Käsemann's interpretation, indeed one may say that 'radicality' is the ultimate value for him, the thing he most wants and needs to find in Paul.[12]

Something similar is to be found in his handling of the passage about 'a law to themselves' in ch. 2 (his pp. 57 ff.). It is not a matter of placing humanity within a scheme of order, but it is a matter of the 'crisis of existence' (p. 59).

Even with full respect to Käsemann's arguments, however, we may question whether they really demonstrate the absence of some kind of natural theology from Romans. Even if creation is not an

---

[11] Käsemann, *Römer*, 36, is clear that one may and must speak of natural theology in Wisd. 13[5], in Aristeas 132, and in Acts 14[15 ff.], 17[22 ff.], but that things are not so simple in Paul himself: 'Ohne jeden Zweifel darf und muss man hier von natürlicher Theologie sprechen. So einfach liegen die Dinge dagegen bei Pls nicht.' For discussion cf. Link, *Die Welt als Gleichnis*, 86 f.

[12] Though Käsemann has much respect for Barth and is much influenced by his thought, in respect of natural theology his approach seems more akin to Bultmann's: see R. Bultmann, 'The Problem of "Natural Theology"', in his *Faith and Understanding*, ed. R. W. Funk (New York: Harper & Row, 1969), 313–31.

'independent theme' in the other genuine letters, this does not entirely prove that it is not a theme here: after all, the argument of Romans 1–2 in general does not find a duplicate elsewhere in the genuine letters. The fact that the argument is one of accusation rather than of abstract discussion does not show that natural theology could not have taken part in such an argument. Paul may not have had a 'theoretical' interest in the beginnings of the world, and may not have been interested in its διοίκησις or τάξις, but it is very likely all the same that the profound and systematic creation story of Genesis was an important source for his thought. And, even if his view is an eschatological one, that does not exclude a close linkage with creation; on the contrary, the two opposite ends of the time spectrum are commonly closely linked. I shall later come back to Käsemann's view and try to suggest an explanation for the difficulties he sees.

Another recent exposition of Romans which offers a further possibility is that of W. Schmithals. In his view (his p. 29), the document which we call the Letter to the Romans is a combination of two quite different writings, Romans A and Romans B. The sections which we have been studying, from the point of view of our discussion of natural theology, lie within Romans A (which consists of $1^1$–$4^{25}$, $5^{12}$–$11^{36}$ and $15^{8-13}$). The first part of this document, the first two chapters of the present book, builds heavily in his judgement upon traditional synagogue polemic against the Gentiles. But—and this is the essential point—Paul is here quoting or rehearsing a customary Jewish argument *in order to use it against the synagogue.* In other words, what he is saying is not his own opinion, but is the argument of others, which he is using against these others. He is thus (p. 92) not at all unfolding any natural theology of the law: 'his interest lies only in showing, with the help of synagogal arguments, that even the possession of the Torah does not provide the Jews with a distinctiveness over against the Gentiles (*nicht vor den Heiden auszeichnet*).' In $1^{18}$–$3^{20}$ Paul's 'representations move in pure synagogue language ... thus he is not putting forward his own arguments, he is reproducing synagogue teaching' (p. 72). To sum up, the first part of Romans A (pp. 72 f.) does not unfold genuine Pauline theology, but puts synagogal idea material into a Pauline field of view (*Optik*) and places it in the service of the apostle's missionary strategy. Thus, Schmithals writes with emphasis marked, a systematic representation of Pauline theology can leave out of consideration the individual lines of argument of $1^{18}$–$3^{20}$, and 'this first part of the doctrinal document sent to Rome thus contains no content of Christian preaching'.

Thus, if I understand him rightly, Schmithals is probably quite ready to accept that there is natural theology in these parts of Romans, and that this represents an acceptance of Stoic teaching on the part of the relevant currents of the synagogue, and its use on behalf of Judaism as against the Gentiles. But its presence in the Letter, our letter, to the Romans does not mean that it was seriously meant as the view of St Paul. Indeed, we may perhaps say, though he does not exactly put it in this way, the presence of natural theology in the words of Romans makes it highly probable that this part, though written by Paul, was not intended to be taken seriously. The effects of this argument—to most of us a rather novel and paradoxical one—cannot be considered further here; for the present it helps to demonstrate the variety of implications that can follow from different exegetical handlings of the New Testament texts.[13]

Before we go further, we may make some general assessments of the exegetical positions described. What I, speaking personally, most gain from this sort of discussion is a depressing feeling of the weakness of the Bible as a guide in fundamental theological questions. On the whole, people are far more heavily influenced by the strong dogmatic convictions which they have inherited or to which they adhere, and only with the greatest difficulty can they find it in themselves to admit that the Bible actually points in a direction different from these convictions. We have noted this in the more specifically Barthian approaches.

We began by acknowledging that it is at least possible to expound the early chapters of Romans in a style more akin to the Barthian approach, and this is what we have seen in highly reputable exegetes like Barrett and still more in Cranfield. But one cannot avoid the impression that the Barthian sort of interpretation, when handling

[13] Cf. W. Schmithals, *Der Römerbrief* (Gütersloh: Gerd Mohn, 1988), 77, where he rightly emphasizes Wisdom of Solomon as the closest parallel, mentions in small print Acts and other works, but claims that the Jew in any case did not depend on this natural revelation, since he did not need to conclude from the creation that God existed, because the Torah provided all this knowledge, cf. his p. 98 on Rom. $2^{20}$. Cf. also the somewhat similar argumentation of E. P. Sanders, *Paul, the Law, and the Jewish People* (Philadelphia: Fortress, 1983), 123 ff., and the comment of K. Syreeni, 'Matthew, Luke and the Law', in T. Veijola, *The Law in the Bible and in Its Environment* (Publications of the Finnish Exegetical Society 51; Helsinki: Finnish Exegetical Society, 1990), 145 n. 43.

the passages that might support natural theology, turned over to that same sort of narrow critical exegesis that was exactly the kind most attacked by Barth in the handling of any other element of scripture. In general and for the most part, Barthian exegesis has been theologically expansive: it was open to the wide and profound theological problems and possibilities, of which it was possible to accuse academic and critical exegesis of having failed to grasp the potentialities. But, in anything touching natural theology, Barth and his followers espoused the narrowest and most negative, suspicious, and critical approach. The kind of exegesis which will refuse any openness to natural theology in Romans 1–2 is the kind of negative exegesis which will also deny a doctrine of incarnation in John or a doctrine of the Trinity in Paul.[14]

But something similar can probably be said about other lines of exegetical discussion. It is extremely difficult for scholars to maintain an open mind about the question of natural theology in scripture, most of all in the Letter to the Romans. In general we may say: at least within Protestantism, scholars do not want to find it or to have to handle it. The twentieth-century prejudice is against natural theology, and therefore against any willingness to admit evidence for it within the Bible.[15] For the task cannot be carried out in a simple proof-text fashion, as if a few words in Acts or in Romans would clearly and incontrovertibly demonstrate the status of natural theology. What is required is not just a few words, or the exegesis of a few words, but a wide vision and perspective within which the status of the question might be seen. Exegesis alone will not alter people's minds, until they perceive an alternative total perspective through which they can see not only the biblical material but also an explanation of how it affects a wide range of personal stands and theological problems. Our purpose here, accordingly, is not to 'prove' or to 'disprove' the validity of natural theology through direct exegesis of the classic scriptural evidences on the

---

[14] I return to expand this comment in Ch. 6 below.

[15] Thus Link, *Die Welt als Gleichnis*, 315, quotes the opinion of Schillebeeckx: 'the crisis today of Protestant and Catholic theology seems to me, seen from a particular angle of view, to be the ultimate consequence of the denial of every form of "natural theology", a result of the breach between human experience and Christian faith. Anyone who starts out from the fact of this breach must sooner or later come to perceive that Christian faith is a useless superstructure over human reality.' What is striking is not so much this opinion in itself, but Link's description of it as 'a diagnosis perhaps astonishing for the Protestant reader'.

matter, but, proceeding from these evidences, to explore the wider field within which the questions stand.

Our next step is to make some comparison between the Areopagus speech, along with the other materials in Acts, and these aspects of Romans. Such a comparison may help us to decide how far the Areopagus speech as reported is historical, and such a decision, if it can be made, may be very important. But the reaching of such a historical decision is not our primary aim in this enquiry. More important is to consider the presence of elements that may be common, that may be partly represented in one of these sources or in the other, or that may indicate common sources from which both in varying modes may have drawn.

The passages seem strikingly complementary: they have a certain common theme, but the modes in which they touch upon it are often different. Acts has, at least on the margin, the mention of Stoic philosophers: Romans says nothing about philosophers anywhere, but has the strikingly Stoic term συνείδησις, and also uses φύσις twice in related connections.[16] To this we may add Paul's use of the adjective φυσικός in respect of sexual relations, and this we have to discuss at somewhat greater length. His terminology implies that for him, in this connection, 'nature' is a theological criterion. Homosexual relations are viewed as a climactic manifestation of evil, but the reason given is not because they are forbidden by God or because they are disapproved in the Old Testament (though these could easily have been shown, cf. Lev. 18[22], 20[13]). Paul doubtless thought both these reasons to be valid and sufficient,[17] but they were not the reason he gave: the reason he actually gave was that these relations are against 'nature'. This terminology was by no means new. Plato himself has it in *Laws*, 636, where the Athenian speaker speaks of heterosexual relations as κατὰ φύσιν, 'according to

---

[16] Note that φύσις occurs thrice in Wisd. and frequently in 3-4 Macc.

[17] It seems necessary to say this, if only to notice and to counter the suggestions of John Boswell, *Christianity, Social Tolerance, and Homosexuality* (Chicago: University of Chicago Press, 1980), who thinks, for example, that St Paul 'never suggested that there was any historical or legal reason to oppose homosexual behaviour: if he did object to it, it was purely on the basis of functional, contemporary moral standards' (p. 106)—especially since his work includes some discussion of Paul's use of 'nature' in our passage. Interesting as his work is in its gathering of material from the later history, in its handling of biblical texts and above all in its arguments from specific biblical words I can only say that I find it to be staggering in the degree of its misjudgement.

nature'.[18] The 'natural' use is approved, that which is παρὰ φύσιν, 'against nature', is seen as obviously wrong.

Of course, this use of the 'natural' as a moral guide leaves open the question of what is natural and what is not. An amusing and ironic comment comes from 4 Maccabees 5[8], where Antiochus is depicted as representing to Eleazar that he would be a better Jew if he ate swine's flesh, since it was 'nature' that had graciously given (τῆς φύσεως κεχαρισμένης) the excellent practice of eating pork. The reply in 5[25] is: 'believing the law to be established by God, we know that the creator of the world feels with us according to nature (κατὰ φύσιν), and that what he commanded us to eat was what would be appropriate to our souls'. The argument on both sides assumes that what is 'natural' will be right and in accord with the will of God.

Thus for Josephus, in this same connection, what is 'natural' is the same as what is recognized by the Jewish law. The sentence should be quoted in full:

μῖξιν μόνην οἶδεν ὁ νόμος τὴν κατὰ φύσιν τὴν πρὸς γυναῖκα καὶ ταύτην εἰ μέλλοι τέκνων ἕνεκα γίνεσθαι. τὴν δὲ πρὸς ἄρρενας ἀρρένων ἐστύγηκε, καὶ θάνατος τοὐπιτίμιον εἴ τις ἐπιχειρήσειεν. (*Contra Apion.*, ii. 199; cf. Lev. 18[22], 20[13])

The law recognizes only one kind of sexual intercourse, the natural one, that [of a man] with a woman, and this [only] if it is to take place for the sake of having children. It abominates intercourse of men with men, and death is the punishment if anyone attempts it.

The similarity of words and ideas with Paul is obvious.[19]

To sum up, therefore, the authority of 'nature' in Romans is not easily to be overlooked. For many Jews, no doubt, 'nature' and the will of God could scarcely be distinguished. Philo, wishing to show that providence must follow from the fact of creation, calls it a 'law of nature' that that which makes should take care of that which has

---

[18] Cf. also 836 ff., and Aristotle, *Nic. Eth.* 1148[b]15–1149[a]20. What is involved in 'nature' in these cases, however, is a subtle matter, on which see K. J. Dover, *Greek Homosexuality* (London: Duckworth, 1978), esp. 60, 67, 154, 165 ff. Dover says (p. 60) that, if the meaning is that homosexuality as such is unnatural, that is 'a standpoint ... expounded only in one strand of the Socratic-Platonic philosophical tradition'. In any case, however, the terminology of 'natural' and 'unnatural' is there. For a more recent discussion on Plato and Aristotle see A. W. Price, *Love and Friendship in Plato and Aristotle* (Oxford: Clarendon Press, 1989), 223 ff.

[19] Boswell, *Christianity, Social Tolerance, and Homosexuality*, though he mentions Josephus elsewhere (p. 346), appears not to take this passage into account in his discussion of Paul.

been made: νόμος γὰρ φύσεως ἐπιμελεῖσθαι τὸ πεποιηκὸς τοῦ γεγονότος.[20] 'Law' and 'nature' could belong closely together.

Again, returning to our comparison of Romans and the Areopagus speech, both passages have the theme of the creator God, but in Acts this is developed towards the theme that such a God does not live in temples and needs nothing from humanity, while in Romans it is developed towards the theme that humans should have known God through the works which he had made but instead went on to replace him with the images of mortals or of beasts and reptiles. It is Romans that makes explicit the idea 'that which is knowable of God', but Acts that makes it vivid with the mention of the altar to the 'unknown' God and the relative 'ignorance' of the Athenians who worship him. It is Romans that continues the subject into an emphasis on the appalling morality that follows from failure to acknowledge the true God; and for Romans this immorality seems to be a punishment rather than an accompaniment, 'nicht Schuld sondern Strafe' as Käsemann puts it.[21] Acts on the other hand is quite easy about Gentile morality, treats it as a matter of ignorance, and derives no shocking effects from past idolatry. It makes it clear that past effects of idolatry will be overlooked so long as repentance now follows. Acts emphasizes the theme of the temple, saying that God does not live in any such building, while Romans leaves that aspect aside. If Romans (perhaps) admits that all persons have access to some knowledge of God and have some resource within them that can do the work of the law, Acts touches on this theme in a more purposeful way, not so much making express that they have these resources, but emphasizing that God determined and guided the situation of the nations with this possibility in view. It is only Acts that here appeals to the verses of a Greek poet and only it that builds into its argument the near-pantheistic thought that we all alike live and move in God and are his offspring. Romans may admit aspects of knowledge of God, and of morality, as accessible among the Gentiles, but does nothing to associate these, even distantly, with forms of their *religion*; Acts on the other hand takes its starting-point in Athenian religiosity. Romans is more predicated on the difference between Jew and Gentile, the Areopagus speech distinctly more universal in its view. Both alike, on the other hand, associate the entire subject with the theme of divine judgement.

And, just to give my own preliminary opinion, it seems to me that

[20] Philo, *Praem.* 42.    [21] *Römer*, 34

this complementary situation of the two passages suggests that a common tradition lies behind them both. They have been developed in different ways but retain a strong family resemblance.[22] And, this being so, it seems to me clear that, natural theology being certain in Acts, natural theology is probable in Romans also. For, though Romans portrays the human situation in darker terms than Acts, Romans nevertheless comes closer to the essential terms of natural theology than Acts does, with its mention on the one hand of how the knowable element of God was known to all, and on the other hand its use of terms like φύσις, 'nature'. There remains however the problem, most sharply expressed by Schmithals, that even if these passages are full of natural theology this may not have been seriously meant by Paul and not be part of his own actual theology. If we are to make it more probable that it does belong to his actual theology, therefore, we have to suggest a total scenario under which this would fit into the argument of the letter and also into the intellectual background.

On the one hand, Romans 1–2 may contain, or seem to contain, elements that are absent from the other genuine Pauline letters. On the other, they seem to contain elements which cannot easily be explained as insights of Christianity at all: in particular, the idea that all moral failings, from gossiping, slander, and disobedience to parents at one end to deceit, strife, and murder at the other end, can be accounted for as a consequence of earlier idolatry. What is there in the Christian message that justifies this strange causative linkage? And no more evident is it why homosexual relations, however one should judge them, should be explained as the result of idolatry too. What is the point of this strange scheme? What is there in the gospel that provides a source, a support, or a justification for it? And, if it comes from St Paul, why is it not repeated in his other genuine writings?

Well, I think one would have to judge with Schmithals that this material is very largely taken over from Jewish polemics or missionary preaching toward the Gentiles. But, if so, why might Paul have used it here? I think one might be able to explain it as follows: the plan of Romans, in this respect, is to compare the status of Jews and Gentiles in relation to God's justice. Both, according to

---

[22] I borrow this term, essential in biblical theology, from John Barton's discussion of the principles of that subject in his article 'Old Testament Theology', in John Rogerson (ed.), *Beginning Old Testament Study* (London: SPCK, 1983), esp. 94 f.

Paul, are under the wrath of God for their failings. Why so? For the Jews, it is easy enough to explain: they had the Law of Moses, but did not obey it. But what about the Gentiles? This was more complicated. They had known that which was knowable of God but failed to honour him accordingly and devoted the veneration proper to him to images of humans or, worse, of animals. God had responded to this by giving them up to impurities, lusts, unnatural ways of living, and finally all sorts of general immoralities. All this was indeed traditional Jewish Hellenistic polemic against the Gentile ways of life. But it provided a necessary balance in the argument about the place of Jews and the place of Gentiles in relation to Christian faith. And, just as Jews, who had the law, had disobeyed the law, so Gentiles, who did not have it, might in effect have obeyed it—a point which not only effected the necessary rhetorical balance but also provided a, somewhat needed, recognition of the fact that Gentile life, even where idols were present, was not wholly and purely dominated by the long list of evils which Paul has provided. And, because this was the argumentative line, one can see why an element of natural theology was not only rhetorically but also logically necessary: the Gentiles were at fault because the realities of God had indeed been revealed to them through his works of creation, and, put in the opposite way, that means that the structures and elements of the created world form in themselves a testimony from which the reality of the creator God could have been and should have been inferred. Not only so, but it *was* inferred: they *did know* God, but did not honour him as God. This is why they are inexcusable. All this, in my opinion, forms a chain of reasoning along which it is understandable that a Christian Paul might have deployed these arguments. But indeed, as I shall argue and emphasize, they are Jewish, and Jewish Hellenistic, arguments.

At this point it will be appropriate to mention the important study of Bertil Gärtner, *The Areopagus Speech and Natural Revelation* (1955),[23] which is one of the few full-length exegetical studies in this century to consider the subject seriously as a problem. In spite of the highly controversial character of natural theology or natural revelation at the time of his writing, Gärtner curiously did rather little in his book to relate his study to that general question or to derive general exegetical implications from his results. On the whole, however, the main trend of his study, it seems, was to deprecate the

[23] Uppsala: Gleerup, 1955.

idea that the Paul of the speech in Acts was simply dependent on Greek ideas, especially on Stoic ideas, and to lay greater emphasis on the degree to which he was informed and inspired by Hebrew and Jewish ideas. And it is my purpose in a sense to follow somewhat further along the same line. For the reader may well be asking why the present writer, who is supposedly an Old Testament scholar, should be writing at such length about the New Testament. If I have a distinctive contribution to make, it is to suggest that Hebrew and Jewish ideas were a highly formative source which did much to form the background of natural theology. As will be obvious to anyone who knows the course of studies during this century, this, if justified, is a reversal of the trend which dominated much biblical theology and which represented Hebrew or Jewish material as intrinsically revelational and essentially antithetical to Greek thought, from which latter, it was thought, the seeds of natural theology and of more or less all theological errors had come.

My argument will therefore embrace two lines of thought which at first sight might appear to be contrary to each other. In the first place I shall argue that the real source from which Christian natural theology sprang is Hebraic. Since its basis is Hebraic, much of the criticism that has been directed against it on the grounds of compromise with the Hellenic spirit is improper. But, on the other hand, I also think, though I shall not attempt to prove it in detail, that much of the New Testament, and especially of the letters, and most of all of the Pauline letters, is much more Greek in its terms, its conceptuality, and its thinking than main trends of modern biblical theology have tended to allow. My own experience makes this to me undeniable. If one has spent most of one's life, as I have, working on Hebrew and other Semitic-language texts, and then returns after some absence to a closer study of the New Testament, the impression of the essentially Greek character of the latter is overwhelming, and especially so in St Paul, much less so in some other areas like the teaching of Jesus as seen in the Synoptic Gospels. The attempt, at one time popular and influential, to argue that, though the words might be Greek, the thought processes were fundamentally Hebraic, was a conspicuous failure. I quote the recent judgement of Link, following Bornkamm:

It cannot be disputed that Paul received the thoughts of the Greek tradition, not only eclectically and through a mere borrowing of their vocabulary, but thoroughly in their inner coherence (*Zusammenhang*) and in their framework of reality. He thus positively accepts an internally cohering thought-framework of Gentile natural theology.[24]

If we take the words of Romans 1[19 f.], which are perhaps the prime terms of our discussion, not only the terminology but the thought-framework of the whole thing is unmistakably Hellenic. If it is also Jewish, which it is, this only goes to show that the opposition between Greek and Hebraic is not significant for our subject. Jewish thinkers who wrote in Greek expressed their Jewish thoughts not only in Greek words but in the Greek thought-forms that were so very customary to them.

If, therefore, our researches were to make it seem that Paul, or other NT authority, was substantially dependent on categories of Greek popular philosophy for his thoughts and arguments, we would not be troubled by this; it would count simply as a reality of the situation. For, by arguing that Paul, or any other NT writer, is essentially Hebraic or Jewish in spirit and heritage, we are not thereby making it more clear that he is opposed to natural theology; on the contrary, we are making it more probable that he is sympathetic to it.

---

[24] Link, *Die Welt als Gleichnis*, 89, quoting G. Bornkamm, 'Gesetz und Natur: Röm 2, 14–16', in *Studien zu Antike und Urchristentum*, ii (Munich: Kaiser, 1959), 111, 117.

# 4

# Natural Theology in the Jewish Tradition

We left it a little uncertain just where St Paul stood in relation to the possibilities of natural theology. In order to make further progress we have to look at Jewish traditions that are akin to natural theology. The study of these traditions may make it easier to decide exactly where Paul himself stood; and, even if it does not decide that question, the study of these traditions will be important in its own right. But, because we have started through Paul, we will give pride of place to one particular document, the Wisdom of Solomon; for it shows an unusually high similarity to aspects of Paul's language and thought.

Now we do not know whether Paul had actually read the Wisdom of Solomon, or whether it counted for him as an authoritative scripture. Since he came so close to its diction at a number of points, the probability is that that he knew the book, and, if he knew the book, that it did count for him as an authoritative religious text. If not, it does not matter much for our immediate purpose, because it means only that Paul belonged, though independently, to a very similar tradition of thought. That this was so can be demonstrated from another aspect shared by Wisdom and by Paul, an aspect which by common consent should belong very definitely to revealed theology: namely the understanding of the first man, Adam, in relation to death and immortality. To this therefore we have to devote some attention.

Within the New Testament the typology of Adam and Christ, extremely familiar to all of us, is actually unique to Paul—or, if we are strict, to Paul and the deutero-Pauline 1 Timothy. It is absent from the teaching of Jesus, from the Synoptic Gospels generally, from the Johannine literature, from Hebrews and Peter, from everything. None of them even mentions Adam except incidentally.[1] It is Pauline property.[2]

Moreover, when we go back to the Old Testament, we find two similarly significant facts. Firstly, after the story of Adam and Eve is first narrated in Genesis, nowhere in the books of the Hebrew canon does anyone go back to that incident in order to use it as an explanation for the origin of sin, evil, and death. It just does not happen. The phrase of Isaiah 43[27], 'your first father sinned', refers to Jacob or some other pioneer of the people of Israel. The Hebrew Bible is certainly deeply conscious of the actuality and pervasiveness of sin and evil. But nowhere in all the books of the Hebrew canon is the existence or the profundity of evil accounted for on the grounds that Adam's disobedience originated it or made it inevitable. It is not surprising, therefore, that Judaism, as we know it,[3] has no doctrine corresponding to the Christian traditions of 'original sin', no idea that sin and evil exist as a heritage passed on from the first human beings.

Indeed, secondly, it is not only that the story of Adam and Eve was *not so used* within the Hebrew Bible, but also in itself that story was not primarily a story of a catastrophic 'Fall of Man' at all. It was a story which had a different style and purport altogether, and the 'origin of sin' was only marginal to it. I will not go into this further here, except to say what in my opinion is the central theme of that story: it is a story of how the first humans through a disobedience, possibly a minor one, came close to two elements of divine status, firstly the knowledge of good and evil, which they

[1] Luke 3[38] has Adam in the genealogy; and Jude 14 mentions that Enoch is the seventh after Adam. These are what I count as 'incidental', i.e. not directly related to the typological relationship of Adam and Christ.

[2] Incidentally, C. E. Raven, *Natural Religion and Christian Theology* (2 vols., Cambridge: Cambridge University Press, 1953), i. 33 ff., deploys the complementary argument that even in Paul the 'Fall' of Adam is 'by no means a fundamental concept'. It is introduced, he says, only in Rom. 5[12ff.] and 1 Cor. 15[21f.,45ff.]; 1 Tim. 2[13f.], he says, 'is probably not Pauline and in any case refers to the primary guilt of Eve rather than to the abiding effects of the Fall'. In particular, he points out, relevantly to our theme, 'in his great indictment both of the pagan and of the Jewish world in Romans 1–3, he [Paul] never suggests that they, like all mankind, are corrupted by Adam's sin'.

[3] I say 'as we know it' because traditions more like the Christian idea of almost universal inherited sin and guilt are to be found in the Judaism of the intertestamental period. The fact remains that the biblical heritage could be utilized and interpreted in the main trends of later Judaism without anything close to 'original sin' being recognized.

gained, and secondly eternal life, from which they were now excluded.[4]

This is of central importance for the whole subject of natural theology.[5] The 'Fall', so-called, was appealed to again and again by Barth in his angry arguments against Brunner: natural theology might have worked all right, if only Adam had not sinned.[6] Barth repeats it frequently, wheeling out from time to time that well-worn catch-phrase *si integer stetisset Adam*.[7] We cannot attempt to follow out the details of this here: suffice it to say that, if the Genesis text does not support the idea of a cataclysmic and catastrophic 'Fall', then the appeal to that story ceases to be useful as a resource for argument against natural theology.[8]

Even more essential, however, was one detail, namely the place of *death* in that same story. Traditional Christianity believed, following Paul, that Eve and Adam by their sin brought death into the world. This implies, or appears to imply, that if there had been no sin there would have been no death. But in Genesis itself, though there are possible variations in the interpretation, something like the reverse appears to be intended. The problem created, and created in particular for God himself, by the disobedience of the man and

---

[4] What is here argued is stated in fuller form in my Read-Tuckwell Lectures from Bristol University, soon to be published as *The Garden of Eden and the Hope of Immortality*.

[5] For a recent discussion, see C. Link, *Die Welt als Gleichnis* (Munich: Kaiser, 1976), 122 ff.

[6] According to the Wittenberg theologian Johann Deutschmann, not only was Adam a theologian but he was an orthodox Lutheran, and his teaching was in full accord with the Augsburg Confession and the Formula of Concord. Before the Fall he may have worked by natural theology, but after the Fall natural theology, though it might have truth in it, no longer worked for blessedness or salvation. See H. J. Birkner, 'Natürliche Theologie und Offenbarungstheologie', *NZST* 3 (1961), 282.

[7] Brunner had left himself defenceless at this point, for he emphasized the 'Fall' in traditional terms, just as much as Barth did. See his hostile correspondence with Ludwig Köhler in 1926, in which he contemptuously sweeps aside the very justified argument of that Old Testament scholar to the effect that the story of Adam and Eve was no story of a catastrophic 'Fall of Man'. The dialectical theology was an ingenious mixture of modern and primitive ideas. Its use of the idea of the Fall belonged to the latter: it was really not even Paul's idea, it was the idea of traditional, essentially of Reformational, Christianity. For the Köhler–Brunner correspondence see *KBRS* 41 (1926), esp. 105f., 121 (Köhler), 113f., 141f. (Brunner). I am deeply indebted to my friend Dr Robert Hanhart of Göttingen for his help in enabling me to gain access to this interesting material.

[8] For a brief discussion, see my article 'The Authority of Scripture: Genesis and the Origin of Evil in Jewish and Christian Tradition', in *Christian Authority* (Henry Chadwick FS; Oxford: Clarendon Press, 1988), 59–75.

woman is that, as a consequence of what they have done, they may come to *live for ever*! This is the reason, and the only reason, why the human pair are expelled from the Garden of Eden. The natural cultural assumption, supported by a mass of evidence in the Hebrew Bible, is that the humans were mortal from the beginning. They would have died, and death as an end to life was perfectly natural, proper, and acceptable, provided that the circumstances were good—in good old age, surrounded by children and later offspring, just as Job died, rightly and well, after his sufferings were over. In Genesis itself, then, there is no reason to understand that the point is that the first human disobedience brought death into the world. The text does not say that and, except through extremes of exegetical ingenuity, it seems to say something quite different.

But all these things, which are lacking in the Genesis text itself, and which *are* found in Paul and are essential to his argument, are found first in the Wisdom of Solomon and found there together.

Thus Wisdom 2[23] has:

> For God created man with incorruption (ἐπ' ἀφθαρσίᾳ),[9]
> and made him in the image of his own eternity,[10]
> but through the devil's envy death entered the world,
> and those who belong to his party (μερίς) experience it.

For the main thought of the passage it makes little difference whether man was created *with* immortality (as if this was a built-in constitutional difference) or *for* immortality (which would have to be gained or merited). Death was, originally, not part of the human scene; only after the devil's intervention did it emerge as a prospect.

---

[9] There are some detailed questions of text and language here. The first is whether the meaning is 'with incorruption', i.e. created with intrinsic immortality, or 'for incorruption', i.e. with the intention or prospect of immortality to be gained or merited. That ἐπί in Wisd. means 'in' or 'with', but not the final sense 'for', is argued by J. M. Reese, *Hellenistic Influence on the Book of Wisdom and Its Consequences* (Analecta Biblica 41, Rome: Biblical Institute Press, 1970), 66 and note. Dr Peter Hayman of Edinburgh has urged the understanding 'for immortality' (to be gained in the future), but seems to me to go too far in saying that this is 'expressly stated'. In view of the different possible shades of meaning of ἐπί, this cannot be claimed, and the contrary is indicated by the passage from Enoch cited here below and kindly mentioned to me by Dr Hayman himself.

[10] Here there is a variation of text. I follow Rahlfs, Fichtner, and others in reading ἀϊδιότητος, 'everlastingness', which gives a good parallelism. Dr Hayman prefers the ἰδιότητος of the major uncials BSA, which gives the sense 'peculiar character'.

Afterwards, according to the thought of Wisdom, humans might gain immortality through the possession of wisdom; but this was after death had entered in. In either case death was not originally part of human destiny. The translation 'in' or 'with' incorruption therefore seems to be right. REB translates well with its: 'God created man imperishable, and made him the image of his own eternal self.'

The idea that possession of immortality is a common point between God and humanity is supported by comparison with 1 Enoch 69[11], 'for men were created exactly like the angels, to the intent that they should continue pure and righteous, and death, which destroys everything, could not have taken hold of them, but through this their knowledge they are perishing'. In any case no substantial difference is made: for, if death is not part of the scene for the original humans, it makes little difference whether they 'were' immortal from the beginning or 'were to be' immortal: in either case they were not going to die. Moreover, the words 'in the image of his own eternity' imply that humanity, being made in the image of God, had from the beginning a share in God's own immortality. Again, Wisdom 1[13] explicitly states that 'God did not create death'—and formally speaking this is true. The Old Testament speaks of God as the living God and the giver of life, and the creation stories, seen from some points of view, do not tell of his creating death. Elsewhere, however, we do hear that God brings death just as he gives life, so for instance in Hannah's song, 1 Samuel 2[6], 'the Lord kills and makes alive', similarly Psalm 104[29] 'when thou takest away their breath they die', corresponding to their revival or recreation in the next verse. Thus God, as the giver of life, is not to be construed as one who gave life without limit, as if no person, animal, or insect would ever perish. Such a conclusion, however, Wisdom drew, at least for humans. It would naturally encourage the view that the humans had immortality, or at least the prospect of it, from the start. Anyway, they lost it, and death entered the world. Wisdom's understanding of Genesis is in this regard the same one that is basic to Paul; and like Paul's use of the passage, it works from a broad generalization and fails to pay attention to the numerous details in Genesis which point very clearly in a different direction.

We shall not pursue further, however, the matter of Adam, Eve, and the origin of sin and entry of death into the world. What has been said is sufficient to suggest a strong affinity or common tradition relating the thought of this document to St Paul.

The second theme that is prominent in Wisdom is the theme of *idolatry*. After Deutero-Isaiah, no Old Testament book devotes more space to idolatry than Wisdom, and if anything it exceeds the great exilic prophet in its concern for the question. The three chapters 13–15 form a solid and continuous polemic against this evil practice. The emphasis the author lays upon it stands out by contrast with the other books of the Wisdom tradition. The original Proverbs seems to make no direct mention of idolatry, though all sorts of other sins are thoroughly castigated in the book. Nor does it trouble Qoheleth. More striking still, the Book of Ben Sira, more nearly contemporary with Wisdom, does not bother much about the subject either.[11] It is well known that Ben Sira represents a combination of wisdom traditions with legal traditions, yet, though the law contains severe condemnations of idolatry, Ben Sira does not take up this subject into his (quite lengthy) book. The book that particularly specializes in idolatry is Wisdom.

And Wisdom not only specializes in idolatry, but it handles it in specific ways which have great similarity to Paul's procedure in Romans. For instance, the view that idolatry is the source from which all moral evils flow is common to them both.

> The idea of idols was the beginning of fornication;
> the invention of them was the corruption of life (Wisd. 14[12])

and so, he goes on, later, after idolatry has taken over, a catalogue of moral perversions follows:

They perform ritual killing of children (τεκνοφόνους τελετάς) or secret ceremonies (κρύφια μυστήρια); or else they conduct the frenzied orgies of foreign rites (ἐξάλλων θεσμῶν). They no longer keep life or marriage pure, but a man lies in wait for another to murder him or torments him by seducing his wife. Everything is mixed up—blood and murder, theft and fraud, corruption, treachery, riot, perjury, disturbance of the good, forgetfulness of kindness, defilement of souls, changes affecting the processes of generation (γενέσεως ἐναλλαγή), disarray of marriages, adultery, debau-

---

[11] Sir. 30[18f.] uses the familiar *topos* of the powerlessness of an idol: what use to an idol is the offering of produce, since it cannot eat or smell?—but this is an analogy, to be applied to a person whose mouth is closed, so that it is useless to pour out good things on such a person. It is not directly an attack on idolatry: rather, it uses the characteristics of idolatry, taken to be familiar, to make a point about wisdom and foolishness.

chery. For the worship of unnameable idols is the beginning, the cause, and the end of every evil. (Wisd. 14$^{23\text{ff.}}$)

Paul in Romans has a similarly extensive catalogue. He does indeed have an important variation, for he speaks as if, in reaction against idolatry, God had actually *inflicted* moral corruption upon humanity. He had deliberately given them up to dishonourable lusts, in which homosexual relations are given prime attention. Apart from this aspect of divine abandonment, there is an analogy to the mode in which Wisdom, as just mentioned, begins its catalogue of evils with the ritual killing of children, something that likewise falls into the category of extreme and unnatural vice. And Paul, having started in this way, goes on to a wide-sweeping catalogue of moral faults, very much in the same style as Wisdom, including in the same bag such various faults as covetousness, murder, gossip, slander, and boastfulness. Persons whose background lies in idolatry, he maintains, although they know the decree of God to the effect that those who do these things deserve to die, not only do them but approve of anyone else who does them. Wisdom similarly works up to a ferocious climax: idolaters not only worship animals, but they worship the most revolting animals that exist. 'They worship the most disgusting animals; for, being compared in point of brutishness, they are worse than all the others' (Wisd. 15$^{18}$). They do not have a trace of attractiveness about them. Indeed, when God (in Genesis) approved and blessed his work (of creation), the author tells us, he did not include these particular beasts—not a bad idea, as it happens, indeed a very reasonable thought: can God really have declared 'good' absolutely *every* living creature? Anyway, it is these horrible creatures that are adored by the idolaters, and this powerful rhetorical climax closes the case against them. Both Wisdom and Paul argue in like manner.

One other point about idolatry that has far-reaching importance. To Jews, idolatry meant, primarily, having physical images supposed to represent the divine. It might include, by a natural extension, any indication of polytheism, such as the mention of the names of heathen gods. But apart from these necessary conditions it did not extend to mere *thoughts* about deity.[12] In much Christian theology the concept of idolatry was extended to the realm of *ideas*: people's ideas of God, if they do not come from divine revelation,

[12] See D. Novak, *The Image of the Non-Jew in Judaism* (New York: Mellen, 1983), ch. 4, 'The Law of Idolatry', 107–65.

are idolatrous, they are human manufacture of likenesses of the divine. Jews generally, perhaps always, did not make this extension of the concept. Philo is a prime example. To show that the Torah was wholly consonant with traditions of Greek philosophy was entirely proper and estimable, and was a most excellent confirmation of Judaism. Idolatry lay in the physical existence of the images, in the treatment of the finite as if it was divine. To share other people's ideas of God, or to use them in order to form one's own ideas of God, there was nothing necessarily idolatrous in that, unless some other characteristic that was repugnant to Jewish religion was added on. This is an additional reason why natural theology had a fertile soil: opposition to idolatry could easily co-exist with the acceptance of large doses of Greek ideas and thought-forms.

Returning to our main theme, Wisdom and Paul alike build their arguments against idolatry on the basis of *creation*. Idolatry is wrong because it puts the created in the place of the creator; it venerates that which God has made instead of venerating the God who made it.

Now this argument is hardly fully present within the canonical Hebrew books. There are several laws that forbid the use of idols in worship, some of them doubtless very ancient, but most of them fail to provide this particular connection. Thus the prohibition of graven images in the Decalogue of Exodus 20 identifies the images as images of things that are in heaven or in earth or in the waters, in terms that recall the creation story, and the connection with the creation story is also made explicit in the sabbath command; but there is no identification that specifies that the fault of idolatry lies in putting the created things in the place of the creator. And other old laws prohibiting the use of images probably made a bald and simple prohibition without giving any rationale at all. Even that great opponent of idolatry and protagonist of the idea of creation, Deutero-Isaiah, did not make explicit the connection between the two which in later documents becomes so clear. He indeed much emphasizes creation: the God of Israel is the creator God and thus vastly superior to the vain and futile non-existent 'gods' supposed to compete with him. And on the other hand he much satirizes the foolishness of idolatry, as already mentioned above. But the particular analysis of idolatry, as allowing the created being to enjoy the place of reverence due to the creator, seems not to be prominent with him. He satirizes more the *man-made* character of the idol: how foolish to venerate something that you have made yourself! God is not equal with other things, not comparable. But the particular emphasis on worshipping the *created thing* in place of the creator seems to be lacking or muted. The specific condemnation of the role of *animals* and animal figures in idolatrous and polytheistic worship is also lacking. And thus in Deutero-Isaiah, and in most of the Old Testament, there is lacking a theory that provides the steps from creation to idolatry, and from idolatry to moral perversion. In both Wisdom and Paul these steps are provided, and are extremely conspicuous. In Romans it is emphasized that:

Ever since the creation of the world his invisible nature, namely, his eternal power and deity, has been clearly perceived in the things that have been made. So they are without excuse; for although they knew God they did not honour him as God or give thanks to him, but they became futile in their thinking and their senseless minds were darkened. Claiming to be wise, they became fools, and exchanged the glory of the immortal God for images resembling mortal man or birds or animals or reptiles. (Rom. $1^{20\text{ff.}}$, RSV)

Paul then goes on to say how God had therefore delivered them to lusts and dishonourable impurities, as already mentioned. This is the first stage; the second is that they are given up to homosexuality; the third is that they are given up, yet again, to all sorts of ethical depravity, some of it more obviously appalling, some of it more of the character, we might say, of misdemeanours. But the whole account takes its departure from creation, and the false placing of the creatures in the position that belongs to the creator.

Wisdom has a different, but analogous, process to relate. Its writer likewise begins from creation:

For foolish by nature were all men, in whom there was ignorance of God, and who from the good things that are seen were unable to know him who exists. Nor while paying heed to his works did they recognize the craftsman; but they supposed that either fire or wind or swift air, or the circle of the stars, or turbulent water, or the luminaries of heaven, were the gods who preside over the world. If through delight in the beauty of these things they supposed them to be gods, let them know how much better than these is their Master. (Wisd. $13^{1\text{ff.}}$, RSV)

Wisdom is more inclined than Paul to give an explanation of what went wrong. It begins from the elements of the created world, fire, air, water, and the stars. If people could admire these, there was some sort of excuse, for they were really beautiful things created by God: the only trouble was that they ought, from seeing these things, to have perceived the creator who was behind them. Much much worse, he goes on, are those who give the name of 'gods' to idols which are just pieces of wood or stone made by human hands. It is preposterous, he points out, to pray about possessions, about marriage and children, to a lifeless piece of wood, to pray for health to something that has no strength, to pray for a successful journey to something that cannot walk a step itself, and so on ($13^{17ff.}$). Again, he says, warming to his argument, what sense is there in a man who goes to sea in a ship and yet prays for safety to a piece of wood more fragile than the ship he sails in, while neglecting the aid of the divine Helmsman whose providence alone can save from danger? This leads on, in very Pauline style, to the sentence already quoted ($14^{12}$): 'The idea of making idols was the beginning of fornication', and here the writer proceeds to offer some more original arguments. Idols got into the world through the vanity of human beings, that is, more or less by foolishness or plain error.

The course upon which he here embarks is that of euhemerism, that is, the explanation of gods as human persons or phenomena which by some error or inadvertence came to be elevated to divine status.[13] A father, consumed by grief at the death of a beloved child, made an image of the child, and came to honour a dead human being as if it was a god. Again, kings might live far away from their subjects, and they, wishing to please the ruler, might make a likeness; the multitude, attracted by the charm of the work, came to venerate as an object of worship one whom they had previously known to be a man. And so, whatever the exact explanation, we come back to the gross immoralities that are the result of these processes. To sum up this point, then, both Paul and Wisdom begin from creation and provide an account of the way in which people, failing to recognize the reality of the creator God, entered into idolatry and thence into the vilest immorality. Both say that God, the true God, was known to people, which is why their idolatry was disgraceful and inexcusable. Both hold it clear that God is knowable through the things that he has made (Wisd. $13^5$; Rom. $1^{20}$). The similarities are very great. And, just as Romans uses this argument in order to establish, among other things, that humanity is without excuse, so the matter

---

[13] For a parallel to this juxtaposition of euhemerism with natural theology, cf. Aristeas 134–7, and M. Hadas, *Aristeas to Philocrates* (*Letter of Aristeas*) (New York: Harper, 1951), 154 f.

of inexcusability is touched on by Wisdom 13[8]: if people mistook air, or fire, or stars, for divine beings, the blame for that might, at first sight, conceivably seem to be slight, because these were real and beautiful creations of the creator; but even so they cannot really be excused (πάλιν δ᾽ οὐδ᾽ αὐτοὶ συγγνωστοί), for, if they had so much perception, how did they not sooner come to know the Master of them all?

But, finally, for this aspect, the Wisdom of Solomon is, by more or less universal judgement, a vessel of natural theology.

> From the greatness and beauty of created things
> the Creator of them is by analogy perceived (ἀναλόγως
> θεωρεῖται).                                            (13[5])

Solomon, who has the gift of wisdom, is a sort of early scientist:[14] chronology, astronomy, zoology, botany, and psychology are all within his range, and he learned them all from Wisdom, who was also his guide in natural theology:

> For it is he [God] who gave me unerring knowledge of
>     what exists
> to know the structure of the world and activity of the
>     elements . . .
> the cycles of the year and the positions of the stars,
> the natures of animals and the tempers of wild beasts,
> the powers of spirits and the reasonings (διαλογισμοί)
>     of men,
> the varieties of plants and the virtues of roots.    (7[17ff.])

Wisdom is a breath of the power of God, a pure emanation of the glory of the Almighty . . . she is a reflection of eternal light, a spotless mirror of the working of God (7[25]). God's immortal spirit is in all things (12[1]). All this comes close to what has commonly been regarded as natural theology and, as I say, scholars show little hesitation in accepting this judgement about the book—a judgement, one must add, not unconnected with the fact that, for many of them, being Protestants, it is an uncanonical book. Naturally, in the Wisdom of Solomon we do not have pure or mere natural theology: it is an element mixed in with all sorts of thoughts that would traditionally count as revealed theology: the story of the Exodus (expanded and elaborated in 16 ff.), the doctrine of creation itself. But this is so of the Letter to the Romans also: no one supposes that

---

[14] We will return to this aspect later on: see below, Ch. 9.

it contains nothing but natural theology, the only question is whether an element of natural theology is mixed in with the rest. We may take the key point as this: if it is natural theology to think that God is knowable through one's perception of the world, and to think that this knowledge has been available or accessible to all, then Wisdom contains natural theology.

But if Wisdom contains natural theology, it becomes much more likely that Romans also contains it. The similarity of the type of argument seems so strong. The community of the chain of thought suggests a common tradition, and makes it more probable that Paul is using this common tradition. The emphasis on the place of idolatry, in relation to the accessible knowledge of the creator God on the one hand, and the descent of humanity into fearful immorality on the other, seems to be particularly strong evidence. The fact of this common tradition, if correct, may also go some way to overcome the objections of those who have been most unwilling to accept that there is any element of natural theology or similar thinking in Romans. For example, Käsemann's argument that for Paul creation was not an independent theme may be weakened when we perceive that creation *is* an essential element in the argument, by now traditional, against idolatry. Equally, his argument that Paul is not interested in the $\tau \acute{\alpha} \xi \iota \varsigma$ and $\delta \iota o \acute{\iota} \kappa \eta \sigma \iota \varsigma$ of the world may be made less convincing in view of the other relations with the book of Wisdom: and Paul's view that homosexual relations are contrary to $\phi \acute{\upsilon} \sigma \iota \varsigma$ (cf. Wisd. $14^{26}$) would seem to suggest a clear implication of a 'natural' *order* in creation which it is wrong to override.

It is interesting also at this point to return to the Areopagus speech, for, as we have seen, many have been willing to concede the presence of natural theology in it when they have denied it in Romans. In this regard we should observe that, paradoxically, the thought of Romans appears to be closer to that of Wisdom than is the thought of the speech in Acts. The Acts speech is also concentrated on the theme of idolatry, and takes creation as starting-point. But—more like the canonical Hebrew books—it concentrates on idols made by human hands and says nothing about humanity having mistaken the created things, such as stars, animals, or the like, for divine beings. The place of the animals in this argument is particularly significant. The older Hebrew polemic against both idolatry and polytheism concentrated on the plurality and vanity of the other gods, and upon the absurdity of the making of images.

Apart from the one case of the Golden Calf (Exod. 32), it said little or nothing of the objects that were depicted in these idolatrous cults. Thus it is one of the striking things about the Book of Exodus that, though depicting the sufferings of Israel while in bondage in that land, it says nothing at all about the theriomorphic character which is so conspicuous a feature of the Egyptian religion and its iconography.[15] Images were wrong just because they were man-made images, it did not matter of what, and gods were wrong because they were plural, and other than the God of Israel. But later this was to change. Very probably, residence of Jews in great numbers in Hellenistic Egypt was a major factor. The Wisdom of Solomon emphasizes this point: the fact that images are of *animals* is a particularly disgusting feature, and they were animals more horrible than usual that were used for this purpose. Romans makes exactly the same point: people had exchanged the immortal God for images, not only those resembling mortal man, which would have been bad enough, but resembling birds or animals or reptiles (Rom. 1[23]), which is a good deal worse.

Moreover, as already remarked, Acts 17 says nothing about idolatry leading to foul immorality, and on the contrary speaks of God's overlooking of past idolatry. On the other hand it shares something of the universalist spirit of Wisdom, while Paul in Romans is much more fixed upon the diversity of the two classes of Jews and Gentiles. Again, Wisdom includes the theme of people 'seeking God and desiring to find him', somewhat reminiscent of the groping and seeking to find him mentioned in the Areopagus speech (Wisd. 13[6]); and so likewise in the theme of the seeking of Wisdom, becoming her lover, and the like.[16] It would seem most natural to suppose that the Areopagus speech rests upon a branch of Hellenistic Jewish tradition related to that of Wisdom and Romans but substantially different in interest and emphasis. Whether this makes it more probable that Paul really spoke a speech of the tenor of that reported by Luke, it is difficult to decide. I would surmise that, if I

---

[15] For a remark that does notice the role of animals in Egyptian religion, see Aristeas 138—not surprisingly in a document from a time when large numbers of Jews were living in Egypt.

[16] On the use of terms for love in the important passage Wisd. 8[2], see my 'Words for Love in Biblical Greek', in L. D. Hurst and N. T. Wright (eds.), *The Glory of Christ in the New Testament* (G. B. Caird Memorial Volume; Oxford: Clarendon Press, 1987), 3–18 and esp. 11.

have been right in the handling of Wisdom and Romans, it makes it slightly more likely that Paul did historically make a speech along these lines, but that Luke in his writing up of it was influenced by traditions which slanted it in the direction of the speech as we now have it. In general, any sort of recognition of natural theology in Romans must have the effect of bringing Romans and the Areopagus speech closer together.

It is not my purpose, however, to prove that the arguments of this part of Romans definitely and necessarily constitute evidence of natural theology. For my purpose it is sufficient to have shown that there is reasonable exegetical ground for the opinion that something like natural theology is there, and that it is entirely understandable and reasonable that the older exegetical traditions of the Churches thought so too. More important for my purpose is that we have moved behind the New Testament and seen the importance of a tradition of natural theology existing within Judaism and operative in the understanding of the Old Testament. We shall have to pursue this possibility back into the Hebrew Bible itself.

As soon as we even mention this possibility, we must mention once again that we are conscious of making a break with the major traditions of biblical theology in this century. To these traditions, very often, indeed predominantly, a major function of the Hebrew Bible and of Hebrew thought was to protect the New Testament from the possibility of infection by natural theology. Natural theology, it was thought, derived from Greek thought, and of the most powerful and developed exemplifications of natural theology this may well be true. The New Testament was a Greek document and might therefore have had some such infection, as its use of Greek words like φύσις and συνείδησις might have indicated, but its world of ideas was Jewish and Hebraic, and that Semitic material was essentially revelational and could be used to explain the New Testament thoughts accordingly. But what if natural theology came into the New Testament out of the Hebrew background anyway? Then all that argumentation becomes vain.

But before we leave this subject something should be added on another and essential factor which affects our understanding of the Jewish natural theology, if we may so call it, of the Wisdom of Solomon. The knowledge of God, let us say, is available or accessible. From the greatness and beauty of created things it can be analogically perceived. But, as the title of the book rightly indicates, the realization of this knowledge is not automatic but depends upon Wisdom. So we quickly come to see that this knowledge, though available, is not quite possessed by all humans merely in virtue of their being human. Humans fall into two classes, the wise and the fools. Idolaters, naturally, form the main body of the latter class: as also in Paul, who points out (Rom. 1[21f.]) that those who failed to perceive God for what he was became futile (ἐματαιώθησαν) in their reasonings, their foolish heart was darkened, and thinking themselves to be wise they became fools (ἐμωράνθησαν). This is a remarkably intellectualistic approach to the matter of idolatry: there are, it seems, no idolaters who had any sense or any brains of any kind.

'For a real knowledge of God and His will, man must receive wisdom.'[17] Only with grave difficulty (μόλις) can one divine the things that are on the earth (9[16]); how then can one ever trace out the things that are in heaven? Wisdom, in the thought of this book, introduces subtle complications. On the one hand wisdom is more mobile (κινητικώτερον) than any other motion, and because of her purity she enters into everything (7[24]); she interpenetrates everything, a thought that reminds us of the Areopagus speech with its God in whom we all live and have our being. Some of the terms used are very Greek in style. But in order to have wisdom one has to ask for it, as Solomon himself did, as he narrates (7[1ff.]). So it looks as if access to wisdom might be difficult. Not so, it seems, for she goes about seeking those worthy of her (6[16]); she makes herself easily accessible (6[12]: εὐχερῶς θεωρεῖται ὑπὸ τῶν ἀγαπώντων αὐτὴν καὶ εὑρίσκεται ὑπὸ τῶν ζητούντων αὐτήν). But on the other hand wisdom will not enter a soul that devises evil, nor will it dwell in a body (σῶμα) mortgaged or burdened with debt (RSV enslaved) to sin (ἐν σώματι κατάχρεῳ ἁμαρτίας, 1[4]). So it looks somewhat as if it is a matter decided by morality in the last resort. Wisdom is accessible, but sinners will not realize this access, while those who seek it sincerely will have no difficulty in finding it.

Is a position of this kind close to natural theology or is it not? In some ways it seems closer to it, in some ways it is more like revealed theology. One principle is clear, namely that from the created world one can discern the infinitely greater greatness of the creator,

---

[17] As B. Gärtner well puts it (*The Areopagus Speech and Natural Revelation* (Uppsala: Gleerup, 1955), 126 f.).

and it is fault and foolishness if one does not do so. But the effect of this argument is somewhat spoiled, for our purposes, because it is so tied to the question of idolatry and the provision of an account of how idolatry got started in the first place. The argument is never an account simply of how God is known or of how one normally gets to know God; it is always part of an account of how, where people *ought to have known* God for what he is, they went astray and followed idols. And, because it is tied to an explanation of the origin of idolatry, it is so concerned about the created world and how one could either (rightly) conclude from it to the reality of God, or (wrongly) take the created things to be themselves divine, thus falling into idolatry. It thus fails to give proper thought to the question whether one might, by other mental processes, come to know something about God, perhaps through simply thinking about God, or through innate intuitions which belong to humanity, or in some other way. The tie to idolatry seems to limit the discussion to some form of cosmological argument. Within this ground, as scholars seem to agree, it does imply a kind of natural theology. But, on the other hand, through the question of attainment of wisdom, it seems to turn away from any idea of a theology working by rational process accessible to anyone, and to turn towards an idea of an access to wisdom determined by moral purpose, purity of heart, and the like. Yet again, however, in keeping with the wisdom traditions of the past, there is no suggestion that access to wisdom is limited by the strict lines of special revelation: in principle anyone can gain wisdom, provided they have morality and purity of heart. But, in spite of the large borrowings made from Hellenistic philosophy and its terminology, the argument suffers in the last resort from a narrow prejudice, in that it seems totally unable to see that any idolater might be a person of intellectual ability or indeed possess any sense or morals at all. And the wholesale taking over of this argument by Paul in Romans seems to be a weakness, for he seems to talk as if all Greeks or Gentiles are complete idolaters, totally sunk in idolatry, which was hardly true and could hardly have fitted with his own experience on his journeys in the Hellenistic world; and not only this, but he seems to extend this by infinite logical consequence to suggest that all of them were full of wickedness, envy, murder, disobedience to parents, and the like, and that they all not only did these things but commended others when they did so. There are therefore some substantial gaps, to put it mildly, between the Hellenistic-Jewish anti-idolatrous rhetoric that Paul inherited and applied, and the realities of life in the Greco-Roman world. Equally, even if we grant that there was natural theology in all this, one can see that it was a very simple natural theology, which covered only a limited range of the problems normally associated with that term.

With our interest in the Wisdom of Solomon, however, we have to consider more generally the place taken by Greek philosophy in the transmission of Jewish thought in this period. Characteristic of the Book of Wisdom is its very substantial usage of terms and ideas familiar to us from Greek thought. We may mention, for example, the clearly marked distinction between soul and body—a concept the indigenization of which in Jewish thought and language is clearly marked in the teaching of Jesus. Even more striking, the idea that the body is perishable and weighs down the soul, an idea which modern theology took to be the most heinous of the errors of the Greek tradition, is here within this, at least semi-canonical, book:

> φθαρτὸν γὰρ σῶμα βαρύνει ψυχήν,
> καὶ βρίθει τὸ γεῶδες σκῆνος νοῦν πολυφρόντιδα

> For a perishable body weighs down the soul,
> and this earthly tent burdens the thoughtful
>      [or: anxious] mind          (Wisd. 9$^{15}$, RSV)

Along with this goes the emphasis on *immortality*, which has already been touched upon. In the Greek Old Testament ἀθανασία occurs five times in Wisdom (3$^4$, 4$^1$, 8$^{13, 17}$, 15$^3$), twice in 4 Maccabees (14$^5$, 16$^{13}$), and nowhere else. We have already mentioned the similar term ἀφθαρσία, and it occurs thrice in Wisdom (2$^{23}$, 6$^{18 f.}$), twice in 4 Maccabees, and nowhere else. The souls of the righteous are in the hand of God, says a familiar passage, and no torment will ever touch them. In the eyes of the foolish they *seemed to have died* and their departure was felt as an affliction; but actually they are at peace. For though in the sight of men they were punished, their hope is full of immortality (3$^{1 ff.}$). In the memory of virtue is immortality (4$^1$). Because of wisdom, Solomon says, I shall have immortality, and leave an everlasting remembrance to those who come after me (8$^{13}$). In kinship with wisdom, there is immortality (8$^{17}$). To know God is complete righteousness, and to know his power is the root of immortality (15$^3$). Attention to wisdom's laws is the assurance of immortality (ἀφθαρσία), and immortality (the same word again) brings one near to God (6[18f.]). 'Thy immortal (ἄφθαρτον) spirit is in all things', says 12[1].

It is not immediately obvious, however, in what way material of this kind should be evaluated. The presence not only of terms of Greek philosophy, but of ideas of Greek philosophy, is too obvious to be questioned. But how far does this mean that substantial elements of Greek philosophy are taken over?

In our argument in these pages we have been conservative in speaking of the adoption or 'taking over' of Greek ideas of natural theology, and we have sought to emphasize the Jewish character of this tradition. Nevertheless one cannot fail to notice the remarkable degree of *similarity* that sometimes appears.

A good example may be found in the emphasis within the Bible on *the created universe* as the evidence from which humans ought to acknowledge the creator God. Very similar arguments exist in the classical tradition.[18] 'You do not see God', Cicero wrote, 'but you recognize him from his works (*ex operibus eius*).'[19] Plato himself had argued that that which has come into existence must necessarily have some cause. To discover the maker and 'father' of the universe is no mean task (τὸν μὲν οὖν ποιητὴν καὶ πατέρα τοῦδε τοῦ παντὸς εὑρεῖν τε ἔργον). From the beauty of the world, however, Plato goes on, we may conclude that its maker looked at an eternal pattern.[20] In the same tradition, within Judaism, Philo points out: some, who have the advantage of knowledge, conclude from the harmonious order of the world 'that all these beauties and this exceptional order have not come into being spontaneously (οὐκ ἀπαυτοματισθέντα), but through the action of a world-making designer (ὑπό τινος δημιουργοῦ κοσμοποιοῦ)' and so these admirable persons 'inferred the Maker *from his works* (ἀπὸ τῶν ἔργων)'.[21] Similarly, in an apocalyptic writing the wicked are blamed for rejecting the understanding of the Most High, 'for what he has done has not taught you, nor has the craftsmanship revealed perpetually in his creation persuaded you'.[22]

---

[18] For the choice of examples here cited I am indebted to seminar notes kindly passed to me by Dr David Mealand of Edinburgh.

[19] *Tusc. Disp.* 1. 28.     [20] Plato, *Timaeus*, 28c.     [21] Philo, *Praem.* (7) 42 f.

[22] Syriac Apocalypse of Baruch 54[17f.]; cited from L. H. Brockington's version in H. F. D. Sparks (ed.), *The Apocryphal Old Testament* (Oxford: Clarendon Press, 1984), 874.

Taken along with the examples cited above from Wisdom and elsewhere, these materials suggest an assessment such as the following. It is of course true, as much biblical theology has insisted, that similarities do not prove much and that an idea within the total context of Jewish religion may function in a very different way from the same idea within (say) Stoicism. This is easy to show, so easy as to be obvious. No one is trying to show that Jewish religion and Stoic philosophy, taken as wholes, are the same thing. But the similarities are evidence that certain structures may be present within one as they are present within the other, and the presence of these common structures is significant and indicative just as much as the distinctive elements are. Whether the common structures are 'borrowed' or adopted, or whether they have grown up separately and in parallel, may be difficult to decide. The common structures may not be the definitive and distinctive marks of a religion or philosophy: we are not trying to say that they are the determinative element. No one thinks that the New Testament is primarily and essentially a document of natural theology. But that structures held in common with Greek thought are common features of Jewish and of Christian intellectual life within the Hellenistic world has simply to be accepted. Thus, though this chapter has emphasized the Wisdom of Solomon, because of its status as a 'biblical' book and its close relationship with Paul, it seems to me that the whole movement of interpretation of the biblical tradition in Greek terms, best exemplified by Philo, has to be positively identified and valued in all this discussion. I quote Henry Chadwick: 'His [Philo's] Jewish monotheism made especially congenial to him both the Stoic conception of the immanent divine power pervading the world as a vital force and the transcendent, supra-cosmic God of Plato.'[23]

It was Jewish religion that made attractive the (eclectic) integration of certain Greek ideas and concepts. Among these, we must add, was the concept of *nature* itself. For many Jews it was proper and seemly to perceive a harmony between 'nature' and the command and will of God. Correct Jewish ways were both obedient to the command of God and in accord with nature; there was no contradiction between the two. There was no need to decide whether

---

[23] From his article 'Philo and the Beginnings of Christian Thought', in A. H. Armstrong (ed.), *Cambridge History of Later Greek and Medieval Philosophy* (Cambridge: Cambridge University Press, 1967), 137-57; quotation from 141.

something was natural because it followed the command of God or whether God had commanded it because it was natural: for both were true expressions of the same thing. Thus, Philo tells us, Moses' account of creation implies 'that the world is in harmony with the law, and the law with the world ... the man who observes the law is ... a citizen of the world, regulating his actions according to the will of nature, in accordance with which the entire world itself also is administered'.[24] Again, Moses 'wished to show that the enacted ordinances are not inconsistent with nature ... the first generations, readily accepting obedience to nature (ἀκολουθίαν φύσεως ἀσπασάμενοι) ... followed the unwritten law with perfect ease ... holding that nature itself was, as indeed it is, the most venerable of statutes'.[25] Before the Law was given by Moses, therefore, it was perfectly possible to live in accordance with it, since nature gave the necessary guidance. This explains how righteousness was possible in the pre-Mosaic period. Thus, again, according to Philo, Moses says that 'this man [Abraham] carried out the divine law ... he did so, not taught by written words, but through *unwritten nature* (ἀγράφῳ τῇ φύσει) he received the zeal to follow ... wholesome impulse'.[26] I do not dispute Käsemann's assertion that 'Paul was no Philo'. Of course they were persons of quite different kinds, and the totality of their ideas was vastly different. But in the particular respects here under discussion it is seriously probable that Philo well represents aspects of ideas that were structurally significant for Paul, as for other parts of the New Testament (e.g. Hebrews, John).

In summarizing what has been said, then, we may emphasize one point which will be significant for what lies ahead. Seen in the light of its Jewish background, it is highly probable that elements of natural theology were used and implied within the New Testament. But it looks as if these elements of natural theology, much as they were tied to the idea of creation and depended on it, were nevertheless not direct reflections of the structure of the created world. Rather, they were internal human constructions arising out of particular problems and controversies of religion in certain stages of its development. The importance of this will have to be considered at a later time.

In conclusion we should add some remarks about the relation between the matter of *canonicity* and the question of natural theology. An approach through a kind of natural theology was, as

---

[24] Philo, *De opif. mundi*, 3.    [25] Philo, *Abraham*, 5 f.    [26] Ibid. 275 f.

we have seen, widespread in Jewish writings in Greek language, but our focus upon the Wisdom of Solomon is particularly important because it is a book that, according to many canons—especially the Roman Catholic and the Greek Orthodox canons—was itself a biblical book. As I said at the outset, we do not know certainly whether Paul knew this book nor whether it counted as authoritative scripture; either he knew the book or he belonged independently to a very similar tradition of thought.[27] In either case, as material for the understanding of Paul, the Wisdom of Solomon is of central importance. Scholarship must take full account of it. At least theoretically this is the case; but, speaking more realistically, scholarship is likely to be much affected by the canonical or non-canonical status of the books used as evidence. Wisdom provides a uniquely important link in terms of natural theology between the Hebrew books and Paul. Where Wisdom counts as a fully canonical book, this linkage is fully displayed 'within the Bible'. Its obviousness is much greater, and the awareness of it within the religious community to which the scholars belong is much more natural and more profound. Where Wisdom is taken to belong 'only' to the Apocrypha, consciousness of it and its ideas within the religious community is very low. Except for professional scholars, few will even read the book. Theologians who have a strong canonical emphasis will tend to ignore it. They will know of its ideas and their connections, but, in the end, people will think, none of these is actually 'in the Bible'. Theological authority will be thought of as belonging to the matter of the canonical books. This being so, if the canon includes the Wisdom of Solomon, it is likely that natural theology will seem to be a more 'natural' and indeed a 'biblical' option, sustained by a strong continuity running through the Bible. If, on the other hand, Wisdom is taken to be 'apocryphal', the continuity of natural theology will be obscured and the rejection of it made more likely. And this fits in very well with what has actually happened.

All this is very relevant to the evaluation of Barth's handling of the relevant scriptural materials. As has been said, where it had been claimed that biblical passages supported natural theology, he tried to show by exegetical means that they did not support it. One of his arguments was that any such passages must be seen in the context of

---

[27] On questions of the nature of 'scripture' and 'canonicity' in this period I have not altered my opinion since the writing of my *Holy Scripture: Canon, Authority, Criticism* (Oxford: Clarendon Press, 1983).

the rest of the Bible, and such context showed their dependence on the revelatory themes which dominated elsewhere. This argument has convinced some people: for example, Wisnefske writes: 'Barth deftly shows how these passages only make sense when related to the "main line" of Scripture which is God's revelation of grace in his covenant with Israel and its fulfilment in the Messiah.'[28] But Barth's arguments along this line are invalid. First, he simply uses a harmonizing procedure, by which the majority material is made to silence the contrary position of the minority. Secondly, in so far as Christological and Messianic understandings of the Old Testament are involved, these, even if possible constructions, are not more than constructions superimposed on the text by Barth and others, and therefore their validity as 'context' is at least questionable. Thirdly, the appeal to the totality of scripture very much depends on what books are included in scripture. As soon as books like the Wisdom of Solomon are included, indeed as soon as the theoretical possibility of their inclusion is even considered, then the totality of scripture tilts somewhat more towards natural theology. And Barth had no more genuine theological reason for holding to the Protestant canon than anyone else had. Fourthly, Barth chose the meaning of 'context' to suit his own case. If one takes it in another way, and says, biblical passages have to be understood in the light of the context of a current of natural theology that has accompanied the creation of scripture from the beginning, then Barth turns out to be a denier of context. In any case, he had closed up the whole question from the beginning through his conviction that the Bible had theological relevance only through its relation to revelation. None of these arguments has validity if taken as an open question where different opinions can be discussed.

I do not say this with the intention of supporting the validity of any existing canon or the desirability of alterations in any such canon. It is said purely with the purpose of illuminating what has actually happened in our theological traditions. For the scholar the Wisdom of Solomon is equally vital evidence whether it is fully canonical or not. But the degree of conviction that scholarly argument can achieve within the theological and religious community is very much conditioned by the existing traditions about the canon of scripture. Thus I would not commit myself to the opinion of Professor Hartmut Gese that the Reformers' decision to confine the Old

[28] Ned Wisnefske, *Our Natural Knowledge of God* (New York: Lang, 1990), 73.

Testament canon to the Hebrew books was a mistaken one.[29] But he seems to be right in saying that they had no *good theological* reason for their rejection of the 'Apocryphal' books. They seem to have reasoned by a confused medley of ancient traditions (especially from Jerome), arguments that authorship proved canonicity, arguments that canonicity proved authorship, and personal preferences based on theological content.[30] And, at least under the older intellectual conditions, a canon of scripture, once established, becomes self-authenticating: people quickly forget the reasoning (if any) by which it was established, and they cease to read anything outside the canon with the thought that it might be authoritative; indeed, generally, they cease to read extra-canonical books or to know anything about them.

The relation between the Wisdom of Solomon and the question of natural theology is a powerful illustration of this. And this leads on to one of the further themes that are involved: natural theology is one of the central issues in ecumenical relations between the Churches.

Before we go further with these matters, however, we have to go behind the thought of Hellenistic Judaism, which we have exemplified from the Wisdom of Solomon, and enter into the area of the Hebrew Bible itself, in order to see how far the seeds of natural theology are to be found there. That will be the matter of the next chapter.

[29] 'Das biblische Schriftverständnis', in his *Zur biblischen Theologie* (Munich: Kaiser, 1977), 13.

[30] See R. A. Bohlmann, 'The Criteria of Biblical Canonicity in Sixteenth Century Lutheran, Roman Catholic and Reformed Theology' (dissertation, Yale University, 1968).

# 5

# Within the Old Testament

In earlier chapters we have looked at the evidence for something like natural theology within the New Testament and from there we have passed back to the inheritance of Jewish interpretations following upon the Old Testament. In this chapter we go on to consider similar evidences within the canonical Old Testament itself. We shall investigate several areas, and because of their size and importance each of them can be discussed only in a very succinct way. These are: Psalm 104; Psalm 19; Psalm 119; the Wisdom literature; the Prophets; and, finally, the law itself.

## 1. Psalm 104

The 104th Psalm is a celebration of the world and of God as its sustainer, more its sustainer than its creator. It begins by telling how God is clothed with honour and majesty, how he stretched out the heavens and makes the clouds his chariot, fire and flame his ministers. Thus the basic elements and structures were established by God. After this it goes on to the earth, and celebrates its fixation, its secure establishment. It does not say he created the earth, rather that he set it on its foundations so that it should never be shaken. Apart from that the main thing is getting rid of water from it. It is expressed in words more like those describing the ending of the Flood than those of the familiar prose creation story of Genesis 1. Once the earth is properly established and the floods removed, we have the provision of water, giving drink to the beasts and the growth of fruit. Grass grows for the cattle, wine to keep man happy, oil to make his face shine, bread to strengthen him. But the emphasis is not on humanity, and more is said about the wild things: the trees, the birds, the wild goats in the mountains, and the changes of times, sun and moon, light and dark, the difference this makes for the lions, also for man, who goes forth to his work from morning to evening. Then it goes on to the sea—it is striking, for a mainly inland-living people like Israel, how much the sea is emphasized—the ships travel there, also the sea monsters play there. All of them depend on the Lord: if he provides food, they are satisfied, if not they shrivel up or die; if God sends out his Spirit or breath, they are revived.

So, it goes on, God looks on the earth and it trembles, he touches the mountains and they smoke. The Psalmist will praise the Lord as long as he lives; and may sinners be consumed from the earth.

Now this poem has often been quoted as part of the biblical evidence for natural theology, but this is not entirely obvious, and can be disputed.[1] Certainly some may agree, with Raven, that this Psalm, along with other similar sources, expresses 'the delight in the physical universe, the appreciation of the majesty of desert and mountain and of the manifold beauty of valley and woodland' which, he thinks, characterize the Jewish attitude towards nature.[2] But there are two objections at this point.

First, it is not clear that the ancient Hebrews had as much of this 'delight in the physical universe' as Raven, like many other commentators, attributes to them, or that it was massively different in degree from the delight in the physical universe that many other cultures have displayed. It seems to be arguable that the utterances that look to us like 'delight in the physical universe' are often expressions of delight at the way the physical universe functions as a theatre for religion. Secondly, in any case, it may be argued that the Psalm is not concerned to perform the function that most normally and directly forms natural theology, namely to suggest that the nature of God can be known through contemplation of the universe and its workings. Taken in itself and as it stands, it seems to go in the opposite direction. It starts throughout from God. It tells us that God has done all this: he has set up the basic structures of the universe, provided the conditions for fruitfulness of the earth, the changes of times and climate, day and night, under which beasts and humans live and die. It is all presented from the angle of God as the sustainer of the world and the life within it.

Thus Psalm 104 is perhaps the prime biblical example for those

---

[1]  For Barth's brief and rhetorical treatment of it, see *KD* ii/1. 125 f.; *CD* ii/1. 114 ff.

[2]  C. E. Raven, *Natural Religion and Christian Theology* (2 vols., Cambridge: Cambridge University Press, 1953), i. 22 ff. Note that on 23 he uses the words 'nature has value not only in itself but as emblem and parable', terms that were to be taken up later by the very Barthian tradition to which he felt himself to be so strongly opposed.

who think that there is such a thing as a theology of nature,[3] which is different from a natural theology. Interest in a theology of nature has greatly increased with our modern awareness of ecology and ecological crisis, and that is, in my opinion, a very right interest. More negatively, on the other hand, one must suspect that many utterances in favour of the theology of nature are really attempts to recognize the evidence that favours natural theology, but to evade the conclusion that natural theology is really there. For it seems to me that no theology of nature can really be purely 'revelational': any such theology must necessarily involve a combination of specifically Christian (or other religious) revelational insights with knowledge of the world gained through other approaches.[4]

In any case the arguments for counting Psalm 104 with the theology of nature and not with natural theology are not conclusive. The Psalm has in fact a number of the characterizing features of natural theology. First, while it may indeed be said, as we have said, that the poem starts from God and sees the world as from God's side, this does not in itself prove that it is entirely revelational, if that term is used to exclude natural theology. For, when you look at the *content* of the poem, and consider what events and configurations in the world are ascribed to God, there is no specific content that comes from revelation as such. If you ask where the content comes from, then you find that either (1) it comes from traditional mythology, the stretching out of the heavens, the draining off of the waters of the flood, the sea monsters, or (2) it is easily available public knowledge. Everyone knew that the springs give water to the wild asses, that the lions roar at night, that men go to work in the morning and come home to rest in the evening. And that all this came from God, this was no new idea either: everyone in that ancient culture took it as obvious. So if it is revelational, as I believe it is, this is not so because of the presence of new information that is not otherwise known; it is rather a matter of new insight into matter that is already 'naturally' known and familiar. So it is closer

---

[3] For example, C. Link, *Die Welt als Gleichnis* (Munich: Kaiser, 1976), 313; but many have made the distinction. So Stephen R. Spencer, 'Is Natural Theology Biblical?', *Grace Theological Journal*, 9 (1988), 63 (of Paul and Barnabas at Lystra) and 72, where his conclusion is that 'although both a theology of nature and natural revelation are biblical, natural theology is not'. George Hendry, in his book entitled *The Theology of Nature* (Philadelphia: Westminster, 1980), seems, rather surprisingly, to say nothing about our Psalm.

[4] See especially Jan-Olav Henriksen, 'How is Theology about Nature Natural Theology?', *St. Th.* 43 (1989), 197–209.

to natural theology after all. To this we add a few brief points: (1)
Psalm 104 has long been known to have striking parallels in content with Egyptian poems on a similar theme, especially the hymn
to the Aten or sun-disc associated with the religious reform movement of Akhenaten. These parallels cannot be dismissed as mere
formal and external similarities, for they enter into the central
sources of the poem's attractiveness. Paul Dion wrote recently:
'much of the evocative power of Psalm 104, and perhaps also of the
intense conviction it radiates, is indebted to old Akhenaten.'[5] We
have seen above that transreligiosity is always something that
brings us closer to natural theology. (2) The approach of the 104th
Psalm has particular similarities to Paul's speech at Lystra, to
which we have already referred: God gave himself witness through
sustenance, with rain, fruitfulness, food, and gladness (Acts 14[17]).
The fact of the sustenance—sustenance rather than creation—is
testimony to the true God.

   To sum up, then, our Psalm is part of that dominant tendency of
Hebrew natural theology, in focusing on the existing cosmos as
evidence and manifestation of the divine beneficence. Interestingly,
it seems to belong to a stage of tradition anterior to that which we
find in Genesis 1. Some of the same elements are there, but seem to
be in a logically prior and more primitive form. In particular, the
emphasis on total creation is less clear. In the Psalm God has
constructed, rather than 'created' ('stretched out' is the term used),
the outer structure of the world, the heavens, and the earth he has
securely founded, removing from it the overwhelming waters,
which remind us more of Noah's Flood than of the waters of
Genesis 1. Of the animals and humans there is no word of creation,
the word is rather of *sustenance*, support, provision: it is the *continuance* of life that is emphasized. In so far as the Hebrew word ברא,
usually 'create', appears, it is used of the *renewal* of life (v. 30), not
the making of something that was not there before.

   Of course the poem is written from a faith-perspective; it knows
that God has done all this. But, conversely, it paints a picture of
God through the collocation of this evidence, which was accessible
and well known to almost everyone. From experience, plus some
reliance on mythology for ideas of the origins of the world, the

---

[5] 'YHWH as Storm-God and Sun-God: The Double Legacy of Egypt and Canaan
as Reflected in Psalm 104', *ZATW* 103 (1991), 43–71; quotation from 69.

playing of Leviathan, and the like, the poet has constructed a very beautiful and effective picture for the rendering[6] of the God of Israel. No other biblical passage so strongly emphasizes that it was the *beneficent effects* of divine sustenance for animals and for humanity that signified the nature of God. Without this emphasis, the idea of creation in itself might never have been so powerful in this direction. Here also likewise is the emphasis on the diversity of *times*, the darkness and the light, the morning and the evening—an emphasis not so much on the regularity of the changes, but rather on the beneficent effect of them all, each in its own way.

Taken together with other passages and with the total development of ideas in Israel, then, Psalm 104 must be counted as a force among others that worked in favour of the rise of natural theology.

## 2. Psalm 19

> The heavens declare the glory of God
> and the firmament proclaims his handiwork.
> Day to day pours forth speech
> and night to night declares knowledge.

There are some linguistic obscurities in the next portion, but the ending is clear: their words go forth to the end of the world. The poem goes on to speak of the sun:

> which comes forth like a bridegroom from his chamber
> and like a strong man runs his course with joy.
> Its rising is from the end of the heavens,
> and its circuit to the end of them;
> and there is nothing hid from its heat.

After this the poem changes style, rhythm, and subject-matter in a striking way, so much so that some have thought we now move into another poem altogether:

> The law of the Lord is perfect, reviving the soul;
> the testimony of the Lord is sure, making wise the simple;
> the precepts of the Lord are right, rejoicing the heart ...

[6] For the use of this word, see Dale Patrick, *The Rendering of God in the Old Testament* (Philadelphia: Fortress, 1981).

and so on, in familiar and beautiful language. Addison, you will remember, paraphrased the first part of the Psalm into the most poetic of all expressions of traditional natural theology:[7]

> The spacious firmament on high,
> with all the blue etherial sky,
> and spangled heav'ns, a glorious frame,
> their great Original proclaim.

and I add his final two verses:

> What though, in solemn silence, all
> move round the dark terrestrial ball?
> What tho' nor real voice nor sound
> amid their radiant orbs be found?
>
> In Reason's ear they all rejoice
> and utter forth a glorious voice
> for ever singing as they shine:
> 'The hand that made us is divine.'

Addison rendered the Psalm very well. Only over 'in reason's ear' might one quibble, as too rationalistic a gloss on the natural theology of the Psalm.

But there are two or three ways in which this Psalm can be read. Much depends on the mode of connection which one sees between the two parts of it. One might say that there is no natural theology here at all, an approach that would have been very acceptable to the Barthian position. In that case, some would say, the heavenly bodies indeed declare the glory of God, but the declaration that they make is one unintelligible and inaccessible to humans.[8] Day to day may

---

[7] The spelling follows that of A. C. Guthkelch's edition: Joseph Addison, *Miscellaneous Works*, i: *Poems and Plays* (London: Bell, 1914), 215–16. The poem was published in the *Spectator*, 23 Aug. 1712. Addison's proem is worthy of quotation: '*Aristotle* says that should a man live under ground, and there converse with the works of art and mechanism, and should afterwards be brought up into the open day, and see the several glories of heaven and earth, he would immediately pronounce them the works of such a Being as we define God to be. The Psalmist has very beautiful strokes of poetry to this purpose, in that exalted strain [here he quotes Ps. 19]. As such a bold and sublime manner of thinking furnishes very noble matter for an Ode, the Reader may see it wrought into the following one.'

[8] So Kraus in H. Berkhof and H.-J. Kraus, *Lichterlehre* (Theologische Studien 123; Zurich: Theologischer Verlag, 1978), 24. In conscious opposition to 'all interpretations', he makes the unintelligibility of the heavenly speech into the one clear and central message of the poem! He writes with emphasis (his italics): '*Die Schöpfung hat keine Anrede für den Menschen*; mit ihren Aussagen, ihren Selbstaussagen ist sie dem Mensch *nicht* zugewandt.' I did not know of this passage when I wrote my article on the same Psalm (cf. n. 9 below), but, on the basis of Kraus's exegesis in the *Biblischer Kommentar*, I pointed out that his explanation depended upon 'philological

pour forth speech, and that is the praise of the creation to the creator, but it is day that is saying this to day, and night to night, so that there is nothing there about a communication to humanity at all. Added to this, one could argue that the second part of the Psalm, concerned with the wonderful life-giving qualities of the law of God, is distinctly revelational, so that any minor impressions of a natural knowledge of God, attained through the first part, would be cancelled out by the emphasis on the revealed law in the second part. Thus Barth emphasized the unity of the two parts, lambasting critics like Gunkel who had interpreted them as two separate poems, 19A and 19B.

But the same point, the unity of the poem, could be understood, and has been understood, in the very opposite sense: namely, God makes himself known in two complementary ways, first through the great works of creation which control the world, and secondly through his special communication exemplified here by his law. The two channels of natural and revealed theology are here very properly to be seen. It is not surprising that the Psalm was seen as a fine manifestation of their complementarity, as was traditional in the older Christianity.

Two major points may be made. First, we should note the emphasis in the first part on the *universality* of the heavenly speech. There are indeed some textual and linguistic uncertainties in vv. 3–4 (Heb. 4 f.), which I have discussed elsewhere[9] and will not repeat here; but in any case the voice of the heavens and its words go out to the end of the earth, and probably, though not quite certainly, that voice is commingled with all human speech and is heard in the midst of it. In any case, the poem goes on, all this—which seems to mean all this linguistic interchange—is like a tent for the sun, whose rising is from the end of the heavens and its circuit to the end of them, and 'there is nothing hid from its heat'. As everyone on earth receives the heat of the sun, we are entitled to conclude, so everyone on earth

recklessness of a high degree' and concluded that 'opposition to the idea of natural theology . . . has led to an injudicious snatching at highly improbable philological identifications and connections'. For comments by Berkhof, see ibid. 32 ff.

[9] See my 'Do we Perceive the Speech of the Heavens? A Question in Psalm 19', in *The Psalms and Other Studies on the Old Testament Presented to Joseph I. Hunt* (Nashotah, Wis.: Nashotah House Seminary, 1990), 11–17. In supplement to what I say there, p. 12, I now think that NEB's 'their music' for *qawwam* of v. 5, literally 'their line', is probably correct: not so much for the reasons adduced by G. R. Driver, but because of the use of *qaw* in the Masada scroll of Ben Sira, 44[5]. It meant 'a string' and hence the music produced thereby.

receives the language of the heavens or some impression of it. Why should the poem not have so implied?[10]

Well, one might appeal to the second portion of the poem, about the law of the Lord and his testimonies, which revive the soul and make wise the simple. This might quickly bring us back to that traditional revelatory medium, the Law of Moses. But in fact the poem says nothing about the Law of Moses. It can be read in that way, of course, for the terms 'law', 'testimony', 'precepts', 'commandment' are all terms that occur plentifully in the Torah. But the poem itself says nothing that can be specifically identified with the Mosaic Law of the Bible. One can of course make that identification but the text does not require it. It is possible to read the text in another way, taking these as general terms for divine 'instruction' which may be available and must be heeded. And such instruction is likely to be universally available and accessible: it is not necessarily limited to the specific materials of the Mosaic Law. It is more like the instruction of the Wisdom literature, where *torah* is commonly the instruction of a parent, notably a mother (Prov. 1[8], 6[20]), or Wisdom's own instruction, directly given. If this is so, then both parts of the poem form a fine unity in their expression of a universal communication of praise of God from the heavens and instruction from the deity for humanity. Taken this way, it definitely looks positively towards something like natural theology. Once again, this fact is only strengthened by the probable relation of the poem with the thought of other cultures and religions, very likely from Canaan and Egypt.

Barth, discussing this same Psalm, makes the point that the 19th Psalm must be seen in the context of the rest of the Book of Psalms, in the context of the Exodus, of Moses, of the story of Israel, and so on. Seen in that wider context, he implies, it is only a small part of a revelatory process, and thus any appearance of natural theology that there may be is overwhelmed. But this argument is not convincing. Nobody is trying to prove that there is nothing but natural

[10] It is significant that Ps. 19 does *not* explicitly comment on the aspect of the heavenly bodies which has actually had most effect on natural theology, namely their *regularity and immutability*. This aspect, incidentally, impressed Calvin a lot: 'But Calvin based his natural theology, like the natural theology of antiquity, above all on the heavenly bodies ... It is "the symmetry and regulation" of the universe, amazing in view of its vastness and the speed of its motions, that particularly display the glory of God. Astronomy, therefore, "may justly be called the alphabet of theology".' So W. J. Bouwsma, *John Calvin* (New York: Oxford University Press, 1988), 104. Cf. further Ch. 6 below.

theology in the Bible. There are, however, units, substantial literary units, complete speeches, complete poems, even if only a few of them, which meditate mainly or even solely on natural theology; and Psalm 19 may be seen as one of these. No Barthian Psalmist would have written the 19th as it is: he or she would not have been content that this wider revelational context existed, the author would have insisted on making it explicit, on putting it expressly within the poem.

### 3. Psalm 119

This interpretation is strengthened when we take into account another important poem which, however, has seldom been thought of as evidence for natural theology: I refer to the longest of all the Psalms, the 119th, notable for its systematic acrostic form and for its concentration on what appears to be nomistic piety. The vocabulary, phraseology, and thinking of this great Psalm have often been noticed to be very similar to those of the second part of the 19th:

> Blessed are those whose way is blameless,
> who walk in the law of the Lord!
> Blessed are those who keep his testimonies,
> who seek him with their whole heart ... (vv. 1 f., RSV)

All the terms for laws, statutes, commandments, and ordinances are very frequent within the text. And yet, surprisingly, the classic elements of divine revelation to Israel are not mentioned at all: neither the patriarchs, nor the promise of the land, nor the Exodus, nor Moses, nor the prophets, nor—above all—the *book* of the law or any of its specific contents. As Jon Levenson pointed out in an impressive article,[11] in spite of the stress laid by Psalm 119 on specific commands and statutes to be followed, no one can tell from its text what these specifics are: they are simply not mentioned; thus nothing about the sabbath, the year of jubilee, the levirate marriage, the sacrifices, not even anything about the avoidance of idolatry. As in Psalm 19, where the words like *torah* are used, the meaning is closer to that of the Book of Proverbs; and, in terms close to those of Psalm 19, the 'word' of God is something set up in the heavens:

---

[11] Jon D. Levenson, 'The Sources of Torah: Psalm 119 and the Modes of Revelation in Second Temple Judaism', in P. D. Miller, Jr., *et al.* (eds.), *Ancient Israelite Religion* (Philadelphia: Fortress, 1987), 559–74.

For ever, o Lord, thy word is set up in the heavens;
thy faithfulness is to all generations.
Thou hast established the world and it stands fast;
by thy judgements they stand this day;
for all things are thy servants.          (vv. 89 ff.).

On this I quote Levenson's judgement:

In other words, the commandments that the psalmist practises, even those
which may be Pentateuchal, constitute a kind of revealed natural law. They
enable him to bring his own life into harmony with the rhythm of the cosmos
and to have access to the creative and life-giving energy that drives the
world.[12]

'A kind of revealed natural law'—these are words that are profoundly significant for our subject. They will echo through the
remainder of this book.

Enough of the 119th Psalm for the moment. But the mention of
this great work of gnomic wisdom must have made it clear in what
direction we are moving. Thus far, both in the New Testament and in
the Old, we have started from the classic passages traditionally cited
as evidences for natural theology. In some of these passages we have
thought that natural theology of some sort is clearly implied or
expressed, in others that it is possibly doubtful, so that a decision
must depend on other factors, in others that the passage might belong to some other category, such as the theology of nature. But we
now have to broaden our perspective a great deal, for our suggestion
will be that these passages, quite few in number, are only the tip of
an iceberg, and that beneath the surface lie much larger masses of
material that may belong to some kind of natural theology. The
presence of these much larger masses will, consequently, make it
much more likely that natural theology is present in the classic
passages than one might think when these passages are taken as
isolated cases.

## 4. The Wisdom Literature

I cannot start on the Wisdom literature without mentioning the
distinguished work of Scottish scholars in this area: I think of Professor McKane of St Andrews in our own time, but especially my
own teacher here in Edinburgh, Professor Oliver Rankin, whom I

[12] 569.

later succeeded. Professor Rankin was by no means in sympathy with the revelational trends in the theology of his time, and we may believe that something of his spirit is hovering beneficently over us as we think about Hebrew Wisdom as a region of natural theology. What I remember best, and with most gratitude, was how we used to meet together, just the two of us—for it was not a subject much in demand—to read Maimonides in Hebrew.

With the Wisdom literature we widen our scope, for we are no longer discussing the individual classic passages, long used as evidences for natural theology, but are turning to large bands of literature, and few will question that, within the Old Testament, the Wisdom literature is the area with the largest similarity to the procedures of natural theology.[13] I propose to treat it fairly briefly at this point, however, for several reasons. First, I have already had something to say about the key position of one of the Wisdom books, the Wisdom of Solomon, and will be returning to it again, and similarly something about the figure of Wisdom herself, and in addition the Psalms we have discussed above contain strong Wisdom features. Secondly, in general, John J. Collins of Chicago, one of the few biblical scholars of recent times to interest himself in natural theology, has already written an admirable study along these lines,[14] and I do not wish to repeat his arguments. Let me quote a few lines from his conclusion:

There are certain fundamental aspects of the sages' approach to reality which are common to natural theology in all ages. Specifically the sages attempted to discern the religious dimension of common, universal human experience without appeal to special revelation or the unique experience of one people. This religious dimension was correlated with the distinctively Israelite tradition but it was not subordinated to it. The history and law of

[13] Thus for instance H. D. Preuß, 'Alttestamentliche Weisheit in christlicher Theologie?', *Bibliotheca Ephemeridum Theologicarum Lovaniensium*, 33 (1974), 174, maintains that the 'Act-and-Consequence Sequence' (*der Tun-Ergehen-Zusammenhang*) of Wisdom literature is 'a piece of natural theology' which represents 'the way in which the so-called natural man thinks and wishes God to be'. In this respect, Preuß goes on, the New Testament here offers a particularly clear 'plus' as against the Old. A view based on the cross of Christ is a clear alternative to any theology of an Act-and-Consequence Sequence, and not a kind of faith that can in any way be combined with the latter. He goes on to give examples of this from the New Testament. To him, clearly, the affinities of the Wisdom literature with natural theology are manifest, but constitute a negative element and thus count against the value of that literature within Christianity.

[14] John J. Collins, 'The Biblical Precedent for Natural Theology', *JAAR* 45/1, Supplement (Mar. 1977), B: 35–67. I am indebted to Dr Collins for kindly providing me with a copy of this article.

Israel did not replace universal wisdom, although the sages claimed that they did complement and illustrate it.

To this I have only certain remarks to add at this point. First, we have noted transreligiosity and transculturality to be features that point towards natural theology. The great territory of the Wise lay in the south and east, beyond Israel's own borders, in areas like the land of Uz, where Job lived. In the Old Wisdom of Israel, as seen in the Book of Proverbs, this is made highly evident through the very close parallels with Egyptian wisdom, amounting to detailed verbal similarities over several chapters. If later Wisdom, as seen in Ben Sira and Wisdom of Solomon, made clearer its close identification with the specifics of Jewish religion, it simultaneously became more transcultural in another way, assimilating characteristic patterns of Greek thought. Reaction against Greek culture only accelerated, rather than diminished, this tendency.

Secondly, many scholars of modern times have sought to legitimize Israelite Wisdom by insisting that it nevertheless came to be integrated with specifics of Hebrew religion. As von Rad depicted it, Wisdom 'was a response made by a Yahwism confronted with specific experiences of the world':[15] in other words, distinctively biblical faith and 'the fear of the Lord' were there first, and created a space within which Wisdom then operated. I agree with Collins[16] that this depiction is both improbable and unnecessary. Though von Rad, so far as I know, nowhere mentions natural theology explicitly, one cannot but feel that his mode of approach to the subject depends ultimately on the sense that nothing too close to natural theology should be admitted to exist within the Bible. This is not without importance in the theological sequel, for Christian Link, one of the theologians who has done most to develop the discussion of natural theology in recent years, is visibly heavily dependent on von Rad in his use of the Old Testament, and indeed generally.[17]

[15] G. von Rad, *Wisdom in Israel* (London: SCM, 1970), 307.

[16] Collins, 'Biblical Precedent', 45.

[17] Thus see Link's ch. 7 entitled 'Gerhard von Rads Interpretation des alttestamentlichen Weltverständnisses', 268–85 of *Die Welt als Gleichnis*. This chapter is strategically important, lying as it does between ch. 6 on 'The Problem of Natural Theology as Search for the Relation of God to the World' and ch. 8 on 'Karl Barth's Doctrine of the Parables of the Kingdom of Heaven'. Link's treatment makes no attempt to describe the variety of scholarly opinions on the Wisdom literature, nor does it take into account the feeling of many scholars that that same literature constituted a difficult problem for von Rad and formed a particularly weak area in his total theological view of the Old Testament.

However, the book I wish to speak about in particular is the work of later Wisdom, Ecclesiastes or Qoheleth, for it is particularly significant in relation to our study.[18] Of all the books of the Hebrew Bible Qoheleth seems, at least at first sight, to be the most akin to Barthianism; I well remember in my student days, heavily influenced by Barthianism, how Qoheleth fascinated me. For it seems to say exactly the things that are wanted by those who deny natural theology. Qoheleth applied his mind 'to seek and to search out by wisdom all that is done under heaven' ($1^{13}$). The result, he reported, was: 'I have seen everything that is done under the sun; and, behold, all is vanity and a striving after wind' ($1^{14}$, RSV). 'Under the sun' or 'under heaven' are key terms of this writer: he has examined everything that is, as we would say, 'in our world', but he cannot find signs of God in it, he cannot find theological meaning. There is no justice, there is not the necessary divine intervention, there is no advantage in moral conduct. The writer, it seems, does not disbelieve in God, he does not deny God, but the honest investigation of what goes on under the sun does not lead to God. All this looks like prime material for the rejection of natural theology. That this book, so often a cause of disquiet to believers because of its apparent negativism, should nevertheless be included in the canon was surely a clear sign of the divine providence that guided the selection of books!

And in a way, yes, but only in a way. Qoheleth's reaction against the expectation that traces of God might be found through study of the world as it is is in itself evidence that the Wisdom tradition had encouraged that expectation—just as Job's reaction against the customary theodicy was evidence that that sort of theodicy had indeed been encouraged. Moreover, Qoheleth does not turn to revelation to solve his difficulties; not at all, he turns to something more like a distant, uncaring God, and a life for humanity which man must regulate on the basis of his own needs and desires, aware above all of the limits of his own knowledge outside his immediate environment. Moreover, here again we have some sort of transculturality: there may not be actual influence from Greek philosophy, in spite of the similarities that have been seen, so evidently with Heraclitus, with the Stoics, with the Epicureans; but if there was no

---

[18] On the older modes of appreciation of this book, see interesting information provided by H. D. Preuß, 'Erwägungen zum theologischen Ort alttestamentlicher Weisheitsliteratur', *Ev. Th.* 30 (1970), 405

actual *influence* from Greek sources then the argument is all the stronger, for it means that Qoheleth out of his Hebrew tradition independently generated thoughts that have so much kinship with theirs. And, finally, among all the writers of the Hebrew Bible Qoheleth is the one who, more than any other, was something like a philosopher, who had, in Martin Hengel's words, the *'critical individuality* of an acute observer and independent thinker'.[19] From all these points of view Qoheleth stands closer to the standpoint of natural theology. The idea that it supports the denial of natural theology is, at least in part, illusory.


## 5. The Prophets

At first sight the Prophets would seem to be, of all portions of the Hebrew Bible, the most revelatory in character and the most remote from natural theology. The prophet is supposed to speak a word that he has received from God, fresh for the present situation. Nevertheless there are aspects of the prophetic movement that are relevant to our consideration.

The first lies in the ethical basis which they assume. Here I speak briefly, because I follow the study of Professor John Barton.[20] The classical prophets, in their announcements of judgement upon the nations for their sins, were conservative, in the sense that they did not propound a new ethical code based on fresh revelation, but assumed standards that were already current. On the other hand they did not generally refer to a written Torah, such as we now have in our Bible. The paucity of reference to the Law of Moses in the prophets until quite late times is obvious. The case of Jeremiah 34[8ff.], referring to the freedom of the slaves after six years, is one of the few exceptions that prove the rule, and even it is hardly a full exception.[21] This becomes specially noticeable where nations other than Israel were involved and comparisons between the doings of nations were made on some kind of common ethical basis, as in the first chapters of Amos. It seems that they commonly assumed a kind of recognized

---

[19] M. Hengel, *Judaism and Hellenism* (2 vols., London: SCM, 1974), i. 116

[20] See J. Barton, *Amos' Oracles against the Nations* (Cambridge: Cambridge University Press, 1980), and his 'Natural Law and Poetic Justice in the Old Testament', *JTS* 30 (1979), 1–14.

[21] Because Jeremiah refers to a covenant made with the fathers in ancient times, but does not say that it comes from the Mosaic books.

national or international morality, which was not in doubt, and on
the basis of this recognized scale of ethical standards they proceeded
to the aspect which was more original with them and more peculiar
to them, namely the announcement of the powerful actions of judgement which the Lord was soon to put into effect. This ethical basis,
then, was natural rather than revelational in character. Similarly,
'poetic justice', as expressed in Isaiah's

> Woe to those who join house to house ...
> until there is no room ...
> The Lord of Hosts has sworn:
> 'Surely many houses shall be desolate,
> large and beautiful houses, without inhabitant'      (Isa. $5^{8f.}$)

is 'a way of declaring that God acts on the basis of the same ethical
principles as those which humans can discover in nature by the
operation of reason'.[22]

Some might question the words 'the operation of reason': but
reasoning is in fact a strongly marked aspect of the prophetic
phenomenon. 'Come now, let us reason together, says the Lord',
were not by chance keywords of Isaiah's prophecy (Isa. $1^{18}$). Prominent in prophetic speech is the so-called *rīb* pattern, in which the
style of law-court argument and reasoning is assumed. Evidence is
collected, arguments are advanced, a conclusion is reached. Correspondingly in a prophet like Deutero-Isaiah this kind of legal-style
argument is developed into a legal case between the God of Israel
and the other gods, for example Isaiah $43^{8ff.}$. Along with this there
goes the prophetic polemic against idols and false gods, mentioned
elsewhere in these lectures, which takes a strikingly rational form.
Prophecy, then, has a number of features that show an affinity with
the operations of natural theology.

## 6. Hebrew Law

On the face of it, biblical law appears to belong almost entirely to
the sphere of revelation. Almost every element within it stands
under the rubric 'And the Lord spoke unto Moses, saying ... '.
According to the mode in which it is presented in the Hebrew Bible,
biblical law is not something that human beings worked out, or that

[22] Words quoted from a paper written by my Vanderbilt student Mr William W.
Graham.

they derived from rational norms or universal principles known to them: on the contrary, it is something that they were verbally *told*, by God through Moses at Mount Sinai. It was God who expressed all these laws, and more or less all at the same time, to Moses on Mount Sinai. It is not expressly said, but it is left open to the reader to understand, that none of this legislation was known to the Israelites before it was revealed through Moses.

There is thus, taking the text at its surface value, very little or no development in biblical law. Practically no law is promulgated after the time of Moses: it is all there already from that starting-point. To this there are limited exceptions, but their limited character is the obvious aspect of them. Now it is very probable in fact that Hebrew law developed very considerably over the thousand years or more during which we can observe it within the Bible, as social conditions altered and it was found necessary to adjust the law and make it more precise in view of newer conditions. It would be widely agreed that much of Deuteronomy is an example of this, and the P legislation, whether earlier than D or later, would be another. But neither of these documents *represents itself* as a post-Mosaic development. Deuteronomy presents itself as coming at a *slightly* later stage, at the end of Moses' life, and in this sense may be seen as hinting that it is a restatement of an original revelation on Mount Sinai. But it is still, on the surface, a Mosaic document, spoken by Moses before his death, and before the tribes entered the land of Canaan. The P material is even more clearly expressed as belonging to the Sinaitic revelation. Thus, in general, there is very little legal material that is not attributed by the text to direct and specific divine revelation through Moses. Or, putting it the other way, *if* there was legal development through the thousand years or so of which we know something, then that legal development was summed up by ascribing its results to Moses on Mount Sinai: this was the convention. Thus, seen on the surface of the text, the legal material seems to express itself as special revelation.

It cannot be doubted, however, that the actual nature of this material is different. All serious scholarship accepts that there was much development and change in Hebrew law, partly corresponding to social changes and partly arising from the need to clarify older laws; and that the various strata, such as the laws of Deuteronomy and of the Priestly document, whatever their age relative to one another, represent this reality. And, on the other hand, the impact which the biblical laws have upon the reader is vastly altered when we take into account the ancient Near Eastern parallels.

Since the discovery of the Hammurabi laws intense attention has been devoted to the connections between Israelite and other oriental legal corpora. It is hardly necessary for me to give details: some of the most important cases in the Bible lie within Exodus 21–3, and good examples are the law of the goring ox (Exod. 21$^{28\text{ ff.}}$) or that of the Hebrew slave (Exod. 21$^{1\text{ ff.}}$). A Hebrew slave, which probably means one who becomes a slave through debt, works for six years and then goes free; in the Hammurabi laws the period is three years, but the basic structure of the law is very similar. Here the relations are the opposite of those discussed above, which concerned the post-Mosaic development of law within Israel. Far from it being the case that the Hebrew law was developed long after the time of Moses, it was in all probability common social property long before Moses could have lived, and social property not uniquely of Israel nor dictated to Israel directly by its God, but social property held in common with other peoples of the Near East, in particular the Mesopotamians, whose actual religion was very different from that approved of in the Bible. Naturally, there are differences: we are not suggesting an *identity*. But there is a common structure and some degree of common ethical values. Israel no doubt introduced modifications into this common legal structure, in the light of its own experience. But, where such parallels exist, it becomes impossible to suppose that Israel received its form of the law by direct and pure divine revelation, producing a result totally different from what was already known elsewhere. To argue so would only be to trivialize the concept of revelation: all that revelation does would be to change the numbers, so that the slave works for six years in Israel, but for three in Mesopotamia.

Realities of this kind do not necessarily endanger any sophisticated doctrine of revelation: the true God, let us say, can reveal himself through materials that are not totally unique but have common elements with general social patterns of the time. Quite so. But, even taking it in that way, we have to say: biblical law, thus understood, comes closer to the operation of natural theology than to that of pure revelatory theology. Biblical revelation, shall we say, took up into itself elements of legal and therefore of moral perception that already existed and were common ground to large human populations, even though these populations had very different religious systems. The Bible, perhaps, *made* this material *into* revelation, it became revelatory in its biblical form and in relation to other biblical elements: yes, maybe, but the building blocks still came out of something that was closer to the operation of natural theology. If revelation took up into itself legal elements that were common property to large populations with differing religious conceptions, then it can take up into itself conceptions of God and of morality that exist in Greek antiquity and elsewhere. Revelation, this suggests, builds upon human insights existing over a wide spectrum. All this is highly suggestive for the continuance of our argument.

Take an illustration of another kind: the activities of Jethro, father-in-law of Moses (Exod. 18). Jethro, with whom Moses took refuge early in the story, when in flight from Egypt, reappears after Israel has escaped from Egypt. Moses has been triumphantly successful, the people have been making their way through the wilderness, assisted by quails and manna, and there has been a successful battle against the Amalekites. Now Jethro appears and hears all that God had done for Moses and for Israel. He rejoiced, and spoke:

Blessed be the Lord, who has delivered you out of the hand of the Egyptians . . . Now I know that the Lord is greater than all gods, because he delivered the people . . .

And Jethro, Moses' father-in-law, offered a burnt offering and sacrifices to God; and Aaron came with all the elders of Israel to eat bread with Moses' father-in-law before God.

Now what happens after this? On the next day Jethro observed what Moses was doing for the people, judging and deciding lawsuits every day from morning to night. Clearly the children of Israel, not long escaped from Egypt, have quickly developed a strong taste for litigation. When they have a dispute, Moses says, they come to me, and I decide between a man and his neighbour, and I make them know the statutes of God and his decisions. Well, said Jethro, What you are doing is not right—the only person in the Bible to say this to Moses and survive. Moses was trying to run the entire country as a one-man administration and would wear himself out in the process. He must learn to delegate, and appoint suitable men to handle the thousands of minor cases; he himself should reserve his energies for the major matters, where God himself had to be consulted. Jethro's advice was, very sensibly, put into effect; and all of us, no doubt, are glad that this was done.

But consider what this means. Whence did Jethro derive the authority to say all this? He admired what Yahweh had done but it is not clear that he himself was a Yahweh-priest. There is no word of Yahweh having spoken to Jethro or revealed himself to him in any way. As the story depicts it, he recognized what the Lord had done for Israel and asserted that Yahweh was greater than all gods, or all other gods, but even that does not make it clear that he had Yahweh's authority in any way. He was priest of Midian, an official therefore of a people whose religious position was at best rather dubious. He was of course related to Moses and that gave some sort of authority, but scarcely constituted a ground for absolute revelation, and indeed Jethro himself offers no authority for his advice other than that it is his own opinion. In fact it is good common-sense advice, and it is good that Moses accepted it. But the story, taken just as it stands, remains very good evidence of a positive valuation of normal human common sense, independent of religious affiliation, as an element in the establishment of the Hebrew legal polity. And this story is in a very prominent position: this element of sensible legal administration is the last major thing to be established before the arrival at Mount Sinai and the great revelation of the Ten Commandments and other legal materials in Exodus 20 ff.

Another case, one of a slightly different kind but that points in the same direction, is the matter of the daughters of Zelophehad (Num. $27^{1\,ff.}$; 36). Zelophehad had died, leaving no sons but a number of daughters, and these ladies said it was wrong that their father's name should be allowed to disappear from within his family of the tribe of Manasseh. Moses took the case to the Lord himself, who pronounced that the daughters of Zelophehad were in the right, so that in the future, if a man died and had no son, the inheritance should pass to his daughter. In Numbers 36 the consequential problem arises: fine, it is good that the ladies should thus inherit, but what if they marry outside their own tribe? This would mean that that inheritance would disappear from the tribe concerned. In this later stage it is not reported that Moses took the case back to God: he himself 'according to the word of the Lord' (RSV) ruled that the integrity of the tribal inheritance should be maintained. The girls could marry anyone they liked, but only within their own tribe.

Now it is very likely that this is a case of development of law under changing social conditions, or under inherent need for clarification. Very likely, the oldest law provided for inheritance in the male line only. But this could lead to the extinction of a family's name. So female inheritance was permitted. But this in turn, if the girls married, could lead to the loss of tribal land. So marriage outside the tribe was not permitted. All this may be said to come from revelation in the sense that God is actually consulted and gives his ruling on the first occasion, and Moses with divine authority rules on the second. But the actual decision taken is not one that calls for vastly superhuman powers. It seems to be a rather obvious common-sense solution such as any competent person might have reached, given some knowledge of the social assumptions of the time. The law, though on the surface revelatory in character, in fact puts into effect rather obvious norms of natural justice.

The law itself, then, in its content has numerous suggestions that point towards operations akin to those of natural law or natural theology. Only by heavy and unbalanced insistence on the *rubrics*, on the encapsulating formulae like 'and the Lord said unto Moses' which encase most of the material, only by unduly emphasizing the setting as against the content, can a traditional view of the law as totally revelatory be maintained. Once we see that the laws are indeed in many respects a product of the society of their time and its inherited notions, the force of this perception dies away.

And in any case the legal material had always had an effect which pressed in the opposite direction. If, in the history of interpretation, the character of the laws of the Hebrew Bible seemed to support the dependence of humanity on pure divine revelation, they seemed also, on the other side, to support the idea of a rational, knowable, accessible foundation for moral judgements that was, at least in principle, available to all humanity. People wanted to say that the biblical laws, however absolute in themselves, had some grounding in knowable principles: they were not totally and absolutely arbitrary. The biblical laws, though given by revelation, could be seen to be in accord with reason of some kind. It could be seen, even if only under the guidance of expert exegesis, that they accorded with some sort of universal principles.

And there is perhaps, at this point, a basic difference between the situation in Judaism and that in Christianity. In Christianity the idea of revelation seems to imply the concept that the content revealed is something absolutely different, something that could not be known or imagined through any other approach. In Judaism, I think, it is not so. The law is of course revealed by God through Moses. But no one is worried if that which is thus disclosed is something already knowable through other approaches: that fact, if it is a fact, rather strengthens the claims of the revelation than weakens them. Medical knowledge shows the dietary laws to be beneficial, natural morality supports the moral commandments, rational philosophy underpins the entire corpus of law. This is widely accepted as a good and valid thing.

And this is of primary importance for our theme. For natural law was in some respects the gateway into natural theology. Even Barth, you will remember, had admitted that both Luther and Calvin had made an unguarded and unconditional use of natural theology in their teachings about the law. It was easier to exclude natural theology from theology than to exclude natural law from law. The laws of the Hebrew Bible gained some degree of legitimization from their relation to universal principles of morality and right. It was, says Christian Link, in the field of natural *law* that natural theology in fact derived its authority out of the carrying out of life (*Lebensvollzug*).[23] We have shown in this chapter that there is at least *some* basis in the Hebrew Bible upon which a natural theology might be built, and out of which some natural theology did in fact grow.

---

[23] Link, *Die Welt als Gleichnis*, 42, and see his entire section 41-55, on Luther and Melanchthon.

# 6

# A Return to the
# Modern Discussion

## 1. Purposes and Intentions

Before we go more deeply into a statement of the position within the Bible, I have to go back to the background of the modern understanding and the principles that have been involved in it. As will be apparent from what I have said, I consider that there is substantial basis within the Bible for the acceptance of natural theology as a reality. Those present at these lectures may therefore have formed the impression: here is a person who is a believer in natural theology or an adherent to it, and he has therefore gone over the traditional biblical evidences for it, arguing that they really do support natural-theology. He is therefore opposed to all that Karl Barth said in denying natural theology, and wants to have it reinstated as a basic feature of modern theology, as it has scarcely been in recent times.

This, however, is not my position or my purpose. I do not have any starting-point within the tradition of natural theology. In principle, my starting-point is rather against it. To me the arguments of natural theology are not a congenial field. Even if natural theology should be a valid mode of procedure, I doubt if I would find it easy to practise it. In this respect, I share many of the doubts and objections that modern theologians have voiced against the whole idea of it. I have thus a certain underlying sympathy with what Barth was trying to do in his rejection of it. I am not at all sure that the new ways in which theologians—even of the Barthian tradition, and even including Barth himself—have come round to a revived natural theology are wholesome. I incline rather to the belief that they well deserve the same angry blast which the Barth of fifty years ago delivered against Brunner.

I am unmoved by the idea of proofs of God's existence, I dislike apologetics, I start out on the whole subject as one who is distrustful of the entire box of tricks that makes up traditional natural theology, and ultra-modern natural theology as well. It may be, indeed, that through the effect of my own arguments I will be forced to become something of a natural theologian, but that was not the intention with which I started out. What really interests me is the effect that the whole question has upon biblical studies and upon the place of the Bible in theology. What I do find, after a long period of struggling with the problems, is that the Bible does imply something like natural theology and makes it impossible for us to avoid the issues that it involves.

As I indicated in Chapter 1, Barth's rejection of natural theology was never really based on biblical exegesis, nor, as he himself, at least partially, admitted, was it really representative of Protestant tradition as it had in fact been, even in the great Reformers themselves. Its real foundation lay in trends and developments in modern theology, philosophy, and society. Of course strenuous efforts were made to show that the Bible agreed with it, but the actual basis lay elsewhere. From beginning to end Barthianism was above all an intellectual, philosophical-dogmatic, system. But it was one that to an unusually high degree claimed to be based upon the Bible, and by its own logic had to claim to do so.

If it is true therefore that natural theology in some way underlies the Bible, if it is used and therefore supported by some significant parts of the Bible, the effect upon Barth's total theological position must be devastating. And this not so much because it means that his position about natural theology is wrong. That may or may not be the case, but is not the point I wish to pursue. What it means is that his doctrine of scripture is wrong. His assessment of the Bible as the Word of God and as the arbiter of theological truth cannot tolerate the perception that natural theology is sanctioned by its presence there. Certainly Barth's doctrine of scripture was such as to admit limited human imperfections—historical inaccuracies and that sort of thing, such as biblical criticism had amply revealed. But it could not tolerate the gigantic theological error of natural theology within key portions of the scripture—for no portions were more key portions than the Law of Moses, the Psalms, and the writings and speeches of Paul—not at a time when it was being asserted that the rejection of natural theology was *the pivotal matter* of discrimination between one theology and another.[1] This was not a matter of minor historical errors or discrepancies between one book and another. It was a matter of the deepest, profoundest, theological principle. It lay at the central conceptual basis of biblical thought. It meant that, at the very point which was now being said to be the central issue of theology, the Bible was at fault and was a mistaken guide. Thus when Barth in his first Gifford Lecture enunciated the principle of the Reformation (as it ought to have been rather than as it had actually been), that:

The church and salvation are founded on the word of God alone, on God's revelation in Jesus Christ, as it is attested in the Scriptures; and this is the clear opposite of any form of teaching that declares that man himself possesses the power and the capacity to inform himself about God, the world, and man.

he would have had to rewrite the passage somewhat as follows:

The Church and salvation are founded on the word of God alone, on God's revelation in Jesus Christ; and this is the clear opposite of any form of teaching that declares that man himself possesses the power and capacity to inform himself about God, the world, and man, even though such a teaching can be found to underlie certain central biblical passages or indeed is definitely expressed by them.

This, of course, he did not do and obviously could not do. The fact remains irrefutable: if you thoroughly reject natural theology, and if natural theology underlies the Bible in any significant degree, then you must judge that the Bible is inadequate as a theological guide. A theology that took account of this might, of course, be constructed on the basis of Barth's principles, but if so it would be a different theology from that which he in fact constructed.

## 2. Barth and Protestant Tradition

And this would have made a big difference. For one thing, it would have severely qualified Barth's claim that his theology was in positive continuity with the Reformation. He did, indeed, as I have

---

[1] Or, to put it in another way, the rejection of natural theology might be validly maintained if it was explicitly based on a principle of *selection* within scripture—a selection which would simply discount the theological authority of the Areopagus speech, the first chapters of Romans, and various other passages. Such a selection is probably implied by a number of scholars, as we have seen, and with reasonable consistency. What cannot be done is to imply, with Barth, that *all* scripture is agreed in such a rejection.

mentioned, note the use of natural theology by both Luther and Calvin, but he could do this without strain because he appeared in other regards to be completely loyal to that movement, and could interpret his own shift of position concerning natural theology as an element of even greater loyalty to it. But to have made this shift of position, and accompanied it with an admission that the shift not only was a move away from the Reformers' own practice, but meant that Holy Scripture itself was mistaken about this key issue, this would have been too much for most of those who heard Barth's lectures with sympathy and appreciation. For of course Luther and Calvin, in so far as they did use natural theology, did so under the impression, which they shared with most traditional Christians, that scripture itself gave sanction to this.

Actually Barth's rejection of natural theology was based, as he himself more or less admitted, not on the Reformation but on his own reading of the intellectual history of the world over the last four centuries. After that more recent development, he said, we can see more clearly than Luther or Calvin could. But what he said, in his Gifford Lectures, about this intellectual history was highly tendentious and misleading. We have here to take account of the fact that Barthianism moulded past intellectual history in its own image, and its efficiency in doing this was one of the reasons for its own great influence. No one perceived this better than Richard Niebuhr, who in 1964 wrote:[2]

Something very nearly approaching a Barthian captivity of the history of modern Christian thought reigns in theology outside of ultra-orthodox circles. It manifests itself in the efforts, sometimes rather strained, to interpret the theology of the Reformation in conformity with the canons of Barth's *Church Dogmatics*, and it also appears in the evident preconceptions with which the nineteenth century and Schleiermacher are interpreted by those who have fallen under the sway of this captivity.

In identifying Roman Catholicism as involving 'a compromise with' natural theology, indeed, Barth had an arguable case, and that opposition to the Roman tradition gave the appearance of validating the claim of his own theological position to be a truly Reformational one. But in saying that 'Modern Protestantism' was likewise based on a compromise with natural theology he was somewhat misleading his hearers. For one of the main features of Modern

---

[2] R. R. Niebuhr, *Schleiermacher on Christ and Religion* (New York: Scribners, 1964), 11.

Protestantism—let us say, since the mid-eighteenth century—was its departure from the tradition of natural theology which had, in fact, been highly influential in Protestantism. Schleiermacher, for instance, had already emphasized the futility of natural theology. Ritschl had polemicized furiously against 'metaphysics' as an element within theology. The Barthians disliked Ritschl and hated to see any suggestion of a continuity between Ritschl and Barth, but the continuity is not to be denied.[3] Barth's own major teacher, Herrmann, was one of the Ritschlian group. And Harnack had made familiar the idea of a 'Hellenization' of the original substance of Christianity,[4] and in most people's minds there was much in common between Hellenization and natural theology. Thus, contrary to the impression that was deliberately made, the denial of natural theology was one of the aspects in which Barthianism was *continuing* the line which Modern Protestantism had initiated,[5] and was alienating itself from the older religious world in which the Reformers and the Fathers had lived. The attraction of the Barthian position lay precisely in the fact that it seemed to fit with the experience of a generation in which science on the one hand and war on the other had seemed to make the world empty of God.

Equally ignored by Barth, in the statements in his Gifford Lectures, was the heavy debt owed to natural theology in *conservative* Protestant theology, as already mentioned above. Now conservative Protestantism is considerably divided in this regard. As one illustration we may mention the nineteenth-century neo-Calvinism of the Princeton theology of the Hodges.[6] Charles Hodge was quite clear about the importance of *reason* in the knowledge of God, and he used all sorts of rational, scientific, and historical apologetics, of just the kind which the Barthianism of the next century was to subject to ridicule. It was not unnatural that those of this tradition were to

---

[3] On this see the remarks of James Richmond, *Ritschl: A Reappraisal* (London: Collins, 1978), 32 ff., who there quotes Richard R. Niebuhr's expression cited above.

[4] Cf. ibid. 69.

[5] Cf. Berkhof's words: 'Karl Barth's battle against natural theology was in respect of content a conflict with the theology of the 19th century; formally and programmatically, however, it was an inheritance from that century.' H. Berkhof and H.-J. Kraus, *Karl Barths Lichterlehre* (Theologische Studien 123; Zurich: Theologischer Verlag, 1978), 39.

[6] For an earlier simple statement, see my *Fundamentalism* (2nd edn., London: SCM, 1981), 272 ff. Hodge insisted that reason was 'necessary for the reception of a revelation', that it 'must judge of the credibility of a revelation', and 'must judge of the evidences of a revelation'.

resent the way in which Barth and his followers not only undercut their arguments, but claimed in so doing to be representing the genuinely Reformational point of view.

Thus some evangelicals, annoyed by Barth's arguments (which the main body of evangelicals reject), point out—in my opinion rightly—that scripture itself contains or at least by implication sanctions natural theology. A good example of evangelical thought that supports natural theology is the work of T. C. Hammond, *Reasoning Faith: An Introduction to Christian Apologetics* (London: Inter-Varsity Fellowship, 1943), which was, I think one could say, the nearest there was to a theological textbook in British student evangelicalism of the 1940s and early 1950s. As the title correctly states, the entire approach is an apologetic one. Although the book says rather little directly or positively about natural theology, a positive valuation of it is clearly implied, and thus its chapter 9, pp. 80ff., reacts against 'Two serious objections to natural theology', in particular, of course, the Barthian one. Hammond has some sympathy with Barth's emphasis on sin and revelation, but cannot accept his anti-apologetic position, which would make vain the entire approach of his own book. On the other hand, though he does not do much to argue that scripture positively supports natural theology, he does imply it, using a verse from Proverbs which may indeed be quite relevant. He writes that 'If "the spirit of man is the candle of the Lord" (Prov. 20$^{27}$), there can be no discredit in employing it to illumine the greater things of life' (p. 88). Recognizing with Calvin the weakness ('imbecility') of this light, and continuing with gloom about human nature, Hammond goes on, in purple prose, to tell us that

yet we can still direct the thoughts of our fellows to those ruins of our former greatness which still bear imposing witness to the great temple which God erected when He made man in His image. Nor does it seem evident to us that, if God designs to restore man to the dignity from which he has fallen, then the relics of greatness which he still possesses must be wholly ignored in the process. It is one thing to say that a man cannot by searching find out God, and quite another to say that the Holy Spirit will never employ his earnest gropings to direct him to still better modes of finding that which his soul desires.

Hammond, and many of his readers, were doubtless quite unconscious how near this 'conservative evangelical' position came to the traditional liberal-idealist use of natural theology.

Other evangelicals, however, impressed by the power of sin over the 'unregenerate' human heart, are against natural theology and deny that it has any biblical basis.[7] Part of this can be explained as follows. Much evangelical argumentation and apologetic uses what, if seen from a Barthian point of view, counts as natural theology, and hence it is understandable that this viewpoint should support a rational natural-theology approach and accept the existence of traces of it within scripture. But on the other hand much evangelicalism does not know what to do, positively, with natural theology. Its emphasis lies more on the contrast of sin and grace; its evangelism stresses the complete darkness of the unconverted heart; and it is terrified by the critical effects which the presence of natural theology might exercise upon the biblical picture of God as evangelicals see it. It is willing to allow reason or natural theology to be a support to revelation, as evangelicals see it, but not that they should have any power to *modify* revelation as thus seen. Thus it tends to stress in practice the ideal of entire dependence on revelation, and at the same time to leave unobserved or unrealized the heavy dependence on natural theology which, as any Barthian would see it, underlies the main theological tradition of evangelicalism.

And similarly, yet again, that modern style of philosophically refined Calvinism, which appears to me to be a philosophical theism uneasily combined with a naïve biblicism, would also surely have counted for Barth as being a form of natural theology, even when its practitioners themselves deny the validity of the latter. But in any case, admitting these complications and possible exceptions, the point I am arguing must remain true, and natural theology had a strong tradition of support within conservative and evangelical Protestantism also.

Barth's dependence on intellectual history can and must be pursued further, both back and forward. Looking further back, we have to ask about his views of the Reformers, and especially of Calvin himself. Here, as Richard Niebuhr saw, the effects of the 'Barthian captivity' are particularly intense. Very different pictures of Calvin's thought in the relevant areas can be seen in the writings, for instance, of E. A. Dowey, T. F. Torrance, and John Leith, and I would not presume to comment on these works, except in so far as

[7] e.g. S. R. Spencer, 'Is Natural Theology Biblical?', *Grace Theological Journal*, 9 (1988), 59–72.

concerns my own areas of Old Testament, exegesis generally, and relations with natural theology. For a general picture of Calvin's thought I am impressed by the work of Bouwsma, and inclined to believe it the more because he is a true historian and not a theologian, and therefore less likely to be grinding a theological axe. Work written from a pro-Barthian standpoint must be judged likely to be biased, as Niebuhr implied: not because Barthians are necessarily less able in history, but because the Barthian tradition did more than any other theological current to attack the ideal of historical objectivity—especially in biblical exegesis, but also in other historical regards—and failed to concede that even the attempt to achieve a limited objectivity was a desirable goal. Applying the same principle to their own historical work, which had an important apologetic function, we have to expect it to be biased.[8] In this they are hoist with their own petard. Barthians asked questions of the older traditions, but they asked them in Barthian form and so they obtained Barthian answers. They cannot complain if others discount their historical work accordingly.

Actually Calvin's debt to natural theology was, I believe, much greater than is suggested by Barth's very grudging admissions.[9] 'Given his intellectualistic anthropology, his respect for valid method and argument, and his conviction that religious truths are accessible to human beings in nature, it is hardly surprising that Calvin was attracted to natural theology.' Much of his use of it was unoriginal: 'he repeated commonplaces long available, especially those of Cicero.' Note particularly Calvin's emphasis on the *immutability* of God, highly fateful for the idea of predestination and other central doctrines; and similarly the importance of the heavenly bodies and their regularity, so that 'astronomy may justly

---

[8] One example: Barth in *Natural Theology* (London: Bles, 1946), 100, indicated that he wished to leave it to his brother, Peter Barth, as a Calvin specialist to inform readers about the problem of natural theology in Calvin. Among English-speaking readers of *Natural Theology* probably few ever looked up the article that was produced: Peter Barth, 'Das Problem der natürlichen Theologie bei Calvin', *Th. Ex. H.* 18 (1935), 1–60. But a glance at it leaves so extreme an impression of partisanship and personal hostility to Brunner as to make dubious the quality of it as a historical work. Cf. Christof Gestrich, *Neuzeitliches Denken und die Spaltung der dialektischen Theologie* (Beiträge zur historischen Theologie, 52; Tübingen: Mohr, 1977), 184, and the valuable appendix III on the Barth–Brunner controversy in E. A. Dowey, *The Knowledge of God in Calvin's Theology* (New York: Columbia University Press), 247 ff., as well as other remarks *passim* in the same work.

[9] See lately W. J. Bouwsma, *John Calvin* (New York: Oxford University Press, 1988), esp. 102–8. Quotations in this paragraph are from these pages.

be called the alphabet of theology', thoughts very relevant in relation to Psalm 19, as we have already seen. The limited role that Calvin, in some of his doctrinal statements, may have assigned to natural theology has to be complemented with a recognition of the influence that it had on his exegetical perceptions, which may well have been much greater. And, in doctrinal statements like the first chapter of the *Institutes*, where Barth admits a 'guarded' use of natural theology by Calvin, I believe that the arguments there deployed by Calvin are much more essential and thus deserve much stronger emphasis than Barth here suggests, because Calvin uses natural theology to prove the *impossibility of atheism*, a point which is not marginal but of central importance.[10] Human beings had an innate religious instinct, which on Barthian terms might not amount to much, but for Calvin himself was a powerful basis of argument. Religion was for him, as it was not for Barth, a significant positive symbol. It was not by chance that his best-known work was called the *Institutes* 'of the Christian Religion'.

Respect for the religious instincts of the natural man, even after the Fall, is also implicit in Calvin's belief in the superiority of Greek religion to other expressions of ancient paganism. The Greeks, who represented the gods with human figures, were less deluded than the Egyptians, who worshipped dogs, oxen, and even cats and herbs. Degrees of natural insight imply, in principle, the validity of natural theology.[11]

The strong classical and humanist interests of Calvin point in the same direction. Early on he had written a commentary on Seneca's *De clementia*, and the atmosphere of Stoicism was familiar to him. Naturally, he deplored the many failings of classical civilization, as all Christian theologians did: but the idea, familiar in modern times, that the classical mentality was intrinsically inimical to biblical revelation was lacking. Reformational exegesis had little perception of the cultural, logical structures especially of Semitic people, which structures have been so strong a subject of attention among modern scholars. What it knew of the thought-forms of ancient humanity was drawn much more from the classical than from the Semitic world. In spite of the total acceptance of the Old Testament by a man like Calvin, and his full enthusiasm for it, there

---

[10] On the later use of this, cf. the apophthegm of Christian Wolff, 'per theologiam naturalem optime refutantur athei'; cf. E. Jüngel, *Entsprechungen* (Munich: Kaiser, 1980), 195.

[11] Bouwsma, *John Calvin*, 103.

is little sign in his work of that appreciation for the distinctive mind and logic of the Hebrews which has so interested the twentieth century. The contrary is the case: in spite of Calvin's strongly pro-Old Testament standpoint, he may be understood rather as one who in considerable measure Hellenized the understanding of it.[12]

All in all, then, there may be good reason to question the links that have been claimed to exist between Barth's theology and that of Calvin in respect of the question of natural theology. Even Barth himself, as has been mentioned, admitted that he had gone beyond Calvin in this respect. He was aware that, in completely rejecting natural theology, he was entering new territory. And the same applies in other theological areas: how much common ground is there between Barth's doctrine of 'election' and Calvin's predestination, other than the use of the same words? I suspect that there is as much truth both in the conservative Calvinistic understanding of Calvin and in the moderate, more humanistic interpretation of him, as there is in the Barthian understanding of him. Not that it matters for us in the long run anyway: our interest here is not in Calvin, but in the Bible, and Calvin's opinion one way or the other cannot decide anything for us. All we are doing is to test and question the supposed foundations of the Barthian position in the past history of ideas, and especially of theological thought.

### 3. Barth and National Socialism

This being so, it is appropriate to direct a similar questioning at the way in which Barth associated natural theology with the pro-Nazi position of the 'German Christian' movement.[13] It is not clear that there is any essential or necessary link between German National Socialism and natural theology. Why should there be? To attach the label of 'natural theology' to the hoarse and inchoate utterances of the DC—who were in any case a limited element within the German Protestant population, had no unitary theological views, and in the long run were not very important historically—is a quite disgraceful smear on the careful, rational, and philosophical discussions which have generally been intended when the term is used. The

---

[12] Cf. my similar remarks in my 'Biblical Scholarship and the Unity of the Church' (R. T Orr Lecture, Huron College, 1989), 16.
[13] Cf. above, Ch. 1.

motives of those who believed in an affinity between Christianity and Nazism were probably a variegated mixture of confused national ideals, hopes of personal profit, and the vague belief that Hitler's coming to power heralded an important moral revival, a belief which was certainly an important part of the atmosphere of the time and was shared by many Christians who did not therefore become DC members.[14] In so far as there was any central theme in it, it lay in what was seen as a 'miraculous' turn in historical events, an 'hour' of a sort of 'salvation' initiated by Hitler's rise to power. Whatever one may think of this, it is not obviously to be identified as 'natural theology'—or if it is, it is something very different from what has commonly been understood to be natural theology. In fact, natural theology may well have been only a small part of it.

Indeed, it may be more correct to say that the average theology of those who supported National Socialism was a revelational theology, in which the new 'events' and the 'crisis' of modern experience formed an extension—or even in effect a replacement—of ancient revelation, than to see it as a form of natural theology. Two aspects of natural theology were markedly absent from these currents: first, its rationality, and secondly and more important, its tendency to the universal. Nothing was more marked in the arguments of Nazi supporters than their hostility to any kind of universality or internationalism. This indeed could be a reason why an affinity between Protestantism and National Socialism was perceived: for Catholicism had an air of being 'international' and 'universal', while it might be thought that there was some reason for the claim that Protestantism was essentially German. To Nazi supporters the particularity of German historical experience was an essential idea. In this respect they were closer to the patterns of revelational theology, with its background in the particularity of Israel as people of God. The *völkisch*, 'folk', dimension was essential. If the *völkisch* dimension could be stated as a structure or 'order' built into creation, which looked rather like natural theology, it could also be understood as a revelational principle valid, as in the Bible, for a particular people with its history. Thus

---

[14] See the careful and detailed discussion by Gestrich, *Neuzeitliches Denken*, 145 ff.; also the brief account of K. Nowak in *Evangelisches Kirchenlexicon*, 1 (1986), cols. 825–7. A striking and vivid account in English is given by my Oxford colleague Jonathan R. C. Wright, 'The German Protestant Church and the Nazi Party in the Period of the Seizure of Power 1932–3', *Studies in Church History*, 14 (Oxford, 1977), 393–418.

the understanding of pro-Nazi theology as basically a kind of natural theology was probably a vast misdiagnosis. And if this diagnosis was mistaken, the consequences were grave: for the insistence that natural theology was the ultimate and decisive factor led to the decision that Church dissent should not be directed in the first place against the racial politics of the government, its persecution of the Jews, or its deification of the state. Attention to these evils must wait, it was implied, until the prime matter of natural theology had been dealt with.

And even Barth himself could use revelational terms to describe the DC theology which he opposed. Its essential dogmatic premiss was that 'German *Volkstum*, its history, and its political present were to be evaluated as a second source of revelation'.[15] Why then did he so insist that it was *natural* theology that was the source of evil? Several reasons may be suggested. First, the dialectical theology from the beginning had emphasized the Word of God and divine revelation, and had been remote from the sort of mental activity that characterized traditional natural theology. Though in the end the tradition of the dialectical theology might find its way towards some sort of natural theology—as might be said to some extent of Bultmann and even, as we have seen, of Barth—the whole character of traditional natural theology was obviously distasteful to the movement in its earlier stages. Thus it was an easy critical tactic to associate the various pro-Nazi theologies with natural theology, but it may well have missed the mark.

Secondly, natural theology was seen as essentially a Roman Catholic interest, and the dialectical theology was strongly Protestant in its orientation. Thus Bultmann, opening his discussion of the matter, explained what 'natural theology' was in the Catholic tradition, but instantly went on to rule it out as 'impossible' for Protestant theology, firstly because it is impossible to provide proofs of God, but 'especially' because 'the only access to God is faith'.[16] Later on, Barth's thought may have become more 'catholic', and Roman Catholic appreciation of him became greater; but there is little sign of this in the earlier debates, for example in his Gifford Lectures, which are narrowly and exclusively Calvinist. The con-

---

[15] Gestrich, *Neuzeitliches Denken*, 145.

[16] R. Bultmann, 'The Problem of "Natural Theology"', in his *Faith and Understanding*, ed. R. W. Funk (New York: Harper & Row, 1969), 313. This essay is stated to be 'unpublished' and I have not been able to discover when the German original was written.

centration on revelation in Christ and the consequent denial of all natural theology were seen by him at the time as the 'long overdue fundamental settling of accounts with the Roman Catholic method of thought in theology'.[17] There was no worse judgement to be made of the aspects of the DC movement, judged by Barth as natural theology, than that it 'must and will make the Protestant Church *romreif*, ripe for Rome'.[18]

A third reason may well lie in Barth's own style in the use of language. To him a term like *revelation* could mean only one thing, that is, the true revelation, or in other words what he himself meant by the term. It was not proper to use a central theological term of this kind as if it could equally comprehend sharply contrasting human opinions. He might occasionally, therefore, speak of the opposing view as implying a sort of 'revelation', but this would be an improper usage, employed to indicate how scandalous a thought it was. 'Revelation' could properly mean only one thing, and any deviation from that one meaning would be a departure from revelation: as such, it was therefore a resort to natural theology.

For my present purpose, I do not have to *prove* this point. Nevertheless, it seems to be supported by a consideration of some of the more prominent theological figures. Thus Paul Althaus, another who belonged like Barth to the general trends of the dialectical theology, seems to have supported the Nazi movement but, it is said of him, he 'specifically denies that he means a natural theology; natural revelation cannot be sufficient by itself, for it will not lead to Christianity. Althaus is also unwilling to espouse a natural theology because of its ties to Roman Catholicism. However, the compromise which he develops does accept a revelation in nature.'[19] Likewise Emanuel Hirsch, a strong opponent of Barth and supporter of the National Socialist movement, seems to have based himself above all on a kind of strongly Lutheran theology, in which the doctrine of the two kingdoms was combined with a rejection of

---

[17] Gestrich, *Neuzeitliches Denken*, 147.

[18] Ibid. 146. One should remember, in addition, that, on the one hand, the DC thought themselves to constitute a 'moderate' element in comparison with more extreme pro-Nazi movements, and, on the other, Barth's own displeasure fell particularly on that 'mediating' theological group who combated the DC but at the same time disagreed with the line taken by the Confessing Church and the Barmen Declaration. In this group he included his former travelling companions in the dialectical theology, Brunner and Gogarten. See ibid. 149.

[19] Quoted from Robert P. Ericksen, *Theologians under Hitler* (New Haven, Conn.: Yale, 1985), 99.

all the principles of modernity supposed to be associated with the German defeat of 1918 and the revolution that followed it. If I understand it rightly, it was less a natural theology and more like a theology of revelation which included a renewal and broadening out of revelation in a modern 'miracle'. This is what one would have expected. There was perhaps some connection, but no direct and necessary correlation, between natural theology and support for the National Socialist movement. Equally, there was no necessary correlation between rejection of natural theology and opposition to that movement. For the question lay rather *within* the field of revelatory theology: if God revealed himself to a particular people and within their history and experience, why should this not be true also of a more modern people and its history and experience?—a question that even today remains difficult to answer.

We have shown, then, that Barth may have been quite wrong in his belief that the events of the Nazi period demonstrated the fatal long-term effects of natural theology. This is not essential for the rest of our argument, but it certainly makes a difference to the atmosphere in which it is likely to be received. More important for our purpose, perhaps, is this other point: that this very example shows the difficulty in making an ultimate distinction between natural and revealed theology. If one believes that God has revealed himself in his creation and continues to do so, why is that 'natural' theology and not 'revealed'? If one believed that God was revealing himself in the German political experiences of a certain era, why was that 'natural' theology and not 'revealed'? If one believes that God was revealing himself in ancient Israel, why is this not 'natural'? Perhaps all theology is both 'natural' and 'revealed'?

There is a further aspect concerning the argument about Nazism. It was used, as we have seen, by Barth himself, within that period and context. In the English-speaking world, however, it achieved a significance that was probably much greater than Barth himself could have known. To associate a theological trend with the misdeeds of Germans and German governments has been a well-tried and generally successful rhetorical technique, fuelled by the experiences of two world wars. Barthian propaganda in Britain and North America used the same, and did so from the very start. From the beginning, when Barth was first spoken of, we were told how shocked he had been when distinguished liberal theologians had been among those who signed the 'Aufruf der 93' which supported the German case over the outbreak of war in 1914. It was often the first thing to be told, when Barth's name was discussed, and was infinitely repeated. One war later, the same thing happened again, and the supposed affinity between natural theology and National Socialism became a foremost element in the Barthian bid for theological power, and again with very considerable effect. In calling it propaganda, I am not saying that the allegations were without truth. Good propaganda has to have some truth in it. But it was propaganda because people used it for its power to persuade. They had not examined the facts: few, probably none, had read the German documents of 1914–15 or knew what they said (they are, in fact, rather inaccessible); they did not consider that there might be contrary evidence—for example, conservative theologians and churchmen supported their German national cause with just as much enthusiasm as liberal ones did, but no one said anything about that side of it; few made a critical investigation to discover how far natural theology was really involved in the DC movement; few bothered to mention the enthusiasm with which Hitler was greeted by groups that in the English-speaking world would have counted as 'evangelical' and 'pentecostal'. The arguments were not based on real knowledge: they were used because they seemed to have power and to bring power.

Barth's opposition to Nazi ideology was fully genuine: but it is not easy, in the atmosphere of such a time, for even the most sincere opposition to avoid taking on certain characteristics of that which is opposed.[20] Barthianism took shape within that same world. Features of aggressiveness and totalitarianism are manifest in the Barthian tradition, and its own rejection of natural theology, which carried with it an inability to use open-minded and reasoned forms of discussion, easily led on to a dependence on rhetorical and propagandist means of persuasion.[21] And, finally, if Christians in Germany then held, along with their Christian faith, a mixture of national and cultural values and ideological inclinations, just as most Christians at all times have done, there is no reason to believe that the rejection of natural theology in itself does anything to remove these values

[20] For one comment in this sense, cf. Stephen Webb, *Re-figuring Theology: The Rhetoric of Karl Barth* (Albany, NY: State University of New York Press, 1991), 168: 'The rhetoric of his dogmatic period ... can only be understood and appreciated, in the last analysis, in this context of the rise of fascism. Barth confronts the unlimited power of fascism with the jealous power of God, playing off one exclusive rhetoric against another; this explains, in part ... his condemnation of natural theology.'

[21] On the aspect of rhetoric see again below, Ch. 10.

and inclinations: on the contrary, as all experience has shown, they continue to coexist equally well with that rejection.

Thus the foundations of Barthian theology in the history of ideas, both when used positively, as in its claim to be the true outcome of Calvinist theology, and when used negatively, as in its claim to offer the one decisive antidote to cultural poisons of modern times, should be treated sceptically and critically. There may be truth in them at certain points, but seldom is it such truth as to validate the claims in full; and in any case all of it is a matter of modern historical judgement, none of it is a product of revelation. And it is the judgement of people who see the entire world and its history very much through the glass of their own particular theology. All this is fallible. The result is that, for the evaluation of these particular theological claims, much more weight must fall on our evaluation of the biblical material itself.

As I see it, Barthianism was an ingenious interweaving of elements that were older, whether biblical or Reformational, with elements that were entirely modern, novel, and innovational.[22] Conceptions entirely modern, related to existentialism, to atheism, to Hegelianism, were cleverly compounded with biblical exegesis and Reformational formulae. If some positions were justified by the assertion that they were held in the Reformation, others were supported by the quite opposite argumentation, namely that they belonged to the most modern trends of thought and that any who did not agree were out of date, were relics of nineteenth-century thought and out of touch with modernity. Barthianism managed to combine the dreariest conservative traditionalism with the same unseemly boastfulness about its conformity with recent trends that it had castigated in the liberals. It is thus not surprising that the outcome of Barthianism should manifest itself, as it has done, in numerous extremely different and mutually contradictory expressions.

## 4. Barth and Modern Biblical Studies

How did all this relate to the specific question of biblical study? Much attention has been drawn in recent discussion to the consider-

---

[22] Jülicher made the point that 'Barth is a man of two worlds, in whose breast two souls wrestle with each other': see H. Räisänen, *Beyond New Testament Theology* (London: SCM, 1990), 37 and note.

able friction that developed between Barth and the tradition of modern biblical scholarship. At times Barth seemed to treat biblical scholarship with mere contempt, and brushed it aside: he could do better himself. And this aspect certainly existed. But, typically of the paradoxes of our theme, there are also aspects in which Barth was very much in debt to the tendencies of biblical scholarship of his time. He *depended on* certain positions which were the result of historical-critical scholarship. One of these was the matter of the historical Jesus: the belief that the Gospels were not biographies, that nothing much definite could be known about Jesus through purely historical analysis—of this aspect we shall say no more.[23] But another such aspect was the alienation from natural theology.

For at least the last century biblical scholars had ceased to work seriously with natural theology. It was no longer part of their work or their interests. They were interested to work with the minds of the biblical people, and they no longer cared whether these minds conformed to the ideas of modern reason, logic, or psychology. They no longer thought that it was part of their work to 'validate' the thoughts of biblical writers by showing that they fitted with modern requirements, or even by showing that they fitted with modern Christian beliefs. On the whole, they chose the opposite path: if the thoughts of biblical people were entirely *different* from what modern rationality might demand, then so much the better for biblical people. The discovery of the mentality of ancient people might uncover a mode of thinking that, while different from modern modes, was valuable and constructive when taken in its own right. Again, unlike the biblical scholars of an earlier period, modern biblical scholars were no longer interested in apologetic arguments, in proving, for instance, from scientific discoveries that it was possible for the earth to be covered with water as in the time of the Flood, or that Jonah might quite probably have been swallowed up by a whale, or in showing from historical sources that the plagues of Egypt had really happened as described in the Bible.[24] Such matters

[23] The subject will, however, reappear briefly below, see Ch. 9. On the general question, see my 'Exegesis as a Theological Discipline Reconsidered: And the Shadow of the Jesus of History', in D. G. Miller (ed.), *The Hermeneutical Quest: Essays in Honor of James Luther Mays* (Allison Park: Pickwick, 1986), 11–45.

[24] Pusey, it is said, went to seaports and interviewed ships' captains, asking them what knowledge they had of incidents in which seamen had been swallowed by whales and remained alive. Doubtless he received many assurances that this really

now lay for the most part outside the realm of serious biblical study. All this was a setting, already existing before Barth, into which the Barthian approach to theology fitted very well.

Barth was in this very much a man of modern times. He perceived and followed their trend. The rejection of natural theology, apologetics, and the like suited very well the way in which biblical scholarship had long been going. This is why, in spite of the strangeness of Barthian theology to most biblical scholars, and in spite of the contemptuous attitude Barth displayed towards their work, there was never any great outcry from biblical scholarship against that rejection. It suited them very well. Added to this is the professional concentration of biblical scholars on the Bible, their 'biblicism' in the sense of their occupational unwillingness to see anything decided by factors without the Bible and beyond the range of their competence or expertise. Contrary to general opinion of recent times, the obvious weakness of the average biblical scholar lay not in his or her bias toward historical approaches, but in his or her lack of philosophical insight or ability. Their professional expertise encouraged this. Most were not sorry to see natural theology forgotten about. Their own natural sympathy with the idea of the Bible as the supremely revelational document made them all the less willing to discern traces of natural theology within it, all the more willing to do like Barth and use exegetical means to obscure these traces.

Much, though not all, of biblical theology was thus the provision of a parallel, set within biblical scholarship and working on its plane and with its methods, to the general trends and objectives of the dialectical theology in dogmatics. Natural theology, it was felt, had its chief expression in Greek thought, and Greek thought thus became the enemy. Unfortunately, the New Testament had been written in Greek, and this, by the ideas of the time, might have made it more likely that the New Testament was infected with aspects of Greek philosophy, of the mystery religions, and so on. It was Hebrew thought that came to the rescue. Hebrew thought, it was supposed, was more or less exclusively revelational. New Testament writers who had written in Greek were nevertheless imbued with Hebrew thought, so that their words were Greek but the mean-

---

happened. Köhler (*KBRS* 41 (8 July 1926), 105) reminds us that Konrad von Orelli (1846–1912), in writing his commentary on Genesis, still felt it profitable to discuss the question whether snakes had at some primitive stage had legs to walk with.

ings were Hebrew. Volumes of apparently scientific evidence were produced to show how this was so. Thus biblical theology, in this aspect of it, functioned as a kind of apologetic for the Barthian tendency in dogmatic theology. It provided evidence, allegedly demonstrable on the linguistic and cultural plane, that appeared to validate that tendency. Its function in this regard, incidentally, demonstrated that Barthianism, great as was its disdain for traditional rational or philosophical apologetics, was very ready to accept the aid of an apologetic of this different kind—and also of yet others, as we shall see. It refused any apologetic through which the non-Christian might be persuaded to become a Christian; but, within Christianity, it desperately needed an apologetic by which it would be able to claim that the Barthian way, and no other, was the right one. Such an apologetic was swiftly manufactured.

Moreover, here again the Barthian theology, far from moving against the stream of modern historical scholarship, was depending entirely on it. Without the historical orientation of scholarship none of this perception of the way of thinking of biblical man would ever have come to light. The matter is well put by Krister Stendahl in a memorable passage, which refers in particular to the *religionsgeschichtliche Schule* but goes on to the general characteristics of scholarship after that period:[25]

What emerged out of the studies of the *religionsgeschichtliche Schule* was a new picture of the men, the ideas, and the institutions of biblical history. Those elements and traits, which did strike modern man as crude, primitive, cultic and even magical, were now given equal and often greater emphasis than those which happened to appeal to enlightened Western man . . . J. Pedersen applied V. Grønbech's studies of human self-understanding in old Nordic religion to an extensive study of OT anthropology, where cherished distinctions between soul and body, magic and religion, cult and ethics, individual and collective, were thoroughly intermingled and lost much of their meaning. It became a scholarly ideal to creep out of one's Western and twentieth-century skin and identify oneself with the feelings and thought-patterns of the past.

That whole emphasis on the different categories and thought-forms of ancient people—especially of ancient people lying outside the philosophical currents supposed to be typical of the Greek world—was a product of the historical orientation of scholarship just as important as its historical analysis, datings, source theories, and the like. It was a distinctively modern achievement, though first

[25] Article 'Biblical Theology, Contemporary', in *IDB* i. 418.

steps in this direction might go back as far as Herder and romanticism. Something of that idea of the mind of biblical humanity was assumed by the dialectical theology and formed part of its strength and attractiveness. Existentialism, it was thought in the earlier stages, provided a modern world-view which retained some of the aspects of it. And the biblical theology movement, again running parallel with the dialectical theology, made enormous play out of this particular heritage which had come out of modern scholarship.

Thus of St Paul, who is in many ways the central figure in this matter, though he certainly used many expressions that seemed at home in the Hellenistic culture of his time, it seemed to people very important to argue that, though these expressions were in the Greek language, the thought behind them was Hebraic—and that fact, if true, it was thought, made it clear that the ideas derived from revelation and were expressions of it. That St Paul of all people sympathized with, used, and actually depended on arguments or concepts of natural theology has been more or less unbelievable to many, and especially those trained in the traditions deriving from the dialectical theology.

But even in that tradition the assurance of these positions has been breaking down. My own criticisms of earlier years showed that many of the arguments used to demonstrate Hebrew meanings in Greek words were linguistically invalid. I have already quoted[26] the judgement of Christian Link, writing in the latest stage of Barthian tradition, to the effect that Paul uses not only the words and terms, but the full coherent idea-framework of Greek thought.

Exegetically, therefore, we have to be entirely open to the presence of Greek thought and to the possibility of natural theology within the New Testament. The zealotic opposition to Greek ideas is something that can now be forgotten. But even so that formulation of the questions points towards a further, and less obvious, move that we ought now to make. As I have begun to hint, the bases of natural theology within the biblical tradition were Hebraic anyway. If Greek thought-forms could be the vehicle of a familiar natural theology, Hebrew thought-forms were only the vehicle of another, perhaps somewhat different, natural theology. That is what made it all the easier for them to find expression in Greek. And this, if at all true, must mean that it becomes all the more probable that natural

[26] See above, Ch. 3.

theology had a significant part to play within the New Testament. A Hebrew background for natural theology reverses the direction of the arguments that have so long been familiar, and considerably strengthens the argument for natural theology in the New Testament, and thus for a continuous tradition of it running from Hebrew Bible times down into the post-New Testament Church.

We may remind ourselves that one of the main arguments against natural theology was based on the centrality of communication through Jesus Christ. I have already quoted the principle asserted by Barth, that:

> The church and salvation are founded on the word of God alone, on God's revelation in Jesus Christ, as it is attested in the Scriptures; and this is the clear opposite of any form of teaching that declares that man himself possesses the power and the capacity to inform himself about God, the world, and man.

Such an argument was certain to carry much weight with convinced Christians: only through Jesus Christ is God known. But how does it fit with the Old Testament, where also God was known?

By pressing upon the discussion his own categories of question: is God known or not?, Barth was intruding his own conceptions into an Old Testament situation where they did not fit. As I wrote some time ago, in the Old Testament 'apart from some quite limited concessions, there is no stage at which God is not known'.[27] Adam and Eve after their disobedience had a less good relationship with God, they were fearful and guilty, but it makes no sense to say that they did not 'know' God: they communicated with him throughout. Cain likewise, though excluded from the near presence of God, in no sense was without 'knowledge' of God. The Old Testament question is not so much whether God was 'known', but when and how he was worshipped. From a very early stage we are told, quite unceremoniously, and without any suggestion that there was a problem of 'knowing' God, that 'then it was begun to call upon the name of the Lord' (Gen. 4[26]). The idea that there was a problem because God was not 'known' is an intrusion of a quite alien set of ideas, and an intrusion which by its nature favoured the Barthian construction of theology.

To say that even in the Old Testament God was known solely through Jesus Christ might be a possible dogmatic construction, but exegetically it simply does not work at all. Any accounts of the

[27] *Old and New in Interpretation* (London: SCM, 1966), 89.

knowledge of God that work from the actual textual material of the Old Testament must necessarily approach the matter, and answer it, in a quite different way. Barth's dogmatic approach to our question, in spite of his full veneration for the Old Testament, took its departure entirely from the setting within Christianity. He handled the Old Testament as if it was a portion of Jesus Christ, not just something that looked forward to him, prepared the way for him, or that provided the most important of the categories in which he would be understood, but as if it was an actual piece of him, in a sense which might be meaningful for the New Testament but was contrary to the actualities of the Old. For the question, by his formulation, was: is there any knowledge of God anterior to the self-revelation of God in Christ? Well, the only answer, by orthodox Christian principles and even by Barth's own, if they are properly considered, is: yes, the Old Testament provides such anterior knowledge. But, if there is any anterior knowledge at all, that breaks the force of Barth's argument. If there is knowledge anterior to Christ, in the Old Testament, it may as well include natural knowledge within it. To put it in another way, the idea of a 'Christological' exegesis of the Old Testament may have been a fatal obstacle to any perception of the reality of natural theology in the Hebrew and Jewish background to Christian faith.

Barth took what appeared to him to be the Christian situation and imposed it upon the whole, just as conversely he and/or his followers imposed the patterns of supposed Hebrew thought upon St Paul in order to keep him away from any suggestion of natural theology. But Paul interpreted certain key passages, and especially, as we have seen, the story of Adam and Eve, in the way he did only because he followed the understanding which had become conventional in the Hellenistic world and in a context which willingly developed natural theology. Correspondingly, Barth's imposition of what to him seemed to be a Christian/Calvinistic/Reformed understanding depended on a Pauline stance which had itself come into being through acceptance of that which Barth denied.

In other words, it was taken to be obvious that *either* Jesus Christ was sole Lord *or* there was other or anterior knowledge of God. Either alternative absolutely negated the other. Time was not wasted on such alternatives as that Jesus Christ was sole Lord but the way in which the scripture both led up to that and stated it took up anterior knowledge within itself. No one considered such possibilities as that, while Jesus Christ was sole Lord, there were *structures* akin to natural theology which were involved in seeing him as Lord, especially when we specify 'on the basis of the scriptures'. It is this alternative that we now propose, and which we see to have very substantial scriptural evidence in its favour.

Another argument used was that against the 'and' of so much contemporary religion: 'Christ *and* culture', 'Christ *and* history', 'Christ *and* nature', 'Christ *and* reason'.[28] All such cases of *and* or *also* were to be got rid of. As an expression of disgust with all sorts of compromise, such an argument is understandable. But on the other hand it is a clear admission of weakness, in that it provides no reason why specifically *natural theology* was to be identified as the thing to be rejected. Even if it was a valid protest against the opinions of the DC, and even if we accept that their ideas really included a kind of natural theology, this still is no reason why all and every kind of natural theology should be singled out as *the essential* element to be opposed. And if Barth and the framers of the Barmen Declaration thought that they were opting for a position in which Christ *only* was criterion and there was no *and* at all, they were either deceiving themselves or misrepresenting themselves. They did not have any such option nor did they take any such option. For they certainly implied: Christ *and* certain accompanying features without which 'Christ alone' would not have been acceptable; thus Christ *and* a clearly Reformational theological approach, and, for our present purposes most important, Christ *and* the Old Testament. But this meant: Christ *and* the Old Testament history. And it made sense only because the Old Testament furnished its own separate fund of knowledge which could not be subsumed within the entity 'Christ alone'. It was genuine anterior knowledge: in Israel God was known. To affirm 'Christ only' and couple this with 'according to the scriptures' was very possibly, as we have seen, to contradict the scriptures. And *if* the statement that revelation was *only* in Christ was meant by Barth and the framers of the Barmen Declaration to deny that creation was a revelation of God,[29] there may be some doubt where Genesis 1 stands on this but there can be no doubt that such a view is in contradiction of Romans 1. Therefore the argument condemning all these 'ands' was a mistaken one. The problem was

---

[28] Gestrich, *Neuzeitliches Denken*, 146 f.; *KD* ii/1. 194 f.; *CD* ii/1. 173 f.
[29] As is maintained by Gestrich, *Neuzeitliches Denken*, 146.

that of sorting out the differences between various kinds of natural theology, as also between different kinds of revelational theology. The condemnation of *all* natural theology meant that these tasks were not attempted.

## 5. Various Arguments against Natural Theology

Certain other customary arguments against natural theology may be mentioned here. One of them was that natural theology was 'the theology of the natural man'.[30] Seen in this way, natural theology is part of the 'natural man's' hostility and revolt against God.[31] The argument is a sort of linguistic trick, in which the 'natural' of the customary expression 'natural theology', implying a theology that can be attained without the use of special revelation, is infected with the suggestions of the Pauline phrase 'the natural man', meaning man unredeemed, deeply sinful, and so on. Nevertheless, there could be something in the argument. But modern experience has made clear the fallacy in it. Thoughts that may be derived from revelation become the possession of the thinker in just the same way as thoughts that originate through human initiatives: they are his own thoughts, they become his 'property', the basis for his self-interest and self-aggrandizement in exactly the same way; indeed, if anything, the confidence that one's thoughts are based in revelation, and are therefore not one's own human product but are given to one by a divine source outside of one, only makes more serious the hubris of the 'natural man'. One of the things that Barthianism has abundantly shown is that revelational theology is just as much the theology of the 'natural man' and plays just as much into the demands of his will and passions as any natural theology ever did. The harsh words of St Paul about the natural man in Romans 1 have many echoes in the impression that the Barthian movement left within modern theology. 'Professing themselves to be wise, they became fools . . . whisperers, backbiters . . .'—such expressions are all too reminiscent of modern realities. And with this argument we

---

[30] So for example T. F. Torrance in 'The Problem of Natural Theology in the Thought of Karl Barth', *RS* 6 (1970), 125.

[31] According to Gestrich, *Neuzeitliches Denken*, 179 f., Barth understood Brunner's proposals about natural theology in this way, and this was a major part of their misunderstanding.

touch upon a theme which will occupy us more extensively as we continue: the possibility that there is, ultimately, no important difference between natural and revealed theology after all. The thought is by no means an original one of mine; let me quote again an Edinburgh theologian:

The methods of natural and revealed theology are therefore the same in form and manner ... There is no special, privileged theological method or epistemology.

Theological order is achieved like any other, and knowledge within it is like knowledge elsewhere, so it has to conform to requirements for truth and justification if it is to gain credibility.[32]

Original or not, the thought is one that certainly makes a difference to our theme. For the moment, however, we shall not pursue this.

Turning in another direction, it has also been argued against natural theology that it was a conservative and obscurantist force that acted against progress and discovery. Natural theology, it has been claimed, has been the means by which ideas from the heritage of the Greco-Roman world have come to be canonized as the true view of 'nature' and given the blessing of Christianity as final and unalterable truth. The Church's persistent support of outdated pre-scientific and cosmological views is too well known to require attestation. Many of the controversial opinions in modern social/political/medical areas, for example, go back to natural theology. Thus religiously motivated opposition to contraception and population control, though often bolstered by appeals to the Bible and divine revelation, commonly has its real basis in a view of 'nature' as something willed by God to be static and unchanging and therefore as something that should be left to take its own course and not be interfered with by human actions, initiatives, schemes, and planning. In this respect the rejection of natural theology appeared to open a way through which modern theology could ally itself with more progressive and dynamic scientific approaches of today.

[32] Ruth Page, *Ambiguity and the Presence of God* (London: SCM, 1985), 102: see Page's whole section, 101 ff. Cf. also B. L. Hebblethwaite, *The Problems of Theology* (Cambridge: Cambridge University Press), 79: 'The old distinction between natural and revealed theology, between what reason can achieve and what requires revelation, breaks down ... Reason and revelation cannot be treated as different sources of knowledge ... Revelation-claims ... are part of the data upon which reason has to operate.'

There may indeed be something in this as an argument against natural theology, although it has doubtless been overplayed in our time. But it contains one obvious mistake: for, in its bias against natural theology, it has omitted to register the enormous degree to which the same conservative and obscurantist effects have been exercised by revelatory theology and the revelatory materials of the Bible. Perhaps not so much in science, but certainly in matters of social organization and relationships, materials treated in the Bible as revelatory, and understood as such by theology, have worked in the same way. Indeed, in so far as these obscurantist effects were exercised, they were probably seldom exercised through natural theology alone, but rather through the combination of natural and revelatory theology.

Another of the arguments against natural theology has surely been this: that, as a means of persuasion toward faith, it just did not work. Andrew Louth, for instance, sympathizing with Barth against his critics, makes this point.[33] 'Is apologetics so successful that we simply cannot ignore it?' he asks, and implies the answer, no, it is not very successful. And this may indeed be quite true: few people are persuaded by the arguments from natural theology, few become active believers as a result of them. Indeed, it can be argued that natural theology acts *against* belief: by persuading people that they are already, by their human nature, aware of the true God, it makes it seem less necessary that they should embrace faith itself. Against natural theology, against apologetics, it is quite a good argument. But, unfortunately, it cuts both ways. It equally provides a good reason for exactly what happened, a good reason why natural theology came to be dumped. For, one could easily say, however effective arguments from natural theology had been or at least seemed in an earlier age, by 1930 or so it was visible that they no longer worked, and precisely that explains why Barth's influence was so effective. Natural theology had had its place in the older world of Christendom, where God (i.e. a recognizably Christian God) could be largely presumed in any case. But by this time changes in philosophy, in scientific knowledge, in biblical criticism, in the entire mental climate meant that the older apologetic arguments had ceased to convince the minds of many people. Abandonment of natural theology was thus an easy and obvious course. Thus it is not surprising that suggestions should be made that the real

[33] 'Barth and the Problem of Natural Theology', *Downside Review*, 87 (1969), 269.

natural theology of Barth was atheism.[34] Here again he ran with the current and not against it. The hoarse, and often unsophisticated, conservative charges that Barth was a modernist, a new liberal, however ill argued, were not without some kind of foundation.[35]

## 6. Was Barth Himself Dependent on Natural Theology?

Moreover, as seen from the viewpoint of the biblical scholar, it was never so clear that Barth was really against natural theology, even at the stage at which he most expressly rejected it. Great as was his emphasis on revealed theology, it always seemed that there was some kind of non-revealed intellectual structure that provided the necessary assumptions. Such a structure might not be a natural *theology*, but it seemed it was some kind of substitute that performed the same function as a natural theology had done for other theological systems. As we have just seen, some have thought that his true natural theology was atheism. Again, it is clear that his theology depended in large degree on an analysis of the history of ideas, especially of theological ideas. This again was not revelation. He might be right or he might be wrong but in either case he had not got his ideas out of revelation. Yet, again, in the area of biblical theology, Hebrew thought was used as if it provided the necessary logical basis on which positive theology should rest. Hebrew thought might be represented as if it was revelational, but in actual function it did for the New Testament what natural theology had normally been expected to do, that is, to provide a framework of logic and connections of ideas upon which the coherence of revelational ideas might depend. In later Barthian times the dependence on some particular philosophical position became even more clear. Again, in literary approaches to exegesis, some have argued that modern ideas of 'realistic narrative' support Barth's understanding. 'Barth is one of the readers

[34] See W. Kasper, *The God of Jesus Christ* (London: SCM, 1984), 76: 'paradoxically, atheism has here [in Barth] become a form of natural theology', and see his entire discussion, 58 ff. Cf. also Gestrich, *Neuzeitliches Denken*, 47.

[35] And cf., from a sophisticated, non-conservative viewpoint, the judgement of J. C. O'Neill, *The Bible's Authority* (Edinburgh: T. & T. Clark, 1991): 'Barth's system is a pure humanism . . .'.

who see in the Bible what Auerbach, Dame Helen [Gardner], and Frei see', writes David Ford, and therefore 'the sort of literary criticism the latter explicitly engage in might illuminate Barth's implicit principles'.[36] Maybe yes, maybe no. But why should we believe that Auerbach and these other critics are right in their opinions? Did their literary judgements depend on revelation? Of course they did not. If they are used to show the coherence of Barth's exegesis, they work as a form of 'natural' knowledge which is adduced because it supports, or appears to support, a theological position. In fact, *all* attempts to argue for Barth's theology on the grounds that it is supported by modern intellectual trends, philosophical, literary, or whatever they may be, necessarily show that it is not what it pretended to be, an independent and purely theological position deriving exclusively from revelation.

And, most strikingly, only a few years before he delivered his Gifford Lectures Barth had written his book on Anselm (German original 1931, ET only in 1960); and there are some who think that his Anselm study is the really dominating element in his entire work, more so even than the commentary on Romans. But the Anselm book, at least as the biblical scholar sees it, comes very close to the operations of natural theology. It was always said, of course: it is all within the context of faith, and Barthians were always ready to quote the slogan *fides quaerens intellectum*, which was also the title of Barth's book. It was faith seeking understanding.[37] Anselm believed in God anyway, and would continue to believe in God even if his argument failed. Yes, but, even if this is true, and I do not wish to argue the point, the appeal is entirely to a public logic, and, if that public logic failed, then it meant that the

---

[36] In 'Barth's Interpretation of the Bible', in S. W. Sykes (ed.), *Karl Barth: Studies of His Theological Methods* (Oxford: Clarendon Press, 1979), 77. For a questioning of the idea that 'realistic narrative' or 'realistic fiction' might provide an answer to the problem of biblical narrative, see Stephen Prickett, *Words and the Word* (Cambridge: Cambridge University Press, 1986), 203 and *passim*. If the salvation of biblical narrative is to depend on its being categorized along with George Eliot's *Scenes from Clerical Life*, how are the mighty fallen! (Cf. Prickett, *Words and the Word*, 77, 186, 208.)

[37] The expression *crede ut intellegas*, as used by Augustine, may well have been remote from natural theology: see E. TeSelle, in Cornelius Mayer (ed.), *Augustinus-Lexikon* (Basle: Schwabe, 1986–), s.v. But the argument entered by Anselm under the same terms seems to be clearly close to, or certainly part of, natural theology.

believer derived no understanding from the argument.[38] And this is exactly why the ontological argument has continued to be a matter of philosophical discussion between those who believe and those who do not believe. Even allowing the utmost to the Barthian sort of interpretation, if the argument failed to work by the publicly available logic that it uses, then it would mean that the believer seeking understanding would not have gained any more understanding than he had at the beginning.

And in any case Barth's presentation of Anselm may well be quite wrong. Barth's view that 'the knowledge which Anselm's proof seeks to impound and impart is the knowledge that is peculiar to faith, knowledge of what is believed from what is believed', has 'overwhelming textual evidence against it'.[39] Anselm wanted to make his proof 'by necessary reasons', 'without the authority of scripture', and even *Christo remoto*, that is to say, leaving out of consideration the facts of Christ's being and the interpretation of these facts. Non-Barthians who had wanted to do the same thing would have been savaged by Barthians for their ignoring of revelation. To talk of anything 'with Christ left out', even to use the expression, would have been the worst of offences.

In other words, Barth's work on Anselm, and that entire side of his thinking, stood entirely opposed to the biblical, revelational, aspect of his work which had so much influence on biblical scholars. If the existence of this work by Barth did not cause disillusionment among biblical scholars, this was because most of them, being (unlike him) truly remote from natural theology, uninterested in its values, and unaccustomed to its

[38] I say this with hesitation, because I find theologians whom I respect insist, along with Barth, that this is not so. But I find I cannot believe them. I am much more inclined to believe philosophers, who normally—if not universally—count Anselm's proof as an obvious element of natural theology. Thus J. L. Mackie, *The Miracle of Theism* (Oxford: Clarendon Press, 1982), 49: 'Contrary to what is sometimes said, Anselm's argument was put forward explicitly as a *proof* of the existence of a god. Anselm's own belief, did not, of course, depend on the proof, but preceded it; equally his first critic, the monk Gaunilo, presumably believed in God though he rejected the proof. None the less, the argument is not at home only in the thoughts of those who believe on other grounds, but is designed to convince someone who is initially uncertain or who does not believe that there is a god, by showing that such disbelief cannot be coherently maintained.' This statement seems to me to be correct.

[39] Jonathan Barnes, *The Ontological Argument* (London: Macmillan, 1972), 6, and on Barth's faults in philosophical analysis see his p. 68.

ways, neither read the book nor paid any attention to it. Its very existence should have been a warning: Barth's apparent biblical emphasis and rejection of natural theology was in part a matter of appearance rather than of reality. His theology was at bottom a dogmatic-philosophical system, in which the biblical exegetical foundation, however many pages it occupied, was logically incidental.

Moreover, the Anselm book undercut much of the same stimulus which Barth had given both to biblical theology and to Reformational ideals. What was the point of the highly exclusive Reformational appeal of his Gifford Lectures, and of the declaration that Roman Catholic theology was based on a compromise with natural theology, when this loyal Roman Catholic monk had managed to enunciate so much that was basic to Barthianism? What was the point of the appeals to biblical mentality and to Hebrew thought when so much could be learned from this medieval theologian who was so totally devoid of insight into either?

In fact most people thought that Barthianism retained a concealed natural theology. All that was uncertain was what that natural theology was. Some, as I have said, thought that it was something like atheism. At earlier stages it was more like existentialism, later it came to be more like Hegel's thought. Some thought that Platonism entered into it—again a contradiction with the furiously anti-Greek spirit of the biblical theology movement which did so much to support the Barthian initiative. The fact that external apologetics were rejected, the abandonment of all use of natural theology to convince the unbeliever, left Barthianism with the problem of *internal* apologetics, of means, within Christianity, by which Christians could be persuaded that the Barthian version of their faith was the right one. This was where the loss of natural theology created a difficulty—not perhaps for Barth himself, who on the whole paid little attention to other people's opinions, but for his followers, who had the task of talking within the larger Christian community. The loss of natural theology meant that they could not really argue with other people on equal terms. There was no common ground upon which to stand. The domineering aggressiveness and militancy of Barthian discourse was familiar in the theological experience of the entire mid-century. Revelation was central and must be accepted, but there were no real arguments to be offered why any particular claims to revelation should be believed.[40] This situation continued all along the line. Certainly there is an epistemological structure in Barth upon which his development of doctrinal ideas depends.

But the most powerful Barthian apologetic was *historical*. This may seem surprising at first, since Barth is often visualized, at least among biblical scholars, as one who disputed the (supposed) domination of historical methods in biblical and theological matters. But in fact Barthianism showed itself heavily dependent on historical constructs. It generated, and depended upon, a mass of historical arguments about how things had gone wrong in the history of thought.[41] The great ultimate disappointment about Barthianism is that, when it claimed to be able to tell us, richly and fully, about God, as a matter of Christian faith, we found that we learned nothing about God from it, but only a mass of historical assertions, or sometimes plain myths, which were intended to convince us that Barthianism as an intellectual system was right. We cannot pursue this further, but the existence and power of a Barthian apologetic is obvious, and is likely to be a sign that a hidden natural theology was there all along. And a natural theology is perhaps not in itself so bad a thing, but a hidden natural theology accompanied by violent attacks on natural theology is a clear sign that something is wrong.

## 7. Concluding Aspects

Another important point of principle in this area is as follows: natural theology itself, in all probability, depends on *religion*. This point might well have been made by Barth or made more strongly, for it is in line with his own approach, which emphasized revelation as against religion; but I do not know that he or his followers made

---

[40] On this see the clear and attractive discusssion of W. J. Abraham, *An Introduction to the Philosophy of Religion* (Englewood Cliffs, NJ: Prentice-Hall, 1985), 77 ff. In another paper he writes, 'Despite its extraordinary impact, neo-orthodoxy did not have the intellectual resources to argue a case for divine revelation, not least because it rejected in principle that arguments could be given for divine revelation': this from 'Revelation Revisited' (forthcoming).

[41] Thus, among countless examples, Torrance, 'The Problem of Natural Theology', 125: 'Barth reached this judgement through extensive examination of the history of German Protestantism which it is extremely difficult if not impossible to refute.' It was always difficult to refute for those who wanted to agree with the conclusions reached by Barth.

as much of it as they might have done. What I mean is the following. Natural theology rested supposedly on human resources, on rational arguments, and on perceptible, observable relations like the beauty and order of creation. But these supports seemed valid to people for the most part *because* of the religious faith that they already had or at least admired and partly shared. Far from natural theology being the basis or groundwork of religious faith, it is re-ligion that forms the basis and ground upon which natural theology is formed. Thus, for example, as we shall argue, the idea, basic to the Wisdom of Solomon and to St Paul, that the harmony and beauty of the created world should have led to the recognition of the creator God, that idea existed and exists because people had already a religion in which there was one creator God, and therefore they *saw* the phenomena of nature in that light. Similarly, one might suppose, a person like Barth denied natural theology because his religion, at that stage in time and history, was one for which it was supremely important that people should *not* be able to know any-thing about anything except through Jesus Christ. This observation, as we shall see, has many ramifications running through our dis-cussion.

Barthianism in its earlier stages treated religion as the negative pole to which revelation was the positive one. But at the end of the day it seemed to go back to religion. Barth himself in the good old days was very interested in the secular, in atheism, in socialism, and the like, and seemed to value these as honest reactions to reality, unlike the reactions of religious people which were dishonest and unreal. But in its latter stages Barthianism forgot most of this. It came to favour piety, religiosity, and the like more than the lively stimulus of critical thought. Its tendency ended up with privilege for pious people.

Several other aspects have to be added. First, we should not allow ourselves to forget the *absoluteness* of the classic Barthian rejection of natural theology.[42] Later, as has been said, there was some kind of turn back towards natural theology, and people began to state a modified Barthian position: it all depended on what kind of natural theology, if it had been this kind or that kind Barth would have gone along with it. These are myths created in order to conceal what were actual changes of opinion. In his controversy with Brun-ner Barth made it clear that his rejection was absolute. There was

[42] Cf. already Ch. 1 n. 18.

little or no attempt at achieving fine distinctions between one conception of natural theology and another. In fact the intellectual
standard of that controversy, seen from afterwards, was low. 'True'
natural theologies were to be rejected as thoroughly as 'false' ones.
Barth left no room for the possibility that there might be *any* kind of
natural theology, Christological, ontological, or anything else,
that might even be considered as a possibility.

Again, it later on came to be asserted that it was not natural
theology as such, and only the *independence* of natural theology, its
existence as a total autonomous *system*, its *completeness* and its
*separateness* from revelation in Christ, that was wrong. This would
suggest that a minor, complementary, or ancillary presence of
natural theology would not be objectionable. And all this, taken in
itself, may indeed be true. But it is not true of the classic Barthian
position. For, as I have shown, Barth fought doggedly, deter-
minedly, and uncompromisingly against the very slightest hints of
the presence of natural theology within the Bible, and in doing so he
deployed critical wiles which in their recalcitrance were worthy of
the most extreme negativities of critical scholarship. In his exegesis
he showed no signs of room for this minor, complementary, or
ancillary role for natural theology. In this respect he contradicted
the styles and features which were characteristic of his exegesis in
other regards. As already pointed out, Barth's exegesis in general
was theologically *expansive*. I mean as follows.[43]

With any biblical passage it is always a question whether it states
'a theology' or not. Critical scholars often find this hard to handle:
their approaches do not provide instruments with which to answer
such questions. Asked, for instance, whether according to Genesis 1
God 'reveals himself' in the creation of the world, they will
commonly feel unable to answer: the question depends on defini-
tions of 'reveal' which have their context in theology and not in
biblical studies. If forced to answer, they may well prefer the negative: no, the text does not say that creation is a revelation. There is,
shall we say, a more narrow and critical way, and a more expansive
and imaginative way, of dealing with that question. Of almost any
biblical passage, even of the most 'theological'-seeming, one can
say, with the critical scholar's meticulousness, with his unwillingness to read too much developed doctrine into a text: this does
not formulate a theology. Taking it this way, one can say: John does

[43] Following what is already briefly stated in Ch. 3.

not express a 'theology' of incarnation, Paul does not formulate a 'doctrine' of justification by faith, Deuteronomy does not have a 'theology' of election, and so on. If one goes by the more expansive and imaginative way, one can say: well, John may not state a doctrine of incarnation *expressis verbis*, he is not an academic theologian, but what he says leads in that direction: it points forward to, and gives suggestions that must lead to, such a theology.

Now Barthian exegesis was in this regard solidly in favour of the expansive and imaginative: the scripture opened out into the wide field of theological formulation. Part of the Barthian irritation with biblical scholars lay in their petty-minded doubts about such theological expansiveness, their fact-grubbing unwillingness to go beyond what the text itself actually said. But *in anything that seemed close to natural theology* Barth went the other way, and turned to the most dogged critical and sceptical negativism. Upon any question in this area he deserted his theological expansiveness and adopted the timid pettifogging and defensive tactics which he in other matters so deplored in biblical critics. Let us then put it in this way: a passage like the Areopagus speech, treated imaginatively as a theological point of departure, comes far closer to pointing towards a natural theology than it does to pointing towards a Barthian-style theology of special revelation. *If* there is a theology of incarnation in John, *if* there is one of justification in Paul, *if* there is a doctrine of the Trinity in the New Testament (and even more if there is one in Genesis, as Barth maintained!), then there is natural theology in the Areopagus speech.

One illustration will make this clear. Conzelmann, discussing the Areopagus speech in his Hermeneia commentary, tells us that the sense of the passage 'cannot be restated in the form of a thesis like "Luke advocates a natural theology", because it will not do to evaluate these statements in an unhistorical manner, whether to accept them or reject them'.[44] Exactly so: a careful critical scholar, Conzelmann wants to hold back from saying whether or not this material favours a 'natural theology', for on exact historical grounds the term itself is anachronistic and introduces ideas which belong to later ages. On the level on which *Barth* is speaking, however, this is no argument for the rejection of natural theology: on the contrary, as we have seen, on *that* level Conzelmann's comments translate

---

[44] H. Conzelmann, *Acts* (Hermeneia; Philadelphia: Fortress, 1987), 148.

very clearly into an *affirmation* of natural theology. By contrast, Barth, who was normally expansive in the drawing of doctrinal conclusions, adopted the utmost of sceptical critical outlooks wherever natural theology was in question. His exegesis, however we may evaluate it in general, was thus selectively and tendentiously applied, magnifying the elements which fitted with the needs of his theology, and minimizing those which his theology opposed. If we were to adopt Barth's own usual expansiveness as a universal principle, then we would have to say: the Bible is *full* of natural theology, it runs through it everywhere and underlies everything.

And this leads on to two other implications. First, Barth's position throughout was that Reformed theology had no reason to bother about natural theology. It did not have to argue against it, or take notice of it at all. It simply ignored it. Reformed theology had no need to make adjustments to its own programme because of the existence of natural theology. On the purely dogmatic level this might have been true, but on the exegetical level it was not so. Here Barth broke his own principles: his whole approach to exegesis was designed, I believe, in order to obviate the possibility that scripture might contain evidence for natural theology. The central point is perhaps this: if you ask the question, from where did these ideas come?, you are pretty sure to find traces of natural theology in the Bible. The way to obscure these traces is to damp down, as far as possible, all questions of from where biblical persons got their thoughts. The Barthian approach is to ask, not from where the ideas come, but: what are the theological realities to which the words refer? And since realities other than revelation are not theologically significant, the chances of recognizing the presence of natural theology are slim. Far from serenely ignoring the question of natural theology, Barth directed and biased exegetical approaches precisely in order to evade the exegetical posing of that question. One particularly relevant example will be discussed in Chapter 8. On these grounds alone, and on others as well, we may conclude: it is not possible for Barthianism to move towards a greater recognition and a more positive valuation of natural theology without a substantial element of revision, that is, without a dismantling of some of the claims that were made at an earlier time. This is the very least of the demands that one must make of it.

Secondly, concerning the independence of natural theology as a totally autonomous system. I have not thus far said anything that supports the idea of such an autonomy. Any natural theology we have seen within the Bible is scarcely independent in that sense. What its presence suggests is the converse: that revelational theology is not a totally autonomous system either. Within the Bible it is mixed up with elements of natural theology. Once again, therefore, we come up against the question whether the distinction between the two is really of ultimate importance at all.

# 7

# Religion, Tradition, and Natural Theology

Let us suppose that we have shown that natural theology is not only sporadically present in the Bible, but widely and deeply involved in it. Even if this is true, it will not be the end of our problems, for a new set of questions will arise, including the following.

The elements we have detected, which we may call a 'biblical' natural theology, seem very limited in character. They do not amount to the fuller natural theology with which we have been familiar. They do not offer philosophical proofs of the existence of God, they do not work by means of pure reason, they do not appear to amount to the total system of classical theism or anything like it. People might therefore object: if it had never been any more than this, no one would have objected so vigorously to the idea of natural theology at all.

It might therefore be said: let us accept this very limited 'biblical' natural theology, but let us refuse to expand it in any way. Let us deny classical theism, rational proofs of God, and all the rest, let us stick within the biblical limits. The idea is a tempting one. It would be nice to say, for instance, that the limited natural theology as deployed by the Wisdom of Solomon, or by Paul whether in Acts or in Romans or in both, integrated with revelatory material and used as a sort of conceptual auxiliary to his missionary purposes, is fully acceptable, but that the full philosophical natural theology, working by reason alone, separated from revelation, leads away from the God of the Bible and of Christian faith and is to be rejected. One is validated by the Bible, the other is not. Why should we not take this path?

In order to start an approach to the question, let us go back to the contrast between what we shall call the biblical God, the God of Abraham, Isaac, and Jacob, and the God of the philosophers, the

God of theism. Biblical scholars, as we have seen, are interested in the biblical God, and not much in the God of the philosophers.

When we begin to describe the character of the biblical God, we have to make a remark that will doubtless be surprising: the God of Israel is, in some ways, not so different from the Greek gods as has been supposed. By 'the Greek gods' I mean, of course, the gods of Homer, not the god of the Greek philosophers. The God of Israel is a clearly defined personality, as they are. He has a personal name, as they have. He speaks articulately, in Hebrew, as they do in Greek. He has many anthropomorphic features, and they are highly anthropomorphic. He changes his mind, as they do, and allows himself on occasion to be persuaded to do so, as is the case with them. He intervenes in historical events, as they do. He favours certain individuals or social groups, as they do. He takes vengeance on those who have offended his will, as they sometimes do. He is interested in atonement for offences, as some at least of them are. These common elements have much of importance about them. It is ironic now to think back on the biblical theology of this century and contemplate the fact that the features which were most valued as constituting Hebrew thought as against Greek were actually features which Hebrew thought in considerable measure held in common with the gods of Homer. What made the great difference to the God of Israel was that, along with this common personality profile, he was the only God and jealous of that unique status; and, in addition, he was the sole creator of the world.

Now when we in modern times talk about the 'biblical view' of things, its distinctiveness, its personal and dynamic character, its grounding in history, its involvement in human events, and so on, we are in large measure basing ourselves upon just these aspects of the God of Israel, and upon the many biblical passages that speak in this way. These form the basis, we might say, for the characteristically 'biblical' emphasis in contrast with the theistic one. But its commonage with the gods of Homer may perhaps suggest that those aspects which are most characteristic of the God of the Bible have some basis in the natural rather than in the strictly revelational.

The theistic emphasis, by contrast, is universal. It seeks consistency. It lays emphasis on the distinction of transcendent from immanent, of eternity from time. It is interested in omnipotence, in omniscience, in perfection. Its God does not change. He controls absolutely everything. Naturally, he makes no mistakes. Nor does he suffer. Anthropomorphism disappears from his character, becoming at the most a pleasant figure of speech, for God is incorporeal, and the concept of being god means the opposite of all the finitude that belongs to humanity. If the 'biblical' emphasis has many similarities to the gods of Homer, the theistic has much in common with the god of Greek philosophy.

Now this contrast has much to do with the problems we have been discussing. Modern biblical studies and theology came to emphasize a view of the human person, and of God, for which terms like 'personal', 'active', 'dynamic', and 'historical' were used. According to this view, the person was an active entity, living in interrelation with other persons, and this interrelation took place in time, with one action being followed by a reaction, a sequence which deepened and developed the very living interrelation between persons. This was true of biblical humanity, and it was true of the God of the Bible. The story-presentation of the God of the Bible is a supreme quality of biblically based religion. Contrary to this view there stands the traditional theistic approach and terminology, which, one might say, stresses the absolute rather than the interactive: eternity, omniscience, omnipotence, immutability, and so on, as we have said. Such a theism appears to bring us closer to the world of natural theology. The personal-activity picture of biblical God and man has been dominant among biblical scholars, had some overlap with personalist and existentialist philosophies,[1] and was actively emphasized by Barth, forming part of his adherence to biblical thought-forms[2] and underlying his rejection of natural theology. Thus theologians emerging from the Barthian matrix tend to regard theism and theistic arguments as outdated and generally intolerable. Listen for instance to Dietrich Ritschl, in his *The Logic of Theology*:[3]

Biblically based talk of God is not supported by classical theism but is rather sucked into a lack of freedom . . . This strait-jacket of the theistic model of God, the postulate of a self-sufficient sovereign God who is con-

---

[1] Here one should bear in mind the very considerable impact of the thought of Martin Buber and of John Macmurray, both of whom were very influential in the upbuilding of Scottish Barthianism in the period 1940–60.

[2] See Wolfhart Schlichting, *Biblische Denkform in der Dogmatik* (Zurich: Theologischer Verlag, 1971)—a work on an important theme, but one that seems unfortunately to be almost slavishly uncritical concerning Barth's success in this regard.

[3] Cf. also E. Jüngel, *God as the Mystery of the World* (Edinburgh: T. & T. Clark, 1983), and J. B. Webster, *Eberhard Jüngel* (Cambridge: Cambridge University Press, 1986), esp. 80 f.

ceivable without reference to humanity in the last resort, allows only [either] compulsory subjection to the rule of a mysterious god or a decision for the supposed freedom of godlessness. To this degree it is right to say that classical theism allows no freedom—it requires the sacrifice either of our own humanity or of belief in God ...

[Only a trinitarian understanding can] suppress the theistic longing for the demonstration of a physical and mechanistic omnipotence of God over a meaningless, suffering world.[4]

And with these judgements I very much sympathize. Where then is the problem? Why can we not reject the entire theistic impulse and confine ourselves to the personal, active, biblical God? The problem is that the theistic impulses appear to have a place within the Bible itself. We cannot be sure that the Bible succeeded in keeping pure the ideal of the personally active biblical God as distinct from the God of theistic universalism. It did not. These tendencies which we have, very inexactly, labelled as 'theistic' are already present in the Bible. They are part of the inner-biblical interpretative process. As far as I can see, they do not belong to any one stratum of the literature but are scattered over all of it. They are, not surprisingly, a tendency that is stimulated when Hebrew thought enters into the Greek world, and again with the move of Christianity into that world, but they do not seem to be confined to late strata in particular, for examples can be found in quite ancient Hebrew materials. From quite early times the interpretative process included some perception of the need for consistency, some sense of a universal perspective which might need to be respected, some sense of the difficulties of simple anthropomorphism, some sense of the difficulty involved with a God who takes part in some earthly events but ignores other events or stands aloof from them.

Let us take some examples. First, change of mind in God. The God of Israel can regret what he himself has done. He regretted, for instance, that he had made humanity at all, and other living animals as well, and decided to wipe out the whole lot of them. It had been a mistake; or, if not a mistake, he was sorry he had done it anyway. He made Saul king, choosing him carefully from among the people, but later decided to reject him. That had been a mistake too. He planned to destroy everyone in the city of Sodom but allowed himself to be persuaded by Abraham, stage by stage, that this would be wrong if there were fifty righteous people, then if there were forty, then if

[4] D. Ritschl, *The Logic of Theology* (London: SCM, 1986), 139 f., 155; German original, *Zur Logik der Theologie* (Munich: Kaiser, 1984), 176 f., 194.

there were thirty, or twenty, or ten. And these are only the better-known places. If we bring in interpretations of God's will by prophets and others, there are a good number more. According to Ezekiel 26, God brought up Nebuchadnezzar king of Babylon against the city of Tyre. The prophet vividly describes the destruction of the city that will follow. The statement was made 'in the eleventh year, on the first day of the month'. Only a few pages later, in a prophecy dated, apparently, sixteen years later (Ezek. 29[17]), Ezekiel starts out from the evident fact that Nebuchadnezzar's siege of Tyre had been a failure. Though he and his army had worked hard, they had gained nothing for their labour. Therefore, the prophet goes on,

Behold, I will give the land of Egypt to Nebuchadrezzar king of Babylon; and he shall carry off its wealth and despoil it and plunder it; and it shall be the wages for his army. I have given him the land of Egypt as his recompense for which he laboured, because they worked for me, says the Lord God. (Ezek. 29[19f.])[5]

This all makes for a very natural 'human' reaction, but it is unlike what one expects of a God who controls the world. In fact God changes his mind, or regrets what he has decided or done, a number of times in the Old Testament. All this belongs to what we think of as the 'biblical' picture of God. But 1 Samuel 15[29] gives us the opposite point of view: 'Also the God of Israel will not lie nor repent; for he is not a man, that he should repent.'[6] Because God is different from a human being, one can be sure that he does not change his mind. He has immutability. Something of the theistic viewpoint is already there. Is not something of the same viewpoint already there in St James when he speaks of God as the 'Father of lights in whom there is no variation or shadow of turning' (Jas. 2[17])?

Similarly with God's power. The God of Israel alone had power, other gods were nonentities who could not do anything; Yahweh alone had created the world and guided what went on within it. The Bible tells us a selection of events in which all this can be seen. But does this mean that God's power is absolute, so that he can do anything at all? The answer is, generally speaking: they had not thought of that, the biblical material is not designed, selected, or

---

[5] Already discussed in my *Escaping from Fundamentalism* (London: SCM, 1984), 26 f.

[6] On this cf. already my *The Semantics of Biblical Language* (London: Oxford University Press, 1961), 252 f. and n. 1.

edited with that in mind. They certainly had no idea of the logical puzzles that emerge, such as whether God can create an object too heavy for God to lift, or whether God can make a table which God did not make.[7] But they were certainly able to produce sayings that could appear to point in such a direction, and which were later so understood.

The same applies to God's knowledge. Human knowledge is very limited but God knows everything that is going on. Yet the main part of Israel's story is very reserved about God's knowledge and planning.[8] These things happen, God is somewhere behind it all, but little is said explicitly about a universal direction of events. In Genesis 19[20] God has heard the outcry against Sodom and Gomorrah for their evil ways, but he is not sure that these reports are accurate, and he proposes to go down there to see for himself; clearly, he did not already know. On the other hand, Jesus' words about how a sparrow does not fall to the ground without the Father's will, or about how every hair of the head is numbered, look like a very absolute and universal statement. Too universal, indeed, for some people, so that, even early on, interpreters had to begin explaining that such sayings should not be taken literally: thus it is absurd, St Jerome argues, to suppose that God knows at every moment how many fleas there are in the world or how many fish in the sea.[9]

Time and eternity produced the same kind of problem. It was not surprising that Oscar Cullmann strove so hard to show that 'eternity' in the Bible was not something different from time, but was the totality of time: it was only part of the anti-theistic reaction of the period, disliking eternity as it disliked immortality. The characteristic Hebrew term, עוֹלָם, in the Bible doubtless means 'perpetuity', and no 'problem of time and eternity' was known.[10] But since עוֹלָם was an area specially associated with God it was an easy passage to the thought of it as something essentially different from time as humans experience it.

The question of the immediate parousia is a good illustration. Matthew 24[34] is quite clear: 'Truly, I say to you, this generation will not pass away till all these things take place' (RSV). An expectation

---

[7] A. Kenny, *The God of the Philosophers* (Oxford: Clarendon Press, 1979), 93, 98.

[8] That the Old Testament contains no idea of a divine 'plan' was shown by B. Albrektson, *History and the Gods* (Lund: Gleerup, 1967), ch. 5, pp. 68 ff.

[9] Kenny, *The God of the Philosophers*, 6; cf. also below, Ch. 9.

[10] See J. Barr, *Biblical Words for Time* (2nd edn., London: SCM, 1969), esp. 117.

of a swift or immediate parousia is not to be denied. But by the later New Testament times it was necessary to argue and reason about this. According to 2 Peter 3[3 ff.], there would be scoffers, asking 'Where is the promise of his coming? For, ever since the fathers fell asleep, all things have continued as they were from the beginning of creation.' This rational objection required a considered reply. As the time-honoured answer goes, for God a day is as a thousand years, and a thousand years as one day. So, it implies, God is not behind time with his promise. Moreover, God has a reason: he is giving time for sinners to reach repentance. The inner-biblical interpretative adjustment is necessary in order to meet a reasoned objection.

To sum up this point: those universalizing, rationalizing terms which we take to be characteristic of theism are not wholly absent from the Bible. On the contrary, they are already present, and represent tendencies already there in the Hebrew text. These tendencies, however, were much strengthened through the task of expressing the Jewish religion in the Greek world, and later of doing the same for Christianity. Those aspects within the Bible which have an affinity with theism are indications of operations within the Bible that are similar to natural theology.

My second main argument is this: that some of the features of the Hebrew Bible which at first sight appear most 'revelatory' may in a certain sense themselves be 'natural'. I have already suggested this for the personal, active, nature of the God of Israel, in that that character is at least shared with other gods like the gods of Homer. To this may be added, however, questions of origin. Whence did Israel's monotheism[11] derive?[12] It is not easy to explain it as emerging from an earlier polytheism, as if people who had for centuries been polytheists became monotheistic, whether by gradual evolution or by some sudden internal crisis. In more recent times, when the centrality of the Exodus as a revelatory event was so much emphasized, it was often said that monotheism in its Israelite form

[11] I accept the caution expressed by Dr Peter Hayman of Edinburgh in his learned article 'Monotheism: A Misused Word in Jewish Studies', *JJS* 42 (1991), 1–15. Within the world of Jewish religion 'monotheism' may well be too simple and universal a term. But from the point of view of *comparison* with, say, the world of Homer, the Jewish religion appears extremely different and 'monotheism' seems a natural word to express the difference.

[12] Cf. my brief discussions in the articles 'Monotheism' and 'Polytheism', in *Harper's Bible Dictionary* (San Francisco: Harper & Row, 1985), 652 and 806 f.; earlier, and somewhat immaturely, 'The Problem of Israelite Monotheism', *TGUOS* 17 (1957–8), 52–62.

emerged as a response to the Exodus experience, or as a result of it, or as a reflection on it or an inference from it. Yahweh alone had delivered the people from Egypt, and so they concluded that there was no other god than he. But none of these explanations is really convincing: they often depend on an inappropriate mixing of different categories of evidence and theory. It is at least equally possible that monotheism came to be established in Israel through inheritance from an earlier stage and from an earlier people or group, where monotheism already existed, doubtless in an inchoate form. And it is not unlikely that considerations that would, in later centuries, have been considered to belong to natural theology were already at work in providing an element of rational structure within the complex world of myth.[13]

The so-called 'Kenite hypothesis'—it can hardly be said to have been definitely proved, and in that sense is a hypothesis, but on the other hand is not at all hypothetical, in that it is based on a clear collocation of material from within the Bible—points very suggestively in this direction. The father-in-law of Moses, whom we just met in another connection, appears under another name when Judges 4[11] tells of Heber the Kenite, whose wife was shortly to do a memorable act of exclusivism for the God of Israel, and mentions that he had 'separated from the Kenites, the descendants of Hobab the father-in-law of Moses'—a different name, but again the father-in-law, and this time in relation to the Kenites. The Kenites seem to have been early absorbed within the society of Judah and their identity disappeared, but they left an important mark on Israelite tradition, the most obvious sign of which is the presence, at a key point in Israel's traditions, of the story of their eponymous ancestor or first man, Cain himself. Cain is famous, of course, for his murder of his brother, but he has many other claims to fame, and the one that will concern us is that his family were, within the canonical books of the Old Testament, the great innovators in technology: Cain built the first city, and his children were the first raisers of animals, the first musicians, and the first metal-workers—something that will be relevant much later in our story, when we think about the place of

---

[13] For relevant thoughts in these regards, see John C. L. Gibson, 'The Theology of the Ugaritic Baal Cycle', *Orientalia* 53 (1984), 202–19: note his words (219): 'The Ugaritic Baal Cycle, so interpreted, enshrines in my estimation a view of reality, a natural theology, if you like, that reflects the greatest credit on the mythic poets who composed it.' See also his 'Language about God in the Old Testament', *Cosmos*, 5, (1989), 43–50.

science. But, for the present, to cut a long story short, the exclusive
and sometimes fanatical devotion to the one God only may have
come into Israel as the existing religious attitude of a group in early
times, a group or more than one such group, for along with Kenites
we see Levites with the same characteristics, such as the Phinehas of
Numbers 25, noted for his fanaticism (קִנְאָה) for Yahweh the God of
Israel, who pierced through with a spear a man and a Midianite
woman and brought an end to a destructive plague. In other words,
what I am saying is that monotheism may have come into Israel as a
conviction that was already 'natural' within a particular group and
eventually, partly through their fanaticism, partly through its intrinsic theological power, came to be dominant, so that in the end
monotheism came to be 'natural' for all Jews everywhere. It became
the given way in which people thought. Jews eventually ceased to
feel polytheism as a temptation. Monotheism, like aniconic worship
and like belief in creation, came to be the particular social and
intellectual inheritance of a group, and their world-view was based
upon it. This was not 'natural theology' in the sense of dependence
upon philosophical thinking with its universal categories, but it was
'natural' in that for the group concerned it already was the normal
human awareness of deity which everyone inherited from birth. Once
established, however, monotheism could quickly form links and
contacts with universal philosophical categories, and this is what
took place, in Judaism certainly in the Greek period but probably
even before. The mockery of the feeble and unreal gods of polytheism, as in Deutero-Isaiah, is an easy and obvious expression of
these tendencies; compare and contrast with this the criticism by
Xenophanes of the anthropomorphic gods of Greek tradition.
Hebrew monotheism was part of the essential data of the Bible
which enabled the subsequent connection with natural theology to
be made; and this was all the more so because Hebrew monotheism
itself had an aspect of natural religion about it. Monotheism and
natural theology are thus connected not only logically but also
historically, and the Hebrew law is one of the central means of
connection between them.

But here we must add one of the obvious realities of the whole
question: as a matter of fact, the Jewish tradition proved itself to be
capable of synthesis with natural theology or something extremely
like it. At one end of the temporal spectrum we may name Philo of
Alexandria, at the other Maimonides. Both these major figures

proved able to dovetail philosophical insights dependent on Greek philosophy into a quite traditional Judaism, and, while Philo came to be largely lost from Jewish tradition until fairly modern times and was preserved mainly in a Christian stream of consciousness, Maimonides in spite of criticism and controversy remained a towering intellectual figure, profoundly authoritative in Judaism. Certainly, it may well be asked in what sense their work really constituted a *natural* theology; but let us say that, in this sense, namely that the authoritative material received from God in the Bible and Jewish tradition could be and should be communicated and expressed in categories that were knowable to humanity and already existing in human life, in that sense their work definitely included and implied natural theology. So simple facts make improbable the idea that the Hebrew mind is innately hostile to natural theology. Our arguments have provided an explanation of why this is so.

There is, however, yet another reason why we cannot 'canonize' the natural theology of the Bible and treat it as the sole and final, good and valid, instance of natural theology argument. Though I think there is much use of natural theology in the Bible, I am not sure that its natural theology is always *right*. It does not seem to me to be definitely or necessarily true. First, I am not sure that it possesses internal coherence, in other words it is not proved by the warrants that are offered in order to prove it; secondly, it is poorly informed about some of the realities of the world; thirdly, it is not really 'autonomous' natural theology, but is itself derived from previous religion and is dependent on previous religion. The only way, therefore, in which the direction indicated by the 'biblical' natural theology can be salutarily pursued is that it be extended into the wider world of philosophical, scientific, and other investigation, which within the Bible itself is scarcely attempted. This, I suggest, may be the rationale for the 'full' natural theology which did in fact develop through history and the legitimacy of which is now in question.

Let me exemplify this from some biblical materials. Nothing is more clear about the classic 'natural theology' passages of the Bible than their starting-point in creation. God created the world and its wonderful and beneficent design should have demonstrated the reality of the creator. This is a proof, one may say, from *nature*, but it does not arise from any dispassionate examination of the natural world. It arises from religion, from the established religious belief that one deity had made the world and made it good. Although the natural theology of the Jews insisted that from the observation of the created world one could and should conclude to the existence of the creator, that was not the way in which their own ancestors had arrived at their belief in the one creator God.[14] They had arrived at it, indeed, not by simple revelation, as if God had just told them, I happen to be the creator of the world. They had arrived at it through an intellectual process caused by the meeting of two forces: on the one hand the mythologies of the origin of the world which were inherited from earlier and environing religion and from earlier stages of their own religion, and on the other hand, and dominantly, their own monotheism, their tradition of the one God which brought about a substantial remoulding of ideas in this area. It was by some such process, and not primarily by actual observation of the universe, that they came to the view of creation which we find in Genesis 1: generally speaking, a world formed by a process of separation and ordering, the result being all good. There were, indeed, snags here and there in this belief—Wisdom, you remember, mentioned creatures so horrid that they were not included in the verdict that everything that was made was good. But by and large the belief was held. And, as we have seen, the development of this belief into natural theology was motivated by a particular problem, that of idolatry, which was a way of explaining why things had gone so badly wrong, and especially why the Gentile world was so awful. But that very use of the argument prevented it from taking any even and comprehensive account of the constitution of the world. And, when one goes on to the application of this argument, the idea that *all* the moral defects and evils of the Gentile world, from malice through gossiping, slander, disobedience to parents, up to ruthlessness, envy, and murder, plus approbation of all these practices, that all this derived from that original act of idolatry is impossible to take very seriously. It was theory, and polemic religious theory at that. It had no reason to offer for why homosexual practices should derive from idolatry, no explanation of why the original inhabitants

---

[14] Schmithals (Ch. 3 above) makes an analogous point when he argues that Jews did not require the theology of creation implied by Romans 1, because as Jews they were fully informed about creation by the Torah. This is an analogous observation, but my point is not about what was, eventually, in the Torah, but about how the view of creation in Genesis came to be formed.

of the planet, seeing rivers, mountains, horses, cows and sheep, snakes, mosquitoes, and scorpions, had the means to conclude immediately that one beneficent God had created all. It was, in fact, very amateurish and religiously very prejudiced natural theology. And this is one of the defects that have often existed in the tradition of natural theology, and forms an argument against it which Barth may have had in mind, and might indeed have used if he had bothered to provide a proper discussion of natural theology at all. What has been called natural theology has often been a mode in which particular social or religious world-views have been justified and perpetuated: a good example is the way in which aspects of the Greco-Roman world-view have been given sanction by the Church, counted as natural theology, and thus enforced on a later society for which these norms were no longer relevant, or indeed had been proved to be defective.[15] And, as I say, some of the natural theology of the Bible itself may suffer from these same defects. For this reason it is difficult to canonize the limited natural theology of the Bible while denying the right of the subject to expand, to exercise self-criticism, to make fresh contact with the subject-matter, and to invite discussion and illumination from those who stand in a different religious tradition or outside the religious community altogether. These, then, are preliminary reasons why we cannot easily succumb to the temptation to accept natural theology within its biblical limits while denying its proliferation beyond them.

This is highly relevant for many social and ethical problems of the present day. On highly disputed questions such as those of population control, legality of abortion, and the like, people may quote biblical utterances of a 'revelational' type like the command not to kill, but it must be suspected that the real underlying reason is an appeal to 'nature': things must go as nature itself provides, and humans should not presume to interfere with nature. But 'nature' has changed from what it was in ancient times, whether in Greek thought or in the Bible. Neither of these sources had any idea that the ecological balance of the world could be damaged or destroyed by human economics, exploitation, consumption, or other activities; nor had they any idea that human life could be medically prolonged

---

[15] The Church's insistence on the authority of Aristotle in scientific matters is an obvious instance; and provides an obvious reason why Reformers and others came to be opposed to natural theology in general.

far beyond the limits that would be set by unaided 'nature'. They thought of 'nature' as something already fixed and set, whether by natural processes alone or by the creator God; they had no idea that human purpose was going to have a part in deciding what 'nature' is and is to be. Quite possibly the natural theology of the Bible can be extended, analogically or in some other way, in order to take account of these very substantial changes, but an extension at the least it must be: just left to stand as it is, it cannot be expected to cope with the problems.

We must pass, however, to another way in which we may think about it. Central to modern study of the Bible has been the theme of *interpretation*. Almost all currents of scholarship emphasize it. Part of the popularity of this emphasis comes from the wish to minimize the claims of objectivity which, it is commonly but erroneously supposed, critical scholarship made for itself. Not only does the Bible have to be interpreted, but interpretation goes on within the Bible itself. Much of the Bible, perhaps all of the Bible, is the product of interpretation. But the consequence of this has not always been noticed: the more we stress the importance of interpretation, the more we render probable the influence of something like natural theology. Influenced by the dialectical theology, people have been inclined to think of interpretation as something that followed and expounded the contours of revelation without going in any way outside this narrow channel of thought. Interpretation, seen in this way, not only interprets revelation but interprets it solely by the use of categories which themselves derive from revelation and are internal to it. Some of the peculiar contortions of modern interpretative theory are probably half-conscious attempts to demonstrate this. But it would really be very strange if there was interpretation which used no categories whatever that were external to the material being interpreted. From the material itself, new categories grew, and these called for expression in terms which the original material had not contained. But as soon as we admit that such categories may have been used, we face the likelihood that operations of natural theology took place. Moreover, we can show reasons of particular strength why this was very likely in the traditions of Israel as well as those of the New Testament. Consider this thought:

If God is God, then he must be understood as a reality that determines everything, not as a spatially and temporally provincial deity who by chance has some adherents, but as a comprehensive power which is to be rationally perceived out of the reality which it rationally determines. [16]

This thought, of a modern theologian, expresses something of the need that Jews may have felt when conscious of the Greek world around them. In interpreting Jewish religion in that world and to that world, the primary category might be, not the God personally active in history—a thought that was certainly still known and affirmed—but, rather, monotheism, opposition to idols, and all that argumentation from the created world which was the central basis for natural theology. All this was already there within the Bible.

What this means is that 'revelational' theology and 'natural' theology were irretrievably mixed up with one another. What had been 'natural' could come to be expressed as if it was 'revelational'. What had been a 'revelational' element could come to be restated as 'natural theology'.

One of the old popular arguments against natural theology was the argument about the camel and the tent. Once the camel gets its nose into the tent, it will soon take up all the space within. Similarly, it was said, if natural theology gets its nose into the edifice of Christian theology, it will soon occupy the entire space and be mixed up in everything, including the purest divine revelation. The only way, therefore, to deal with natural theology is to keep it out entirely. And, so long as one thinks of natural theology as a totally foreign body, and revelatory theology as something quite different, it looks as if the argument might have some force. But we have seen how it may be circumvented. The natural theology within the Bible is not a foreign body intruded, but an interpretative stage through which the revelatory material passes, or—sometimes—it is material inherited 'by nature' which then recasts itself as revelatory material.

And, in conclusion, this argument from interpretation offers an answer to another of the apparently strong traditional arguments against natural theology. Natural theology, it was always said by its opponents, produces idols, thoughts and ideas generated out of the human mind, as distinct from revelation, where the thoughts and ideas come from God himself. The emphasis on the interpretatory element, within the Bible and in the handling of the Bible, overturns this argument. That argument makes sense only if the entire Bible is a univocal expression of one unitary theology. As soon as we accept

[16] H. Dembowski, 'Natürliche Theologie—Theologie der Natur', *Ev. Th.* 45 (1985), 225.

that there are different theologies within the Bible, and that only interpretation can lead us back to the one God who is the object of its witness, then we see that revelational theology is, in this respect, on the same basis as natural theology. Even if there is no natural theology in the Bible at all, but only revelational theology, it cannot produce a total picture of God except through the activity of the theological interpreter. But that interpreter must use his own thoughts, reason, instincts, and experience in order to grade, to select, to bring together, to order, and to raise to higher levels the material with which he or she works. The interpreter will have to draw conclusions from the scripture which it itself does not make express; and this drawing of conclusions will depend on the categories, methods, and anterior preferences of the interpreter. Thus the theologian who fully denies natural theology may nevertheless be constructing an 'idol' out of scriptural materials just as much as the natural theologian is constructing an 'idol' out of other materials. That this has been so, the history of theological thinking, and notably of those theologies which minimized the role of natural theology, makes sufficiently clear.

Another point to be added is this. It is often thought that the effect of natural theology is to tone down revelation, to decrease its strangeness by assimilating it to accepted human experience and the tolerances which it will permit. And sometimes this may well be so. But the opposite can also be the case. Natural theology can also work to exaggerate the differences between the human and the divine. God is, people say, 'by definition' perfect, eternal, infinite, in all respects removed from the limitations of human existence. Thoughts of this kind, by emphasizing the infinite distance of God from humanity, strike people as being particularly 'revelatory', just when they are actually produced by operations of natural theology. Some things that are in the Bible may have come about in this way. Take miracle stories, at first sight an obvious area of revelation. But why do we find that one version of a story shows an enormously increased degree of miraculous character as compared with another story of the same kind? Why, for example, does Chronicles sometimes show enormously inflated numbers of soldiers and of casualties in battle, as compared with Samuel/Kings?[17] Part of the explanation may lie in the belief that, God being God, matters of

---

[17] See my *Escaping from Fundamentalism* (= *Beyond Fundamentalism* (Philadelphia: Westminster, 1984)), 88 f.

historical probability and even of theological balance cease to matter at all. Natural theology operates not only through the severely rational philosophic discussion but also through the mythopoeic capacity of biblical authors. Or, to take a case from more modern experience, is not the basic conviction of fundamentalism, the idea that the Bible is infallible or inerrant, a piece of natural theology: God being (by standard arguments of natural theology) absolutely perfect, if the Bible is his Word, it must be absolutely perfect also—a piece of natural theology which, because it carries sufficient conviction, comes to have the status of revelation?

Finally, another word or two about atheism, which has already been mentioned above. As we saw, the refutation of atheism has often been accepted as a major role of natural theology. Calvin in the first chapters of his *Institutes* used it in this way. All human beings, he believed, had an awareness of God, and an awareness that God was their creator. This was of strategic importance for all that followed, establishing in particular the blameworthiness of people for their sins. Knowing all this, they did not glorify God and that leads on to their all-embracing sinfulness and guilt. To some extent this rested on biblical passages, especially of course the first chapter of Romans; though it rested in considerable degree on debates among the classical philosophers, which were very important in Calvin's mind.

But what sort of value does this have? And what about the famous words of Psalm 14[1], 'The fool hath said in his heart, There is no God'? Scholars tend to assure us that these words imply no 'theoretical' atheism: they are not so much denying the existence of God, rather they question his active presence, his power in action. Maybe so. But I do not really see why this *must* be so; I do not see why the fool should not have thought, as the words directly say, that there is no God at all, that no God exists. Why not? In the world of Israel's interaction with the neighbouring cultures, the primary question was not whether there was a god or not, but how many gods there were; and, along with that, whether male or female, and in particular the question, when one had one major deity, whether that deity had also a female consort—a question that now, from archaeological discoveries, has become a very central one for studies in the Hebrew Bible. In Israel, where the dominant current of tradition had insisted on the one God, and insisted that all other supposed deities were vain or non-existent, the elimination of gods was so obvious and dominant a principle and achievement that it could seem an obvious further step to eliminate them all, and to say that there was none. I do not see why persons could not have taken this step. The Psalmist does not argue with them, either by natural theology or by revealed: such a person is a fool, he says, and he goes straight on into moral condemnation. Perhaps that was all that could be done. All I want to say, at this point, is that atheism as an option is hinted at in the Bible. It is a part of the direction in which Hebrew religion could have been taken to point.

Returning to Calvin's argument—whether based on Romans or on natural theology—we come to this question: how did he know that his views were true for all humanity? People like Calvin lived within the culture and traditions of European Christianity and knew very little outside it. Their sources were the Bible, the later traditions of the Church, and classical Greek and Roman literature. Within Christendom everyone was readily classifiable: there were Roman Catholics; there were Protestants; there were various kinds of heretics; there were Jews; on the edge of the world there were Muslims, or Turks as they were then generally called. All these people had some kind of God and some word for God, almost all believed they had been created by God. Starting from this, it was easy to put into words the judgement that all human persons knew that there was a God (meaning one single personal and transcendent God), who was also their creator. But if they thought this, and if the Bible suggested it, perhaps they were wrong! For, once explorers and missionaries began to travel into Africa, among the Pacific islands, and among the native Americans, they were puzzled to find persons who did not conform to the outlook that dogma considered to be universal to humanity. God? Never heard of any such being. Sin? No idea what you are talking about. Creation? No one here ever bothered about that. In other words, the view of humanity in traditional Christianity, whether built upon biblical grounds or upon natural theology, was the product of a particular religious history and cultural situation. If it is to be tested for its final validity, we know, perhaps, how to do this from the biblical side; from the side of natural theology, it is not clear that the natural theology of the Bible itself can be sufficient. Once again we see: natural theology is supported by the Bible, may be made to combine with the Bible, but is also an aspect of the cultural limitedness of the Bible. The Bible, especially the Old Testament, built upon the Near Eastern cultural patterns of the Semitic-speaking peoples. It knew nothing about the way in which the world had actually originated or how the earliest human beings had lived. It knew nothing about what was going on in China or South America, where considerable civilizations already existed in Old Testament times. All this, needless to say, is relevant to questions of the Churches in the Third World today, and the question of whether, and how far, there is an indigenous basis of thought in their own cultures, as distinct from the taking over of ideas from the Western Churches. But here we shall have to leave it for the present.

# 8

# The Image of God and
# Natural Theology

Thus far little has been said about the image of God in which, according to Genesis 1²⁶ᶠ·, humanity was created. But the passages about the image of God have commonly been taken to be relevant evidence for the question of natural theology, and we have to devote some discussion to them.

Let me remind you of the passages themselves.[1] At Genesis 1²⁶, after the other elements of the world have been created, God says, 'Let us make man in our image, like our likeness', and, it goes on, 'let them have dominion over' the various animals and the world in general. The word rendered as 'man' is, of course, אדם, humanity, not just male persons—or so it seems.[2] The next verse, 1²⁷, goes on to say that God created man in his image; 'in the image of God he created him, male and female he created them. And God blessed them and told them to be fruitful and multiply, and have dominion over all the living creatures, etc.' This is the first, and the most obviously important, place where the image terminology appears.

Secondly, in Genesis 5¹ we read: 'in the day when God created man, in the likeness of God he made him', and then it continues by telling how Adam, the first man, was 130 years old and 'he begat a son in his likeness, like his image, and called his name Seth'—note that the same words are used, but their order is reversed as against that of 1²⁶. Thirdly, in Genesis 9⁶, after permission has been given for man to kill animals for food, God forbids the killing of man and, in

---

[1] Cf. my article 'The Image of God in the Book of Genesis: A Study of Terminology', *BJRL* 51 (1968–9), 11 ff. On the subject in general, a good survey of the older discussions is provided by another Scottish theologian, David Cairns, in his *The Image of God in Man* (London: SCM, 1953). For modern scholarly and exegetical discussion the fullest survey is that provided by Gunnlaugur Jónsson, *The Image of God* (Lund: Almqvist & Wiksell, 1988), and because of his work I make no attempt to cover that discussion in all its many aspects.

[2] Not all have seen it in this way—see below on 1 Corinthians 11⁷.

a phrase which in its Hebrew poetic form combines succinctness and assonance, goes on:

> He who sheds the blood of man, by man shall his blood be shed;
> for in the image of God he made man.

These are the only passages in the Hebrew Bible that use the phrase 'image of God'. Many have added, however, as something of the same general kind, the words of Psalm 8[6f.]:

> What is man, that thou rememberest him, or the son of man, that
> thou attendest to him?
> Thou makest him a little lower than the divine [or: angelic]
> beings, and thou crownest him with honour and glory.
> Thou makest him rule over the works of thy hand; thou hast
> put everything under his feet ...

This poetical passage does indeed have similarities with Genesis. It does not, however, use the actual term 'image' of God, but speaks of honour and glory, combined with a status only a little lower than that of the heavenly beings. This seems to point in the same general direction; nevertheless the term 'image' remains peculiar to the Genesis passages. All of these appear to belong to the same source 'P', and may thus be dated in the time after the Babylonian exile.

Now over the centuries there has been a plentiful supply of interpretations which have sought to tell us what exactly the image of God in humanity was, or is. Only a sketch can be attempted here.[3] In a very simplified way we may mention:

1. 'Spiritual' interpretations. The image of God is related to the spiritual or rational character of humanity, which forms a distinction from the animal world.[4] As a special case within this category we may mention St Augustine, who explained that the divine image in man consists in a trinity like that in God. The human trinity consists in memory, understanding, and love (*memoria, intellectus, amor*), or the human capacity to remember, know, and love God.[5]

2. To this we must add interpretations that *differentiate between aspects* of the image. Irenaeus is noted for distinguishing between the *image* and the *likeness*, the two words that occur in Genesis:

---

[3] I here follow the sequence of the survey by Barth, *KD* iii/1. 216 ff.; *CD* iii/1. 191 ff.

[4] Barth, ibid., quotes St Ambrose, *Hexaemer.* 6. 7 f., for the view that the image lies in the *soul*, while Athanasius goes on to place it in the rationality of man, corresponding to the Logos (*De incarn.* 3).

[5] Jónsson, *The Image of God*, 13. See Cairns, *The Image of God in Man*.

thus, it was supposed, one could perceive a distinction between what is lost through human sin and what remained in humanity even after the Fall. 'According to one common variety of this interpretation, "the *imago* means the human nature which cannot be lost; the *similitudo* means man's original relation to God which may be lost, and since Adam, has been lost".'[6] Thomas Aquinas similarly distinguished between the natural image which was retained by all and the supernatural image which no one possessed until it was restored in Christ. Luther on the other hand rejected the distinction between two elements. For him the image of God in Genesis referred to the original righteousness of humanity, which had been lost. The image which we bear, therefore, is the image of the *fallen* Adam.[7]

3. The third viewpoint contrasts drastically with all the above: namely the *physical* interpretation. Humans are like God because God has a human appearance, they walk upright as he does, and exactly in this way they differ from the animals. The God of the Old Testament is a strongly anthropomorphic God, and the idea of the image of God is the other side of this same coin. Moreover, this interpretation fits well with Genesis 5$^3$, where Adam had a child 'in his likeness, like his image', in other words, one who looked very much like his father. By any account, this passage about Adam and his son Seth is a powerful support to the physical interpretation and a serious difficulty for all others. It enjoys the adherence of the great exegete Gunkel, of the Swiss scholars Humbert and Köhler, of some modern Jewish scholars, and, among theologians, of the profound thinker Eberhard Jüngel.

4. Doubtless the most influential opinion today, however, is what Jónsson calls the 'functional' view: the image of God consists in human dominion over the world. And there is no doubt that this dominion accompanies the reference to the image in its most prominent occurrence, in Genesis 1. It also fits very well with Psalm 8, although there, as has been said, the terminology of

---

[6] Quoted from Jónsson, *The Image of God*, 12, who is quoting Brunner, *Man in Revolt* (New York: Scribners, 1939), 505; German original *Der Mensch im Widerspruch* (3rd edn., Zurich: Zwingli, 1941), 523.

[7] One might well ask what Old Testament evidence could be adduced in favour of this construction, in view of the fact that no passage speaks of a loss of the original image or damage done to it. The path that could be followed was to appeal to the birth (Gen. 5$^3$) of Seth in the image, not of God, but of Adam, i.e. Adam as he now was, after his disobedience.

'image' and 'likeness' is not actually used. It fits less well, or not
at all, with Adam's image in his son, and with the blood of the
killer being shed because God had created man in his image. The
advocacy of von Rad in particular did much for the functional
interpretation, and it was widely accepted and became popular,
at least for a time. More recently, people's interest in ecology
and the conservation of the environment has made them less
willing to accept the ideal of human domination of the world,
and consequently more critical of this interpretation.[8]

5. Karl Barth's interpretation. Barth showed sympathy for the
functional understanding but his own interpretation went in a
different direction.[9] He pointed very definitely to the collocation
of the two phrases: 'in the image of God he created him; male and
female he created them.' The second of these phrases, Barth
declared, was obviously the key to the exegesis of the first.[10] The
image of God was the fact that humanity existed in *close and
inseparable relation*, the relation between man and woman. This
was not a direct trinitarian relation such as Augustine had
discerned, but it was a relation, which by being a relation was
analogical to the relation of the three persons of the Trinity in
God. The image of God in mankind was the relational mutuality
of man and woman, and this was loosely analogical to the
relational existence of the persons in the trinitarian being of
God.[11] It thus had a certain similarity to St Augustine's interpretation, but without being so spiritual and intellectualistic as it
had been; it provided a connection with thoughts about the
man–woman relationship, which was to be important for Barth
in other regards also; and it did claim contextual validation
within the wording of Genesis itself.

---

[8] On this see my article 'Man and Nature: The Ecological Controversy and the
Old Testament', *BJRL* 55 (1972–3), 9–32. There is a mass of other literature touching
on this theme.

[9] Here he acknowledged precedents in Vischer and Bonhoeffer, *KD* iii/1. 218 f.;
*CD* iii/1. 194 ff.

[10] 'Diese geradezu definitionsmässige Erklärung des Textes', *KD* iii/1. 219; *CD*
iii/1. 195.

[11] On Barth's relation to the understanding of the image of God, see especially
Jónsson, *The Image of God*, 65 ff. Barth's connecting of the phrase with a trinitarian
view of God implied a dependence on the plural of 'Let us make . . .' in Genesis 1[26],
an aspect of his argument already adequately rejected by J. J. Stamm, 'Die Imago-
Lehre von Karl Barth und die alttestamentliche Wissenschaft', in *Antwort* (Karl
Barth FS; Zurich: Evangelischer Verlag, 1956), 93 f., and I shall not waste time in
discussing it further.

Now Barth's interpretation has still, perhaps, not become widely known. It was indeed welcomed in some feminist circles, who thought that it at least put woman on an equal level with man, as against ideas that the image of God resided in the male only and not in the woman.[12] But on the whole most people did not become aware of it, which has, perhaps, been a good thing for Barth's reputation, for the fact is that it is a particularly ill-judged and irresponsible piece of exegesis.

This is so for two reasons. First, Barth argued from juxtaposition. Because the statement that God created man in his own image is immediately followed by the phrase 'male and female he created them', Barth argued, the latter phrase must obviously contain the explanation of the former. But this is a manifest fallacy. If phrase X is followed at once by phrase Y, it is only one among many possible functions of Y that it should be the explanation of X; it could equally well be the sequel or the consequence of X, or an addition of a new factor to X, or indeed a qualification or modification of X. Syntactically, Barth's argument was obviously fallacious. It was ingenious, but linguistically could not be taken seriously. As Phyllis Bird says, in the best discussion of the matter thus far written, 'At its most fundamental level Barth's exegesis fails to understand the grammar of the sentences he so ingeniously manipulates.'[13]

Secondly, he provided not the slightest culturally based backing for this exegesis. There was nothing in the conceivable cultural background of the passage that could make plausible the idea that the image of God *actually consisted in* the existence of humanity as both male and female. Barth adduced no evidence that anyone in ancient Israel had thought this way or that the words could have been meant in this way. To quote Phyllis Bird once again,

Despite close reference to the biblical text as his primary source, he [Barth] has failed to discern *its* anthropology—and theology—and has advanced only a novel and arresting variation of the classical trinitarian interpretation, an interpretation characterized by the distinctly modern concept of an 'I–Thou' relationship, which is foreign to the ancient writer's thought and intention at all three points of its application.[14]

[12] On this aspect, see esp. P. A. Bird, ' "Male and Female he Created them": Gen. 1: 27b in the Context of the Priestly Account of Creation', *HTR* 74 (1981), 133 f., and literature there cited.

[13] ' "Male and Female he Created them" ', 132.

[14] Ibid. One may amplify Bird's opinion, however, in the following sense. On the one hand, as she says, it is 'only a novel and arresting variation of the classical trinitarian interpretation'. On the other side, however, and typically of Barth's exegesis,

His interpretation of the image of God was thus a prime example substantiating Paul Lehmann's judgement: '[This] elaborate interpretation ... offers an impressive correlation of ingeniousness and arbitrariness, which allows Barth to ascribe insights and affirmations to ancient writers which, as historical human beings, they could not possibly have entertained.'[15] In fact Barth's exegesis meant that the words of the passage are a set of ciphers that derive meaning only from the framework of one completely modern series of dogmatic assertions, namely his own.

And this was not surprising, for it is highly likely that Barth's whole exegesis was fuelled and motivated by his controversy with Brunner over natural theology, and this is a major reason why the passage deserves to be discussed here. In traditional natural theology it was thought that, because human beings were made in the image of God, this made some natural knowledge of God possible; this was a major aspect of, in Brunner's phrase, the 'point of contact'. In the dialectical theology, however, the image of God in this sense received pretty unfavourable treatment. It was not a very positive factor. Barth and Brunner were agreed in this. Brunner wrote: 'I agree with Barth in teaching that the original image of God in man has been destroyed.'[16]

But even so he did not want to go quite as far in this as Barth. According to Brunner certain aspects of the image of God remained even after man's Fall. As we have seen, there was nothing new in this, many interpreters had said something of the same sort. Brunner expressed it by distinguishing between the formal and the material aspects of the image of God. The formal sense of the concept was the distinctness of humanity as against the animals. This position of superiority is not abolished by sin, indeed (ibid.) it is the presupposition of the possibility of sin, since man is a subject, a rational creature, and responsible. Materially, on the other hand, the image is completely lost: 'man is a sinner through and through and there is nothing in him which is not defiled by sin' (p. 24).

in respect of its identification of the image with the man–woman relationship it is a totally modern invention, wildly remote from anything that the Fathers or the Reformers would have thought, and in this respect worthy to be classed with the many anti-traditional and theologically irresponsible opinions of historical-critical scholarship, against which Barth so frequently railed.

[15] 'Karl Barth and the Future of Theology', *RS* 6 (1970), 113; quoted by Bird, '"Male and Female he Created them"', n. 9.
[16] *Natural Theology* (London: Bles, 1946), 22. Cf. 20.

Thus, according to Brunner, Barth thought that:

Since man is a sinner who can be saved only by grace, the image of God in which he was created is obliterated entirely, i.e. without remnant. Man's rational nature, his capacity for culture and his humanity, none of which can be denied, contain no traces or remnants whatever of that lost image of God.[17]

Well, this might have appeared to put Barth in a tight spot, because, notoriously, in all the passages in the Bible about the image of God there is none that says anything about the loss of the image of God or indeed about any damage to it whatsoever. Indeed, Genesis 9[6], which says that the shedding of human blood will be requited by the shedding of blood, because God made humans in his own image, makes sense only on the assumption that the image of God continued, in all human beings, after the Flood and throughout all history.

Well, while the earlier Barth may well have taken the line that the image was totally obliterated,[18] the classic Barth of the *Church Dogmatics* developed a different interpretation, which I have described above. In the image of God he created humanity, male and female he created them: thus, just as the triune God means an inner relationship of persons within God, analogically there is an I–thou relationship within humanity, between male and female. This satisfies the fact that the image is never destroyed: for it never is a 'thing' or quality that belongs to humanity; they never lost it because, strictly speaking, they had never 'had' it.[19] It also satisfies very well the developmental needs of Barth's theology: it makes an apparent contact on the one side with the exegesis of the older Church, which had seen a trinitarian aspect here, and on the other hand it empties the image of all actual contact between humanity and deity, leaving

[17] Brunner in *Natural Theology*, 20.

[18] Already in *Natural Theology*, 74, Barth is resentful of Brunner's supposing that he, Barth, thinks that 'the image of God in man is totally destroyed by sin'. Yet it would not be surprising if Brunner had so supposed, partly in view of the other aspects of Barth's theology, partly because Calvin himself, whom Barth was likely to have followed, had made it clear the image had been destroyed: 'Since the image of God has been destroyed in us by the Fall, we may judge from its restoration what it originally had been'—*Commentary* on Gen. 1[26]; cf. Peter Barth, 'Das Problem der natürlichen Theologie bei Calvin', *Th. Ex. H.* 18 (1935), 30, and J. H. Leith, *John Calvin's Doctrine of the Christian Life* (Louisville, Ky.: Westminster/John Knox, 1989), 71. On the other hand, Calvin can also speak of 'the divine image within us, which was defaced, and almost obliterated, by the transgression of Adam' (Leith, *Calvin's Doctrine*, 70).

[19] 'Was der Mensch nicht besitzt, das kann er wie nicht vererben, so auch nicht verlieren', *KD* iii/1. 225; *CD* iii/1. 200.

only a relationship within humanity which has some analogy with a relationship within God. It is not a property or quality of human beings, it is not a state of a person in relation to God. The fact is, the interpretation is stimulating, interesting, and ingenious, but totally incredible. It is achieved only by tricks with words and the overriding of syntactical constraints, and it is completely devoid of contextual and cultural possibility. It was, in Phyllis Bird's words, an ingenious manipulation. The contextual support derived from the juxtaposition of 'the image of God' with 'male and female he created them' rests on nothing but juxtaposition, and juxtaposition illegitimately used; and it fails completely when set against wider context, for no sense can be made of the passages of chapters 5 and 9 if the image is supposed to be the relation of male and female to one another. It is an exegesis that could be thought out only by someone for whom the thoughts and intentions of the writers and the cultural situation of their work were irrelevant to the reader's decisions about meaning. The fact is, the whole thing was dictated by the needs and pressures of Barth's own theological situation, and, we must suspect, above all by the need to overcome Brunner.

In saying this I am not denying the possibility of Barth's ultimate theological insight, namely that the relation between man and woman is in some way analogical to the relation between the 'persons' within the Trinity. There might be grounds of support for this in other biblical areas, for example in the familiar concept that there is an analogy between the love of Christ for the Church and the love of man and woman for one another. Or it might be argued on general grounds of the doctrine of the Trinity.[20] But to set it forth as an actual exegesis of the Genesis passages is only to invite ridicule. As often, Barth spoiled his own profound theological thoughts by pretending that they could claim close exegetical support. The idea that the man–woman relationship within humanity actually constitutes the image of God cannot be taken seriously.

Nor can Barth escape from this criticism by appeal to the New Testament: for, on the contrary, the New Testament evidence seems to lie strongly against his interpretation. In this there are several different elements.

[20] See for example the sympathetic treatment of Barth's thought on this subject by Paul Fiddes, 'The Status of Woman in the Thought of Karl Barth', in Janet M. Soskice (ed.), *After Eve* (London: Collins/Marshall Pickering, 1990), 138–55—which however is wisely reticent about the Hebrew basis for the interpretation of the divine image.

First, it is sometimes said that in the New Testament the image of God is Jesus Christ, but this is very misleading when applied to our present question.[21] The New Testament does indeed contain expressions like 2 Corinthians 4⁴, 'the light of the gospel of the glory of Christ, who is image of God' (τοῦ Χριστοῦ, ὅς ἐστιν εἰκὼν τοῦ θεοῦ) and Colossians 1¹⁵, '[of his beloved son] . . . who is image of the invisible God' (ὅς ἐστιν εἰκὼν τοῦ θεοῦ τοῦ ἀοράτου). Christ is the likeness of God, his manifestation. It is difficult or impossible, however, to say that these terms, though verbally almost identical, refer directly to the same image of God in which humanity was, according to Genesis, created. The New Testament provides ample evidence of uses of εἰκών in other connections, e.g. Romans 8²⁹, 'to be conformed to the image of his Son' (συμμόρφους τῆς εἰκόνος τοῦ υἱοῦ αὐτοῦ), or 1 Corinthians 15⁴⁹, which contrasts the 'image' of the earthly with the image of the heavenly, or Hebrews 10¹, where we hear that the law has a 'shadow' of good things to come but 'not the very image' (οὐκ αὐτὴν τὴν εἰκόνα). Note especially in this last case how close εἰκών comes to being the actuality, the reality, rather than an image in the sense of a partial though perceptible similarity. Usage of this kind is well known from Hellenistic sources such as Philo. Thus, not to prolong this point unduly, phrases which talk of Christ as being 'the image of God' are not necessarily intended principally, or even at all, to explain what was meant by the terms of the creation of humanity in the image of God, as known from Genesis. Thus New Testament editions, which commonly print in dark type any phrases understood to be quotations from the Old Testament, avoid doing so in the passages I have quoted, and I think rightly: the editors perceived, correctly, that this was not the same thing.

Secondly, there are some passages which talk of the εἰκών as something like a *new nature*, something into which we shall be changed or are being changed: Colossians 3¹⁰, 'you have put off the old man [nature, RSV; Gk. ἄνθρωπος] with its practices and put on the new, which is being renewed in knowledge after the image of its creator.' Note the connection of the image with *knowledge* in this passage. Again, 2 Corinthians 3¹⁸: 'we all, with unveiled face, beholding the glory of the Lord, are being changed into the same εἰκών from glory into glory.' Both of these passages suggest an image which is part of the *new* nature, in contrast with the old, and

---

[21] See Barth, *KD* iii/1. 227 ff.; *CD* iii/1. 201 ff.

both have doubtless been influential in supporting the idea that any original image of God in man had been lost or diminished. Only the former of the two, however, makes a fairly clear terminological connection with the Genesis passages, and neither of them takes account of the many features of the Genesis passages which point in a different direction. In other words, when Barth declared that Paul was making a 'daring equation' of Jesus with the image of God (in Genesis),[22] this was only another of his ingenious manipulations of words: Paul made no such equation.

The passage which comes closest to a definite exploitation of the Genesis passage is 1 Corinthians 11[7], where Paul, discussing the covering of the head while praying or prophesying in church, makes it clear that, according to his opinion, it was the *male* person, the man, who *was* the image of God (εἰκὼν καὶ δόξα θεοῦ ὑπάρχων), while the woman was, as he puts it, 'the glory of the man'.[23] The image of God, therefore, far from consisting in the man–woman relationship, applied directly to the male and only by indirect reflection to the female. Such an opinion may well be unwelcome to many in these days of emancipation, but there does not seem to be any doubt that this is what Paul said. Moreover, it is easy, on the basis of the Genesis text itself, to see how he came to understand things in this way.[24]

As we read it, most of us see the first chapter of Genesis as a self-contained story, different from and complementary to the story of chapters 2 and 3; in this respect Barth read it as other modern scholars do.[25] But Paul probably read it as one consecutive narrative. We will see the importance of this in a moment. To this we add however the ambiguity of the terms אדם, *'adam*, and ἄνθρωπος. It is normally said that these terms could mean humanity in general but could also mean an individual human person. I have said it myself but it is only in part correct. In biblical Hebrew, *'adam* does

---

[22] *KD* iii/1, 228; *CD* iii/1. 202.

[23] Cf. Barth, *KD* iii/1. 229 f.; *CD* iii/1. 203 f. Barth's attempt to make this passage fit in with his view of the image of God is hopelessly weak.

[24] For fuller discussion see J. Jervell, *Imago Dei* (Göttingen: Vandenhoeck & Ruprecht, 1960), 292 ff.

[25] Cf. *KD* iii/1. 259 f.; *CD* iii/1. 228 ff. The P story of creation and the J story of creation are quite separate stories and should be read independently: each has its own harmony, and we should be content with the higher harmony which is achieved when we allow the one to speak after the other. Quite admirable sentiments; but such as may mislead us when we try to see how their meaning was perceived by someone like Paul.

not really mean 'human being'. An individual woman, identified as such, would never be called an *'adam*, nor would it be used of a group of women apart from men. The word is more correctly understood as 'man', with the additional specifications 'which may include woman/women if with man/men or if identity as between man and woman is unnoticed'. If only a woman or women are involved, then the specific term 'woman' would be used; women are human beings, but would not be called *'adam*. The significance of this also will emerge in a moment. In addition Adam was the personal name of the first man, though there is some question in the Hebrew of Genesis at what point אדם still means 'man' and at what point it begins to be the proper name 'Adam'.

Now at Genesis 1²⁶ God said:

Let us make אדם in our image, like our likeness ...

נעשה אדם בצלמנו כדמותנו

Ποιήσωμεν ἄνθρωπον κατ' εἰκόνα ἡμετέραν καὶ καθ' ὁμοίωσιν

And then, in the crucial 1²⁷, it goes on:

And God created the אדם in his image; in the image of God he created him, male and female he created them;

ויברא אלהים את־האדם בצלמו בצלם אלהים ברא אתו זכר ונקבה ברא אתם:

καὶ ἐποίησεν ὁ θεὸς τὸν ἄνθρωπον, κατ' εἰκόνα θεοῦ ἐποίησεν αὐτόν, ἄρσεν καὶ θῆλυ ἐποίησεν αὐτούς.

Now Paul, or more likely a preceding tradition of interpretation which he followed, reasoned thus: from the second chapter of Genesis we know that no woman was created until later on, when Eve was taken from the side of Adam. The phrase 'male and female he created them' must therefore be a proleptic statement of something that is to be done later on. This being so, it follows that the original creation in the image of God was of the man only. This is confirmed by the fact that in 1²⁶, where God states his purpose, there is no mention of creation of male and female together. The terms אדם and ἄνθρωπος, being somewhat ambiguous, were therefore read as referring to one individual human being, who as it happened was also a man, not a woman. Thus Genesis 1²⁶ was read: 'Let us make *a man* in our image, like our likeness', and 1²⁷ was read: 'and God made the man, in the image of God he made him; male and female he [subsequently] made them.' (I say 'made' rather than 'created' because of the Greek ἐποίησεν). In the Hebrew the masculine singular object pronoun 'him' (אתו) in 'he made him', in the Greek the masculine articles, seemed to confirm this. (In Greek it was possible to say ἡ ἄνθρωπος, with the feminine article (Isocrates 18. 52), but the article provided no such distinction in Hebrew.) Personally, I apologize for all this: it is not my own opinion, nor do I think it was so meant by Genesis, but I do not think there is any doubt that it was so understood by Paul. That Paul was quite able to make this sort of exegesis, which depends among other things on the confusion between collective and individual meanings of a noun, is clear from Galatians 3[16], where he speaks of a promise given to Abraham 'and to his seed' and goes on to reason that, since the text says 'seed' and not 'seeds', it is speaking of an individual, and that individual is Christ. To take the 'man' in Genesis 1 as individual rather than collective is much more natural and has better and more contextual support than to interpret this word 'seed' as individual, when it is obviously collective both in Hebrew and in Greek.

Well, enough of this, but Paul's interpretation shows us several interesting points. First, he has no idea whatever that the image of God *consisted in* the man–woman relationship: on the contrary, he thinks it is something that applies to the man, and only by secondary reflection to the woman. Secondly, as far as this particular interpretation goes, it seems to side with a *physical* understanding of the image in Genesis more than with any other. The image is a sort of luminosity which radiates from the man.

It might be thought that any opposition to Barth's exegesis must depend upon so-called 'historical-critical' principles, and that by a less critical, perhaps by a more 'canonical', approach, his exposition would be justified. In the matter of the image of God the case is quite the opposite. Critical scholars, as it happened, were, if anything, much too respectful and welcoming towards his approach: compare the highly respectful, if also critical, discussion of Stamm as far back as 1956.[26] Barth's approach depended on the elementary

---

[26] 'Die Imago-Lehre von Karl Barth', 84 ff. On the general reception of Barth's interpretation among Old Testament scholars see Jónsson, *The Image of God*, 75 ff., which seems to me to be a correct evaluation in general terms. As in matters of biblical theology in general, Barth's work on the image of God was a stimulus to exegetes. But did any exegete, anywhere, believe that he was right in his actual interpretation? Stamm, in his respectful critique, rejected the essential points of it. Some of the general features of Barth's approach may have been in agreement with the

'critical' insight that the stories of Genesis 1–2$^{4a}$ and of 2$^{4b\,ff.}$ were different pieces of tradition, which he used for his grand scheme under which the first provided evidence for 'creation as the external basis for the covenant' and the second story did the same for 'the covenant as the internal basis for creation'. Going along with the style of modern critical scholarship, therefore, he thought that the sentence 'in the image of God he created him, male and female he created them' is one thought and refers to one action of creation. 'He created him' means 'he created humanity'—quite correctly. But the older exegesis did not necessarily see it in this way.

One further point has been recently brought into the discussion by Link in his treatment (his pp. 107–12), following a point made by Westermann. Westermann writes that:

All exegetes, from the Fathers down to the present, proceed from the assumption that the text makes an utterance about humanity, that is, that man is created according to God's image and therefore is in God's image [*und deshalb gottesebenbildlich ist*].[27]

On the contrary, Link goes on, following Westermann, the text says nothing about man (*macht keine Aussage über den Menschen*): it is all about God's act of creating. Thus (p. 111): 'The image of God is neither something present (*Vorfindliches*) in humanity, nor something that is as it were added to humanity later on. Through this concept the Old Testament is interpreting an act of creation, which is *on the way* to its own reality.' All this is much in the style of Barth. The text says nothing about man, it makes an assertion rather about God's action. But I cannot take this seriously. It seems to me that there is no difference. Saying that God made man in his image, and that man as a result is in the image of God, seem to me to be the same thing. This is a result of the obvious semantic character of the terms used. I feel I have to notice this opinion because of the distinction of those who have put the point, but I cannot see what value it has for our discussion. It seems to be part of the plan to push the basis of natural theology *into the future*, of which something will have to be said later.

The chief aspect which we have to discuss, however, is whether the matter of the image of God really has anything definite to tell us

tendency of Old Testament scholars, as Jónsson says, but the most characteristic aspect, namely that the image resides in the man–woman relationship, surely received little acceptance.

[27] C. Link, *Die Welt als Gleichnis* (Munich: Kaiser, 1976), 109.

about the question of natural theology. Some of those who have thought that the image of God in humanity was obliterated or destroyed by sin thought also that, on this account, there would be no place for natural theology; and conversely some, perhaps many, of those who think that humanity continues to live in the image of God think that this validates the human activity of constructing natural theologies. It seems to me that neither of these opinions is definitely right. For both of them depend on the supposition that the image of God is meant as the means, or channel, or agency, through which man can know something about God. It may well be that in the ancient Hebrew situation this had nothing to do with the matter. In that situation the figure of the image of God was not particularly connected with the question whether humans 'knew' God or not: that was just not a problem with which they were concerned.

What then was the point of the expression 'in the image of God'? I will repeat here some of my own thoughts about the matter, as they were published in the *Bulletin* of the John Rylands Library in Manchester in 1968.[28] The image of God in humanity is not something that can be *defined*, as if we could point to this or that characteristic which clearly exists and to which the phrase expressly refers.[29] But we can say that it belongs to the confluence of a group of nodal theological issues: monotheism, creation, anthropomorphism, condemnation of idolatry—exactly the issues out of which, as we have seen, the tradition of natural theology emerged.

As I wrote then:[30]

There is no reason to believe that this writer had in his mind any definite idea about the content or the location of the image of God. There were reasons in the past development of Israelite thinking about the relation between God and man, and in the particular kind of literary work upon which P was engaged, which made it important for him to express the existence of a likeness between man and God; but there were also, in the same development and especially in the whole delicacy and questionability, according to Israelite thought, of any idea of analogies to God and representations of

[28] Jónsson is so good as to say, on the basis of my thoughts in this article, that 'If Karl Barth is the most important name for *imago Dei* studies during the period 1919–1960, it may with some justice be claimed that James Barr is the most important name during the period 1961–1982'—*The Image of God*, 146 n. 6.

[29] For similar thoughts, see J. F. A. Sawyer, 'The Meaning of בצלם אלהים in Genesis i–ix', *JTS* 25 (1974), 426; W. H. Schmidt, *The Faith of the Old Testament* (Oxford: Blackwell, 1983), 197; Jónsson, *The Image of God*, 224.

[30] This and the following passage are quoted from my 'The Image of God in the Book of Genesis: A Study of Terminology', *BJRL* 51 (1968–9), 13f., with the kind permission of the John Rylands University Library, Manchester.

God in the world, very powerful reasons why the subject could not be more narrowly or more exactly expressed without the danger that the whole attempt might be ruined.

I then suggested that the P writer, in his developing of the expression 'image of God', was much influenced by the work of Deutero-Isaiah. To quote again:

There are deep similarities between Deutero-Isaiah and P: the emphasis on creation, the universality of vision, the emphatic monotheism, the assurance of the incomparability and uniqueness of the God of Israel. P would also have shared his hostility to all worship of graven images. But the great prophet of the exile pressed this hostility so zealously, and denied so emphatically any analogy to God from the side of the world ('to whom will you liken God, and what likeness will you set against him?'), as to leave it possible that nothing existed in the world which had any relation or analogy to God. He thus posed a question which he himself did nothing to answer; and he himself did not require to answer it because, being a prophet, he was by no means trying to give an ordered or reasoned account of the world, of man, or of the origin of man. To give such an ordered or reasoned account was, however, just what the P document undertook to do, and in this context, where man as man was being described within an organized world, the question could not be avoided whether there was anything in this world—in this world which, it was granted, could not furnish out of itself any comparisons or analogies with God—which had any special or peculiar relation with God. The placing of man in such a special position is the function of the term 'image of God'.

It may thus be possible to say that, though the image of God is attached to the story of the creation of humanity, its primary function and purpose is to say something about God. Its dynamics develop from the need to clarify speech about *him*. Precisely for that reason one cannot necessarily locate the elements in human existence to which it applies. Nevertheless, by its own nature as a statement of *likeness*, this particular kind of speech about God necessarily says a great deal about humanity.

The image of God is thus a theologoumenon produced out of the forces and tensions of Israel's religious traditions. It is not directly to be 'defined', and it is not immediately or directly clear whether it says anything about natural theology or not. In this respect the older debates about the existence, survival, obliteration, and so on of the image of God were, as a mode of entry into the question of natural theology, a waste of time. As we have seen, the basis for natural theology within the Old Testament is not dependent on any particular explanation of the image of God terminology, and is valid on other grounds and independently of that question.

Nevertheless the idea of the image of God may have had a place in the development that led towards natural theology. For one thing that seems clear about the image of God is that it is attached to humanity and humanity only: the animals do not have it. This, incidentally, is an additional reason why Barth's interpretation should be rejected: for 'male and female he created them', out of which Barth constructed what was in his view the essence of the image, is quite obviously something that is not peculiar to humanity but is fully valid of the animal world also. The distinctiveness of humanity from the animal world is not only emphasized in the story of creation in Genesis 1 but is also reinforced in Genesis 9, where the killing of animals is sanctioned but the killing of humans is to be punished, expressly because God had made humanity in his own image. The male–female relationship cannot possibly be the key to the enigma of the image of God.

Psalm 8 also emphasizes the distinction between human and animal:

> Thou hast put all things under his feet,
> all sheep and oxen,
> and also the beasts of the field,
> the birds of the air, and the fish of the sea,
> whatever passes along the paths of the sea.

But, as we come down into the Hellenistic age, what was the image then taken to be? As we have already seen, the Wisdom of Solomon, which we have consulted so often, gave a first pointer:[31]

> God created man with incorruptibility
> and made him as an image of his own eternity   ($2^{23}$)

—and, like Genesis itself, the Book of Wisdom does not make it clear what happened to that image after Adam's disobedience. But the same book also celebrates wisdom as something that comes near to God in the possession of immortality; and wisdom, on the other hand, is something that humans may possess. On the other hand, the emphasis on the absolute transcendence of God makes less attractive any understanding of the image as a physical showing forth or manifestation of the divine.

The contrast with the animals was very probably a force that

---

[31] Cf above, Ch. 4.

propelled the image of God with great ease into the *intellectual* area. How did man dominate the animals? Not by sheer strength, for the animals had the advantage in strength, in speed, in adaptation to their environment. Human domination rested upon use of technology, however primitive then compared with now, and technology rested upon human powers of thought, reason, language, and abstraction. Thus we hear about the unthinking, unreasoning character of the beasts, which are ἄλογα, mindless (2 Pet. 2¹², Jude 10); and Paul speaks contemptuously of the τετράποδα, four-footed things, among the objects of idolatry (Rom. 1²³). Does God care about oxen? he asks dismissively (1 Cor. 9⁹). But this sense of distance from the unthinking, unreasoning animal has its reflection also in the Old Testament: the בער or brute beast is a standard image of the totally stupid, unreflecting person, for example Psalms 73²², 92⁷, Proverbs 12¹, 30².

Such an 'intellectual' understanding of the divine image in man is found also in the Book of Ben Sira, 17³ ᶠᶠ.:

> He made them according to his own image,
> and put the fear of him upon all flesh;
> and [gave them] to have dominion over beasts and birds;
> Discrimination (διαβούλιον)³² and tongue and eyes,
> ears and heart he gave them for them to think.
> He filled them with knowledge of understanding
>     (ἐπιστήμην συνέσεως)
> and showed them good and evil ...
> he bestowed knowledge upon them,
> and allotted to them the law of life.³³

The powers of thought and knowledge are thus prominent in Ben Sira's exposition of the values of creation in the image of God.

We have argued, then, that the idea of the image of God in humanity does not immediately or directly answer the question of the validity of natural theology. If, however, we extend the purport of the expression beyond its immediate or direct sense in its own context, and consider its wider implications, then we can say: on this ground, and in these terms, Brunner was certainly right, as against Barth, in saying that the image of God in humanity, even in sinful humanity, functioned as a 'point of contact'. In fact, if Brunner was

---

³² 'Debate, deliberation' is the gloss given by LSJ. Since this word is absent in the Syriac, some, like RSV, consider it not to belong to the text. But the word is not unlikely, occurring once in Wisd. and in two other places in Sir. Even if it is absent, however, this makes little difference to our argument.

³³ No Hebrew text exists at this point.

wrong, it was in not claiming more than this. As I remember John Baillie pointing out at the time, Brunner's trouble was that he accepted too many of Barth's own assumptions to permit him to press home his own arguments properly. For in using a term like 'point of contact' he was admitting that the image of God was very largely damaged, only a tiny point of contact being left. Actually, if the idea of the image of God is relevant for this discussion at all, it must mean much more than a tiny 'point of contact', it must mean something like a deep and wide interface containing and providing numerous aspects of community or analogy.

Lastly, there was one other aspect in which Brunner had right on his side as against Barth. Brunner's plea for a new natural theology included an emphasis on the *orders* or *ordinances* (German *Ordnungen*) of creation, and Barth was correspondingly dismissive towards these structures.[34] But to modern Old Testament scholarship there can be no question that the idea of a world *order* is extremely central. It is evident especially in the Wisdom literature and in its relations with ancient Near Eastern culture; and through these it spills over into many other aspects of Old Testament thought, especially the idea of creation, which on the one hand takes the form of separation and ordering, and on the other hand, as has been emphasized, develops into the central base for natural theology. It looks as if Brunner was right at this point also.

[34] See *Natural Theology*, 85 f.

# 9

# Science; Language; Parable; Scripture

As I have been arguing, it seems that the Bible does imply and contain a considerable input from the side of natural theology, and that the basis for that natural theology lies not in 'reason' alone, as the more modern tradition represents it, but in religion and the history of conflicts and developments in religion. In this chapter we shall go on to consider four areas of general implication to which the question of natural theology may be related. These are: (1) the idea that it has something to do with the relations between theology and *science*; (2) the connections between natural theology and the *linguistic* medium of the Bible; (3) the use of parables by Jesus in his teaching; (4) the implications of our discussion for the general idea of 'Holy Scripture'.

## 1. Science

Here we have to give some thought to a view that has been propounded, namely that the relations between theology and *natural science* provide something like a kind of natural theology. The development of such a view has been a feature of certain later phases of the Barthian tradition in which some kind of natural theology has come to be tentatively reaffirmed.

How far, however, can any such view claim to have *biblical* support? On the face of it, only to a very slight degree. Within the pages of scripture, scientific questioning and scientific investigation are very thinly spread. We do know, indeed, that King Solomon, by convention the patron saint of biblical wisdom, composed proverbs and songs, several thousands of them, in which he 'spoke of trees, from the cedar that is in Lebanon to the hyssop that grows out of the wall; he spoke also of beasts, and of birds, and of reptiles, and of fish' (1 Kgs. 4[32 f.]; MT 5[12 f.]). And it is probable that this work, whether it really existed or is merely legendary, had some affinity with the so-called 'list science' of ancient Mesopotamia and had in it some very elementary attempt at the classification of realities of our earthly environment.[1] But the actual books of Hebrew Wisdom contain no serious trace of such material. The Book of Proverbs does include a number of simple analogical statements:

> Like snow in summer or rain in harvest,
> so honour is not fitting for a fool.
> Like a sparrow in its flitting, like a swallow in its flying,
> a curse that is causeless does not alight.
> A whip for the horse, a bridle for the ass,
> and a rod for the back of fools.    (Prov. 26[1 ff.], RSV)

Or again:

> Four things on earth are small,
> but they are exceedingly wise:
> the ants are a people not strong,
> yet they provide their food in the summer;
> the badgers are a people not mighty,
> but they make their homes in the rocks;
> the locusts have no king,
> yet all of them march in rank;
> the lizard you can take in your hands,
> yet it is in kings' palaces.    (Prov. 30[24 ff.], RSV)

These involve simple, pre-scientific, observations of nature, but no more than this. They are illustrations which comment on human customs and mores, and this is their purpose and interest. They are no more science than La Fontaine's fables are science.

More might be made, perhaps, of the creation story of Genesis itself. For generations people have become accustomed to say that the first chapter of Genesis did not purport to be a scientific account of the origins of the world, and this was an understandable apologetic response to the fact that the account is not scientifically true. But to say that Genesis does not purport to be scientific may be

---

[1] On list science, see A. Leo Oppenheim, 'Man and Nature in Mesopotamian Civilization', in *Dictionary of Scientific Biographies*, vol. xv (New York: Scribners, 1970–80), 634–66, and W. von Soden, 'Leistung und Grenze sumerischer und babylonischer Wissenschaft', published together with Landsberger's 'Die Eigenbegrifflichkeit der babylonischen Welt' (Darmstadt: Wissenschaftliche Buchgesellschaft, 1965). I am grateful to Dr Erica Reiner of the Oriental Institute, Chicago, for help in connection with these materials.

a mistaken sort of apologetic argument. In its own context and purpose, for the people who elaborated it and composed it, it *was* a sort
of scientific account. Something akin to the thinking of Mesopotamian list science may have lain behind it, and this, with the
implication of transreligious and transcultural understanding,
lends a certain tinge of natural theology. The writers of Genesis
meant it as a cosmological organization of the world, in which a
place and role are given for the great outer elements, light and dark,
sky, earth, and sea, sun, moon, and stars, and also for the closer,
inner environment, vegetable and animal, and finally for humanity
at the centre of it all. Its seven days, linked by the subsequent genea-
logies with the chronology which runs down through the following
centuries, deliberately inaugurate the exact temporal and calen-
drical framework for later history. To us none of this constitutes a
science; it is closer to legend or mythology.[2] But to them it was as
close as they could come to a sort of science. However, none of the
base on which it was worked out was scientific. They had no means of
knowing how the world had begun, no means of experimentation, no
methods of research other than the most obvious human experience.
Their view of the world rested on religious tradition, both without
and within Israel, and on the refashioning of these traditions in order
to fit with the monotheistic deity of Israel. And thus, though, as we
have seen, the Israelite doctrine of creation was one of the major
influences out of which natural theology was to come, nothing
worthy of the name of science was involved in the evolution of that
doctrine or in its exposition. At the most we may hazard the supposition that the peculiar monotheism of Israel, and other accompanying
features of its religion, had some effect on people's perception of the
natural world; but, even if we give the utmost weight to this, it comes
far short of being evidence that the nascent natural theology of the
Bible had any element of the scientific in it. The idea, sometimes
fashionable, that science had its roots in the Bible must be considered
to have been an oddity of our century.[3] Only in Greek culture—and

---

[2] Chronology in one sense is the essential scientific framework for history. But for
the schematic, mythological, or legendary character of biblical chronology, see J.
Barr, 'Biblical Chronology: Legend or Science?' (Ethel M. Wood Lecture; University
of London, 1987), and Jeremy Hughes, *Secrets of the Times: Myth and History in
Biblical Chronology* (JSOT Supplement Series 66; Sheffield: Academic Press, 1990).
[3] See my discussion of the ideas of M. B. Foster, and others who have seen a sort of
inner unity between natural science and Jewish-Christian faith, in 'Man and Nature:
The Ecological Controversy and the Old Testament', *BJRL* 55 (1972–3), 13 ff.

Mesopotamian!—can something like the beginnings of science be seen; and, in so far as signs of it can be seen in biblical Hebrew culture, it shows no evidence of being more advanced than that of the mythological and polytheistic society of Mesopotamia, indeed quite the reverse.[4]

We should note however that something closer to the interests and the language of science appears in the 'intertestamental' documents, in much greater measure than in the canonical Hebrew scriptures. It is highly likely that contact with Greek culture was the catalyst of this interest. And here once again the Wisdom of Solomon, in a passage already cited, provides one of the best examples:

> For it is he [God] who gave me unerring knowledge of
> what exists (τῶν ὄντων).
> to know the structure of the world (σύστασιν κόσμου)
> and the activity of the elements (ἐνέργειαν στοιχείων);
> the beginning and end and middle of times,
> the alternations of the solstices and the changes of the
> seasons,
> the cycles of the year and the positions (θέσεις) of the
> stars,
> the natures of animals and the tempers of wild beasts,
> the powers of spirits [winds?] and the reasonings (δια-
> λογισμούς) of men,
> the varieties of plants and the virtues of roots;
> I learned both what is secret and what is manifest;
> for Wisdom, the fashioner of all things, taught me.
> $(7^{17\,ff.}$, RSV modified)

Similarly the Book of Enoch, from a comparable period, shows a much greater interest in astronomy, chronology, and the origins of technology than the books of the Hebrew canon do.

Equally central is the matter of *sickness and medicine*. It is interesting that the older traditions about creation in the Hebrew Bible have little to say about disease. If all that God created was good,

---

[4] According to W. M. O'Neil, *Early Astronomy from Babylonia to Copernicus* (Sydney: Sydney University Press, 1986), 'Early Babylonian astronomy, as we know it in the second millennium and the first half of the first millennium BC, was pre-scientific or at best proto-scientific. By about 500 BC it was approaching a genuinely scientific status' (p. 35). He lists two factors. The first is 'the accumulation of observational records', the second 'the early search for regularities', in which 'say from about 300 BC onwards, quite sophisticated mathematical techniques were used to generate from a modicum of observational data very precise and usually very accurate ephemerides, tables like the modern almanacs giving accurate positions at specified times, for the Sun, the Moon and the five star-like planets' (pp. 35, 37).

what about the organisms that transmitted plague and the like? Well, of course, they had not thought about that. The things that were created good were (supposedly) tangible and visible realities like sea and sky, trees and plants, sheep and cows. Disease was not an existent thing, it was a condition rather than an element in the created world. On the one hand, it could produce ritual problems; on the other hand, it could form the means of divine intervention or punishment. But it was not a created reality like a horse or cow. Thus in the Old Testament there is little fundamental wrestling with the problem of disease in relation to the place of God as creator. Occasional miraculous healings, as narrated in the Elijah–Elisha cycle, do not contradict this. The New Testament, by contrast, is far more replete with stories of sickness and healing, which matters are seen as a contest between God and the demons, and as a means whereby God's healing of the sickness of the cosmos is depicted.

It is interesting therefore that the first biblical passages that really concern themselves with the fundamental position of medicine in relation to the God of Israel come in Ben Sira. He produced some original thoughts which showed an awareness that ill health might put in question one's confidence in the goodness of the created order; thus:

> Better is a poor man who is healthy and in strong condition
> than a rich man who is tortured in body;
> health and good condition are better than all gold
> and a strong body is better than measureless wealth . . .
> Death is better than a life made bitter
> and eternal rest than continuing illness.    (Sir. 30[14, 15, 17])

Given these thoughts, it was natural to go on to the consideration of medicine, and I quote from his discussion of doctors in chapter 38:

Honour the doctor with the honour due to him, according to your need of him; for the Lord created him. For healing comes from the Most High . . . The Lord created medicines from the earth, and a sensible man will not despise them. Was not water made sweet with a tree, in order that his power might be made known? . . . My son, when you are sick do not be negligent; but pray to the Lord and he will heal you. Give up your faults and direct your hands aright, and cleanse your heart from all sin. Offer a sweet-smelling sacrifice and pour oil on your offering . . . and give the physician his place, for the Lord created him . . . There is a time when success lies in the hands of doctors, for they too will pray to the Lord that he should grant them success in diagnosis, and in healing for the sake of preserving life. (Sir. 38[1 ff.], selections, based on RSV)

It is, visibly, in the Greek period that the place of medicine is perceived as a problem for traditional Israelite religion. Greek medicine presented one of the most tangible advantages of Greek culture, an advantage that might be utilized even by those who would in other respects be opposed to the ideas and principles of that culture. But how did the use of that medicine fit with the older religion? Ben Sira offers a solution which brings the two together. Doctors and medicine come from God, they are an instrument of divine healing; God himself had used a tree as an instrument of healing (the reference is probably to the incident at Marah, Exodus 15$^{25}$, though strictly that is a case of bitter water rather than of actual disease). In any case, it is clear that the reality of medicine in Ben Sira's time stimulates new developments in Hebrew thought akin to natural theology. These same steps may also lead forward to the increased emphasis on disease and miraculous healing in the New Testament.

Now these interests, as expressed in these books on the margin of the biblical canon, are not without significance. Far from jealously limiting their view of the world to the older Hebrew cosmology, Jewish writers allowed themselves to be stimulated to wider speculations on the basis of the increasing knowledge which was afforded by the Hellenistic period. Problems were seen that the older cosmology had left undiscussed, ideas were raised that had been unknown at that earlier stage. We see an exploration of areas formerly unknown. The cosmos had to be mapped anew. The profound interest of the New Testament in disease and the overcoming of it may owe much to this development.

In so far as faith continues to attach itself to the world as the creation of God, it seems to me that this process has to be continued and expanded. The natural theology of the Bible attached itself— perhaps unduly—to the goodness of the creation as a sign of the character of the creator. There are weaknesses in this approach which need to be noticed, and especially by that current of Christian natural theology—well represented by Raven—which relies heavily on the goodness of the created world. Its goodness is not so clear in the Genesis text as might appear at first sight. The emphasis on the absolutely revolutionary change effected through Christian salvation appeared to imply the completeness of depravity in sin, and this in turn suggested the perfection of that (brief) original period before sin came into the world: and hence the emphasis on the world's original goodness. But perhaps that goodness was not completely perfect. This depends on the syntactical hierarchies within which the parts of Genesis 1 are read. Everything that God made was good. But it is not absolutely clear that everything in the world is therefore good. Is darkness good, according to Genesis 1? God made light, and separated it from the darkness; it does not tell us that he created the darkness. But darkness is part of our world. The same applies to the water—notoriously a chaotic and menacing force. God separated the waters 'above the firmament' from those below it, and he separated the waters from the dry land, but it is not said that he created the waters themselves. They were there, an ominous menace of possible disaster. Jon Levenson refers to the belief in the total perfection of the original created world as only 'a gross overgeneralization from the conventional optimistic reading of Genesis 1'.[5]

In saying this, I do not dispute the value of the conception of the goodness of God's creation, and it may be that it must remain an ultimate essential in religion. But it is not something so clear and obvious that it can be simply evoked, without some critical discussion, as a foundational principle. The biblical evidence for it has to be considered afresh. The natural theology of the Bible, as I have said, attached itself too easily to the goodness of the creation as evidence for the creator, and therefore tended to fail to give sufficient thought to other ways in which God might be supposed to be known. In any case, and this is our main point at the moment, in so far as this particular line of natural theology is to be continued, it must take within itself the total realities of the universe as science has made them known, including, in particular, the extreme age of the world, the reality of evolution, and the high degree of ambiguity of so many features in nature, an ambiguity which the natural theology of the Bible, in many of its formulations, tended to pass over too lightly. It must take within itself the fact that 'nature' itself may be in the course of change, and that human agency through scientific and technological skill has the power, and also the duty, of moulding to some extent what 'nature' is to become. Questions of human action in ecology, in medicine, and consequently in matters of social and political ethics are necessarily involved. The goodness of the

---

[5] See his interesting discussion of these problems in Jon D. Levenson, *Creation and the Persistence of Evil* (San Francisco: Harper & Row, 1988); quotation from p. 50.

creation is not only a datum from the past, it is also a reality still in process and in potentiality.

To sum up this point, then, there is a certain biblical interest in the development of science and technology, though undoubtedly in a very primitive mode. Accounts of the world which were mythological or legendary came to be adjusted to make room for the results of experience and observation in a limited degree. But it cannot be said that this represents a central interest within the biblical tradition. The story of the children of Cain and their technological advances is a sideline which leads nowhere much in the canonical scriptures, and the Book of Enoch certainly did not achieve centrality in the long run either; indeed the detail, verbosity, and obscurity of its 'scientific' speculations may have militated against the acceptance of this otherwise important work. Within the biblical tradition, for the most part, people's view of the universe was determined much more by religion than by anything like science.

This is not to say that the relations of theology with science are not extremely important. I am sure that they are. But, if there is reason to suppose that the place of natural theology in Christianity has something to do with its relation to science, then we must be clear that this position rests upon modern philosophical and dogmatic foundations and is not one that can claim biblical support, nor should it seek it. In so far as there is a sort of natural theology in the Bible, it comes into the stream of biblical faith in a quite different way. On the other hand, in so far as the tradition of natural theology has linked itself so closely to the idea of the world as a reality that somehow speaks of God and makes him known to us, if that tradition is to be continued into the modern world then that task cannot be performed except in so far as the vast new information about the natural world attained by science is taken into consideration by theology.

This does not mean, however, that theology in itself is modelled on the world of science. I do not think that theology has or should have much of the character of science, or of a science. Theologians who argue for its scientific character are usually not arguing for the scientific character of *theology*, but for the scientific character of *their own theology*; in other words, it is an assertion of their own superiority, a typical phenomenon of the intratheological power struggle.[6] To me theology seems to have more the character of an art

---

[6] See the discussion of T. F. Torrance's position by Ronald F. Thiemann, *Revelation and Theology* (Notre Dame, Ind.: University of Notre Dame Press, 1985), 32 ff.

than that of a science. It belongs with the human disciplines, not those of natural science. It belongs with literary appreciation, with the history of ideas, with history in general, with philosophy, and with language and linguistic studies. It has to handle human speech and human texts. Where it has claimed affinity with 'science', it seems to me too often to have achieved affinity rather with politics and propagandist rhetoric. Lectures on 'scientific rigour', supposedly based on the analogy of physics, come badly from those who have published some of the worst and most ludicrous misuses of biblical language in this century.[7] But we shall say no more about this aspect of the subject, and we turn to our second topic of this chapter, the relation of biblical language to natural theology.

## 2. Language

Central to the question of natural theology within the Bible is the position of the languages of the Bible. First, the linguistic terms even of revealed religion are terms that function outside the sphere of what is accepted as revelation. Secondly, the languages in which biblical faith is expressed are languages which are also used to express other religious (or philosophical) positions. Thirdly, these languages are languages inherited by the biblical people from other cultures and earlier stages of their own culture, and these previous stages involve the attachment of meanings to the linguistic symbols, meanings that are by no means univocally identical with the specific meanings found within the circle of 'biblical revelation'.

In other words, the phenomenon of the biblical languages in itself suggests something akin to the insights of natural theology. Or, to use the rabbinic expression so rightly cherished in these matters, דברה תורה כלשון בני אדם, 'the Torah spoke as [or: in] the language of the sons of men' (B. Berachot 62, and elsewhere).[8] There is no holy and separate language for revelation. Or there may be, theoretically, such a 'language', a soundless, wordless means of communication by which God makes himself known to persons; doubtless something of the kind is what people have in mind when they think of God 'speak-

---

[7] As indicated in the writer's *The Semantics of Biblical Language* (London: Oxford University Press, 1961). For a review of the subsequent discussion, see Richard J. Erickson, *James Barr and the Beginnings of Biblical Semantics* (Notre Dame, Ind.: Anthroscience Minigraph Series, Foundations Press, 1984).

[8] I am grateful to my colleague Dr Peter Haas for information on this.

ing' to human beings. But such a superlinguistic communication is something other than the matter of the Bible. Everything in the Bible is in words of Hebrew, Aramaic, or Greek, and has meaning only through the linguistic systems and the lexical stocks of these languages. But meanings are socially preserved and psychologically stored and our knowledge of meanings is socially inherited from the immediate past. The reason why we call a dog 'dog' is that that—or strictly speaking an ancestor form of it—was the usage of the previous generation. Of course language continually changes but the changes are intelligible and usable only because they take place in a mode that retains some adequate continuity with what was there before. Thus when the Hebrews called their own God Elohim, meaning by that the one and only existent god, they were able to do this because that usage, however new it might seem, had recognizability and sense through continuity with a usage where it might have meant 'gods', 'totality of gods', 'transcendent, superhuman beings', and the like. And some of these usages continue in use in the Hebrew Bible alongside the more distinctive Israelite usage under which Elohim is the one true God and incomparably above and beyond all other beings: thus the same term is still used for 'other gods', very likely for intermediate beings surrounding the primal deity, and also for ancestral spirits like Samuel when the Witch of Endor brought him out out of the earth. And the same goes for the special divine name Yahweh. This is a different type of designation but the convention of the use of such designations was widespread if not universal in the relevant cultures. That a god should have his or her proper name was normal: in Mesopotamia Marduk or Ninurta, in Greece Poseidon or Hephaestus, in Egypt Thoth or Anubis, and in the Bible itself 'Kemosh the god of the Moabites' (1 Kgs. 11[33]) and the like.

Take another example: the idea of *covenant*, a concept that has been much in favour in modern biblical and theological discussion. God made a covenant with Abraham, one of the basic events of the whole Bible. But how did people in ancient Israel know what this meant, what a 'covenant' was? Because covenants were something that was already familiar to them, a part of the way in which they organized their conceptual world. Moreover, the emphasis on the covenant as a key concept of the Bible in modern scholarship was greatly increased through studies in the Hittite treaties: God's covenant with Israel followed a pattern, with historical preamble, stipulations, oaths, and the like, which was already widely used in vassal treaties. It may indeed be that the importance of these analogies has been exaggerated; I myself have always been reserved about this side of the matter. But even if the recourse to non-Israelite materials like the treaties is not decisive, within Israel itself, within the biblical text, the normality of covenants as a form of social arrangement is well established, and there is no suggestion that the covenant is something unique to Israel. Abraham made a covenant with Abimelech king of Gerar in a dispute over ownership of a well (Gen. 21$^{27, 32}$); Solomon made one with Hiram king of Tyre (1 Kgs. 5$^{12}$, MT 5$^{26}$); the Gibeonites, fearful for their fate under Israelite occupation of Canaan, came by subterfuge to try to do the obvious thing, to make a covenant with them (Josh. 9$^{6f., 15}$). Thus the covenant itself, one of the key ideas, is something that was 'natural': it was inherited from social experience, probably held in common over a wide area with peoples of a different religious organization. Now of course covenant becomes in the Old Testament a central feature of what we could call 'revelatory' type, a theme of revelatory theology. This is done because of the collocations and contexts in which it is used, the persons of whom it is used, the situations in which it is used, and so on. But in all these revelatory aspects it is intelligible because of meanings that were already, i.e. previously, known. Anterior knowledge is everywhere present, and definitive.

Similar arguments can be deployed over a wide area. The situation with Hebrew language is thus ironical. As I have mentioned several times, the heritage of Barthian theology sought to deploy Hebrew language and Hebrew concepts as a guard for revelation, as an antidote for the Greek of the New Testament which might have suggested Greek ideas including natural theology. This approach proved disastrous in two different ways: first because the linguistic arguments deployed were massively incompetent,[9] and secondly because, if the evidence of language is relevant for the question at all, and if Hebrew language in particular is to be brought into the discussion in this way at all, it strongly favours the affirmation of natural theology. Even if the ideas of the Hebrew Bible count as revelatory, the building blocks which are used for their expression

---

[9] It is probable that the devastation of these arguments from Hebrew and Greek by my book on semantics was a reason why this same current turned, soon afterwards, increasingly to theories of science as a source of intellectual support for Barthian theology.

are very definitely 'natural'. It was truly ironic that Hebrew language, invoked in order to support the revelatory character of the New Testament, actually functioned as a sort of hidden natural theology which served to support the overt rejection of natural theology: seen rightly, it would have been a substantial support for the direct acceptance of natural theology.

The idea that the Hebrew language had concealed within it a sort of hidden revelational conceptuality really rested on a superstitious veneration for the language of ancient scripture plus a lack of serious analysis of that same language. Purely accidentally, ancient Hebrew existed almost only in a corpus that spoke for Hebrew religion. Such limited materials as existed outside this range were generally unknown to theologians or inaccessible to them. Barthian theology, with its vast over-confidence in the dogmatic approach, served only to convince them that they knew better than biblical scholars.

In particular, the attempt to build upon its differences from Greek depended upon superficial contrasts poorly analysed. Commenting on Boman's view that Hebrew was an 'exceptionally unusual' language, the well-known linguist Henry A. Gleason, Jr., wrote:[10]

It [Hebrew] was the first non-Indo-European language that I ever studied, and I too was struck by its strangeness at many points. But now when I turn back to Hebrew after a variety of African, Asian, and American languages, I find myself in familiar territory. Hebrew is by no means extremely divergent from a European point of view.

In fact, in the areas relevant for comparison of theological thought, there are sometimes striking similarities between mechanisms of Greek and those of Hebrew. I have already shown this for the definite article. The definite article was one of the elements long ago identified as significant for the relations between language and thought.[11] Both Hebrew and Greek have a definite article, but not, in effect, an indefinite one. Both belonged to language families which had provided no explicit article type. In both the article has morphological relations with demonstratives and relatives. In Greek, as in Hebrew, the older and poetic usage employed the article rather little, and determination did not require the article. For noun plus

[10] 'Some Contributions of Linguistics to Biblical Studies', *Hartford Quarterly*, 4/1 (1963–4), 52. Cf. Erickson, *James Barr and the Beginnings of Biblical Semantics*, 53.

[11] By A. H. Basson and D. J. O'Connor, 'Language and Philosophy: Some Suggestions for an Empirical Approach', *Philosophy*, 22 (1947), 49-65; see my *Semantics of Biblical Language*, 26.

adjective, both languages commonly repeated the article on both elements. Particularly striking is the Hebrew 'relative article', used mainly with a participle, giving the sense 'the one doing this = the one who does this', a construction highly characteristic of Greek: so LXX at Psalm 17[33], ὁ θεὸς ὁ περιζωννύων με δύναμιν, 'the God who girds me with strength', corresponds exactly to the Hebrew construction (MT Ps. 18[33]). And so on. On the scale of typological possibilities, Greek was enormously closer to Hebrew in respect of its article than it was to its sister language Latin. And both Hebrew and Greek developed their characteristic definite article patterns within roughly the same historical epoch, say the first millennium BC, with Hebrew, one might guess, having some priority in this respect.[12]

In saying this I do not wish to deny reality in the contrast between Hebrew thought and Greek thought. For that contrast there may be good reason. But, since the pattern of the definite article is remarkably similar as between the two languages, the contrast between Hebrew thought and Greek thought, in so far as this particular phenomenon constitutes evidence, can be maintained only by accepting that the parallelism between language and thought is not at all a close one.[13]

And the same sort of thought can be produced in other realms: for instance, the nominal sentence, whereby in Hebrew to say that X is Y no verb 'to be' is used, is of course common in Greek though not as universal as in Hebrew (and even in Hebrew the verb is used whenever a carrier of tense or mood is required), and common in some other Indo-European languages, such as Russian. Numerous parallels in semantic ranges can also be adduced, for example the presence of different words for 'man' in the sense of 'human being' and 'man' in the sense of 'male person'. The fact is that, on the scale of world languages, Hebrew and Greek do not stand at opposite ends of the spectrum, but in a position of some proximity and contiguity. This fact made it easier to translate biblical ideas from Hebrew into Greek, within the (very rough) stylistic limits within which the translators worked, and to express Jewish thoughts in Greek.

Discussion of language in relation to the problem of natural

[12] These sentences are taken almost verbatim from my article '"Determination" and the Definite Article in Biblical Hebrew', *JSS* 34 (1989), 307–35, and in particular from the conclusion, 334. On the relative article, see 322 ff.

[13] See recently S. E. Porter, 'Two Myths: Corporate Personality and Language/Mentality Determinism', in *SJT* 43 (1991), 289–307.

theology has often concentrated on metaphor. And it is true that metaphors can be said to depend on anterior knowledge: to understand that God is a mighty rock, one has to know what a rock is, what characteristics it has, why it might be advantageous that God would share some characteristics of such a thing. This seems to me to be obvious. But it seems to me equally that, for ancient Hebrew, this is not the most important thing. Terms for God were in many cases not metaphorical.[14] When Adam and Eve heard the sound of God walking in the garden in the daily (evening) breeze, God was really walking in the garden. This is the sort of thing that gods did. It is part of the anthropomorphic picture of the God of Israel. It is often said that all terms for deity are metaphorical, or almost all, but I cannot see that this was true in the ancient Semitic world.[15] The language contained numerous important terms which were primarily, basically, terms for divinity and relations with the divine. 'God' itself, or the ancient terms which it translates, like אלהים in Hebrew or, say, *ilani* in Akkadian, were direct terms for God, nothing else. In Greek it was not different: θεός did not mean anything other than 'god'.

In general, nevertheless, there are plenty of metaphors in the Old Testament. Some of them may be neutral to our question of natural theology: when we speak of God as a 'rock', one would hardly say that it was natural theology to know what a rock is. But many biblical metaphors definitely support the idea of natural theology. 'The Lord is my shepherd' was a highly traditional metaphor, for the idea of the shepherd-king was extremely familiar in the ancient Near East: it suggests transreligiosity, and thereby natural theology. Such terms involve anterior knowledge, or at least anterior opinions, about God, about the cosmos, about religiously controlled norms of life.

Thus Janet Soskice writes: 'even the abstractions of natural theology are based, in the long run, on experience—although of a diffuse kind.' Again, 'experience, customarily regarded as the foundation of natural theology, is also the touchstone of the revealed'.[16]

---

[14] I agree here, if I understand him rightly, with Westermann in his remarks about Jüngel's views of metaphor: C. Westermann, *The Parables of Jesus in the Light of the Old Testament* (Minneapolis: Fortress, 1990), 175.

[15] 'All, or almost all, of the language used by the Bible to refer to God is metaphor (the one possible exception is the word "holy")': G. B. Caird, *The Language and Imagery of the Bible* (London: Duckworth, 1980), 18.

[16] J. M. Soskice, *Metaphor and Religious Language* (Oxford: Clarendon Press, 1985), 150, 160.

Or perhaps, not wishing to make experience alone so ultimate, we might say: the terms are part of the organization of a world of ideas, concepts, narratives, and experience, in the meaning of which experience always has a part. In any case, it works in the same way, as Soskice says, for natural and for revealed theology alike.

### 3. Parables

The mention of metaphor leads on to the question of parables, but only a short discussion of this complicated matter can be fitted in here. Raven, you will remember, cited Jesus' teaching in parables as a sort of natural theology.[17] Moreover, it was in connection with parables that Barth himself in his later work came as near as he ever came to an eventual recognition of natural theology.[18] He wrote:

[These parables] are to be witnesses of something new to all men, and to be newly apprehended by them all . . . recounted by Jesus, these everyday happenings become what they were not before, and what they cannot be in and of themselves . . . the New Testament parables are as it were the proto-type of the order in which there can be *other true words* alongside the one Word of God, created and determined by it, exactly corresponding to it, fully serving it and therefore enjoying its power and authority. (my italics)

This may be, as Webster puts it, a 'somewhat meagre source in the search for a natural theology';[19] but, even if meagre, it may perhaps be something. But 'other true words', other than, and alongside, the one Word of God: how can this have been intended? The larger context is Barth's attempt to state a doctrine of 'Lights', a theme which derives from Calvin.[20] According to Calvin, every human person has a 'seed of the fear of God', so that the world can speak eloquently to everyone of God and his virtues. The knowledge of God shines in the creation of the world and in its continual government. Though the actual world is filled with darkness, at least sparks (*scintillae*) of God's glory remain lit. There are 'burning

---

[17] Above, Ch. 1.

[18] *KD* iv/3. 126; *CD* iv/3. 113; and cf. the preceding argument, e.g. *CD* iv/3. 97; *KD* iv/3. 107 f.

[19] Words of J. B. Webster, *Eberhard Jüngel: An Introduction to His Theology* (Cambridge: Cambridge University Press, 1986), 119, in his quotation of this passage.

[20] I follow Berkhof's excellent presentation, H. Berkhof and H.-J. Kraus, *Karl Barths Lichterlehre* (Theologische Studien 123; Zurich: Theologischer Verlag, 1978), 30 f.

lights' in the world, *accensae lampades*, even though these remain partial and fragmentary in this life.

Now Barth seeks to follow in Calvin's track, but, as Berkhof sees it, and I think rightly, his picture of the world is more negative. 'For Calvin the world is self-testimony of God, for Barth it is not.'[21] 'The lack of light in the world is for Barth not the result of an evil blindness of humanity, but the result of a fundamental speechlessness of the good creation of God. . . . For Barth the "lights" are the self-testimony of the creation, for Calvin they are the self-testimony of God in the creation.'[22] For Barth the world in itself is speechless, it is only from Christ that it receives the power of speech.[23] From this, Berkhof continues, 'we see why for Barth *religion* . . . is not among the lights of the world, while for Calvin religion is the direct subjective converse side of the light-giving of the creation'. But, if Calvin is in the right as against Barth in this respect, it is hardly to be doubted that this is because the influence of natural theology—both biblical natural theology and Stoic and other Hellenic—upon him was considerable, and greater than his own dogmatic remarks on the subject may suggest.

Anyway, into this context Barth introduces the case of the parables of Jesus; it is not quite clear why.[24] It seems strange that, when these are the parables of Jesus himself, they should conjure up thoughts of 'other true words' at all. However, on this basis Link (and others, but principally he) seeks to build a new formulation which will take care of the valid reality and interests of natural theology but will do so as a continuation of the lines which Barth has already set out. 'The World as Parable' is the, very deliberate, title of Link's book. And he seeks to sum up Barth's thought succinctly when he writes that 'The world *is* not a parable of the Kingdom of Heaven, it can only *become* one.'[25] It is easy to see why this path is an attractive one. It seeks to find an affirmative value for the biblical material that may point toward natural theology, but to place the realization of this in the future. Thus natural theology has a reality not as anterior knowledge but as future potentiality. Elaborate arguments are deployed in order to show that natural

---

[21] Ibid. 32, thesis 2.     [22] Ibid. 33.

[23] Notice the connection of this with our discussion of Ps. 19, above, Ch. 5.

[24] Berkhof says (*Karl Barths Lichterlehre*, 33): 'There is something enigmatic to me in this. I can understand it only as an indication that Barth really wanted to say more than he actually said.'

[25] Quoted already, in slightly different words, by Webster, *Jüngel*, 119.

theology, in its traditional sense, looks at a static world, without history, and that the parables make sense only for a world in process of becoming, a world with a history (and this is where von Rad's arguments about Wisdom play a part).

But one cannot help seeing the matter in another way, and saying: is not all this a mass of difficulty which the Barthian tradition has loaded upon itself?[26] For all its rejection of natural theology, in the last resort its Calvinism forced it to talk about these 'Lights', and its biblical material forced it to say something about the parables; but it was its own original negativism towards natural theology that made this all so difficult to solve. Barthianism has not only to be continued, refined, and extended: it has also to be clearly admitted that, if any such creative process is to take place, much in the original Barthian structure was misconceived and will have to be dismantled. The biblical evidence *does* point towards natural theology as anterior knowledge, and Barth in rejecting this was simply wrong. He was forcing the biblical material into his own dogmatic mould, he was using every possible means to deny what the texts appeared to say. The parables may or may not point towards future potentiality, but, even if they do so, there is no good reason why this in itself must be made the base for any new understanding of the problems of natural theology, when so much biblical evidence points in the opposite direction.

The parables seem to me to be an outstanding case for the transcending of the contrast between natural and revealed theology. In this respect, far from introducing a totally new element, they are a supremely good illustration of something that has been going on all along, even if Jesus' teaching brought it to expression in a style idiosyncratic and quite original. Few would doubt that, if the word 'revelation' has meaning, the parables are revelatory; and yet so much that is in them is grounded in common experience. And yet not quite 'common'—should we say rather 'mundane'? I find it remarkable that Barth talks about 'these everyday happenings'

---

[26] For the sake of simplicity I devote only a footnote to the mention of another, and related, approach, that of Jüngel. His approach, if I understand it, seems among other things to perceive more validity in traditional natural theology than Barth has done but to classify it in Lutheran terms as *law*. The approach gives more freedom for the recognition of natural theology within the Bible, in the same way as the (Mosaic) Law is within the Bible, while denying it positivity for salvation. As I see it, however, the natural theology of the Bible *is* built into the revelational and salvific material. See Webster, *Jüngel*, 118 ff.

(admittedly, his previous argument makes it clear that he does not seriously think of them as 'everyday') while Raven similarly claims that Jesus bases his teaching on 'the ordinary and commonplace': for surely this is misleading. Certainly there are commonplace elements: the lilies of the field, the patches on the garment, the woman sweeping the house or putting leaven in bread, the fishermen separating the good fish from the bad; but other elements are far from commonplace and seem, on the contrary, to be colossal exaggerations: the man digging a hole in the garden to keep a huge sum of money, or the king who, when guests did not turn up at his son's wedding, sent his forces and destroyed the whole lot, burning their city. This suggests something more like poetry[27] or unrealistic fiction than like everyday experience, or natural science, or the philosophical side of natural theology. The basis is not so much common experience but notions that, whether familiar or rather fantastic, as they often are, can make contact with common experience, can at least be understood by people who have no more than common experience to guide them, or can be seen to enlarge it and enrich it. It is well stated by Sallie McFague:[28]

[The parables] work on a pattern of orientation, disorientation, and re-orientation: the parable begins in the ordinary world with its conventional standards and expectations, but in the course of the story a radically different perspective is introduced, often by means of a surrealistic extravagance, that disorients the listener, and, finally, through the interaction of the two competing viewpoints tension is created that results in a reorientation, a redescription of life in the world.

At least for a number of the parables this states the matter well.

In this respect Raven, in his attempt to bring the parabolic teaching close to his own ideas of science and its gradual disclosure of a world close to incarnation and ready for it, seems to me to have been on uncertain ground. I am not sure that we can ascribe to Jesus the total appreciation of nature and grace as 'sacramentally related as outward to inward', so that 'an incarnation of the divine is in keeping with the whole character of the physical world, since "God

---

[27] C. E. Raven notices this: 'Jesus does not lecture about nature or mankind or the deity: He conveys an immediate experience of our relationship to the world and to one another and to God, using the method of the poet rather than that of the mathematician, the sociologist or the philosopher' (*Natural Religion and Christian Theology* (2 vols., Cambridge: Cambridge University Press, 1953), i. 31): but he might have added that he did not use the method of the scientist either.

[28] S. McFague, *Models of God* (Philadelphia: Fortress, 1987), 50.

so loved it" '.[29] For it seems to me that Jesus took examples, some from nature, like the lilies and the birds, more from human life, masters with servants, sons with fathers, but what he did not do was to attempt grandiose generalizations, either about 'the natural order' or about human life. Raven writes as if the parables used individual items, like the lilies of the field, to point attention to the totality of 'the natural order'; he thinks that Jesus' emphasis is 'upon the elemental and universal, the colour and texture of the flowers, the germination and vicissitudes of the seed-corn, the natural fertility of the soil, the secret working of the leaven in the dough'—in other words, the underlying processes that science understands. But can this be meant? The lilies of the field belong to the world of botany; but mention of them does not imply that a systematic, scientific study of botany will provide an equally good parable, still less a better one. Jesus' teaching has no interest in the comprehensive collection of data about the world and nature that would bring it near to science, or in the level of logical cohesion that would bring it near to traditional, philosophical natural theology either. Some of the things said, after all, are in the strict sense untrue, even if suggestive; they are powerful and effective as communication: a seed does not really have to 'die' in order to grow. As Jerome saw, it is an embarrassment if God has, or is, a gigantic computer registering at every moment the number and whereabouts of all fleas in the world. Rather, Jesus was continuing that line of biblical thoughts about the world which had seen and isolated important structures but had by no means pressed towards comprehensiveness. What he sees are *examples*, to be seen here and there, if one has the perception; and only if one has the perception will one see what it means, a point which Jesus himself makes explicit. Humanity has the resources to understand, shall we say, but it remains a question whether it will in fact understand. The parables may not point towards a total scientific understanding of the world which will inform us of God, nor do they point towards the rational and philosophical discussion of him; but they do have a clear grounding in publicly available knowledge, and in that sense they do come close to natural theology.

[29] Raven, *Natural Religion*, i. 38. I am not sure that, in the familiar phrase of John 3[16], God's 'so loving' the 'world' was directed primarily towards the physical world in Raven's sense. The latter is certainly involved, but I suspect God was more concerned with the people and with the 'world' (the κόσμος) as a sinful environment. Raven takes the implied background sense and applies it as if it was the primary sense.

On the other hand Raven was right in emphasizing the fact of the parables as the characteristic form of Jesus' teaching, and one that was quite different from the interpretation of the traditional sources of revelation. This, very obviously, was a main reason why the parables were an embarrassment to the Barthian tradition. Interpreting a parable is very different from interpreting St Paul. The Pauline model is of one who speaks explicitly about Christ, explaining and interpreting him. This is the 'Christological' model for revelation. If Jesus himself had spoken only about himself, explaining and interpreting himself expressly, his teaching would have fitted into this model very well. But he chose, so often, to speak in parables, which, at least on the surface, taken expressly, were not about himself, rather were about things or events, commonplace or somewhat fantastic, set in the world around. The teaching by parables is important because it is a clear choice to appeal to a source different from the revelatory chain communicated through pre-existing authoritative scripture.[30] Jesus' teaching was visibly his own, and differed in this respect from that of the scribes, who depended on previously given authorities. This is not accidental but is an important clue to the basis and approach of his ministry. And this fits in with another fact: in spite of all the light that may be thrown on his parables by the study of the Old Testament background, by metaphors, similes, parables, and so on,[31] the outstanding fact seems to me still to be that the parables, in spite of their clearly Jewish ambience and atmosphere, seem very different from anything within the Old Testament that might even be thought of as comparable—nor do the rabbinic parables come very close either. The primary impression that one gains is of the *originality* of this aspect of Jesus' teaching.

Interesting also is another point: in view of the argument emphasized in Jewish natural theology, and followed by Paul, namely that from the perception of the created things the knowledge of the creator should follow, it is striking that Jesus hardly uses this argument. There is no question, for him, about the knowledge of the creator God. The questions, like those about the lilies or the birds, are not a means of advancing to belief in the creator. Or, we may say,

---

[30] I have used this argument already in my *Escaping from Fundamentalism* (London: SCM, 1984 = *Beyond Fundamentalism* (US title; Philadelphia: Westminster, 1984)), 11f.

[31] Recently especially Westermann, *Parables*.

they enable us to know a little more about the creator who is already known. They support a confidence in the careful provision God will have made for the smallest details, which is not exactly the same thing as gaining the knowledge that a creator God exists in the first place. It is more a question of continuing trust in the midst of other preoccupations, rather than a question of coming to know the creator through the created. On the other hand, there is absent from Jesus' teaching that continual worry about *idolatry* which, as we have seen, underlies so much of the biblical development of natural theology. Are idols or idolatry mentioned in the Gospels at all? The Jesus of the Gospels seems here to be treading near the risky fringe of Jewish religion, just as he did with statements about his own relation to God and with his associations with the wrong people. Surely the continual linkage of so much express natural theology with the polemics against idolatry constituted a weakness in the theological exploitation of natural realities, a weakness which Jesus was daringly able to defy?

The parables of Jesus seem, then, to support our argument that the distinction between natural and revealed theology breaks down within the biblical material. If something is said by Jesus, that may constitute it as revelation. But if one asks what he said and where he got it from, some of it looks more like observation of things in the world, and that is rather more like natural theology.

The ultimate problem about relating the teaching of Jesus to the question of revelation versus natural theology seems to lie in the modern approach to the understanding of Jesus in general. The failure, as it was supposed to be, of the quest for the historical Jesus left the impression that Jesus could not be accounted for as a historical person. A biography of him could not be written, no entry into his inner life or psychology could be attempted. He was of course human, as orthodox doctrine required. In spite of the enormous concentration on Christology, so-called, everything seemed to be a statement *about* him, from outside, as it were. Utterances like parables are seen as interpretations, doubtless authoritative, of this figure, this 'Christ-event' as people said. Theology was about him but it did not come *from* him. He did not think, he seemed to have no mental processes, one could not ask from where he had got his ideas. Was he perhaps only a mouthpiece for divine revelation passing through him? Or was the teaching attributed to him simply an indirect statement about him, made by others? 'Christology', really a term for a sphere of operation by theologians and much favoured as a term among them, fails to bring us near to any answer, or even to the posing of a proper question. Given these uncertainties, it may have seemed unrealistic even to attempt to discuss whether his teaching inclined to the realms of revelatory or of natural theology. That Jesus even says a thing may seem to many to mean that that thing is divine revelation. Yet what if what he says is a calling to attention of something that is public knowledge available to anyone? Does that not make it closer to natural theology?

The dilemma seems to support our conclusion that there is no absolute distinction between revelation and natural theology. In particular, revelation is not a completely separate body of information or channel of material, totally different in substance from what is publicly known or publicly accessible knowledge. Revelation, if we must still use the word,[32] is not a completely separate entity but is a mode in which things already known are seen in a quite new way, and also a mode in which things previously unknown are added to things already known, making a different pattern but including many elements that were the object of anterior knowledge.

## 4. Scripture

From the beginning we have indicated that, if the presence of natural theology within the Bible is recognized, it may mean that common ideas of the doctrine of scripture have to be revised, and some suggestions in this regard will now be offered.

As I remarked above (Ch. 1), in Barth's theology the Bible was subsumed as one of the three forms of revelation, three forms of the Word of God which comes to humanity: (1) in Jesus Christ, the living, personal Word, (2) in the scriptures, the written Word, which testifies of him, and (3) in the preaching of the Church, in so far as it speaks of him and speaks in accordance with the testimony of scripture. Coupled with the opposition between revelation and natural theology, this doctrine is bound to break down if natural theology is

[32] I continue willing to use this term, although I think it lacking in biblical sanction, as I argued long ago (*Old and New in Interpretation* (London: SCM, 1966)), 65 ff. and *passim*. I welcome the criticisms of W. Pannenberg ('Revelation in Early Christianity', in G. R. Evans (ed.), *Christian Authority* (Henry Chadwick FS; Oxford: Clarendon Press, 1988), 76–85) but think they can be overcome, though I shall not undertake this here.

to be found within the Bible. This indeed is not the only reason why it is defective, but it is the one that most concerns us here.

In essence, the Bible does not belong to this pleasant-looking triadic structure; it is a different sort of thing altogether, and the way in which Barth strung them together, partly because the term 'Word' is used of all three, depends on similarities that are theologically accidental. To call the Bible 'the Word of God' is one of these traditionalisms of the dialectical theology: it is in fact a metaphorical expression, and one which can be perfectly well used so long as it is not taken too literally or taken as an absolute principle. For, as I have argued in various connections, and as is quite obvious if one thinks about it, there is much that is in the Bible that is not there because it is a word spoken by God, something uniquely revealed by him which would otherwise have been unknown, but is there because it was already public knowledge. This is obvious in historical matters. When we read in 1 Kings 22[51] that 'Ahaziah the son of Ahab began to reign over Israel in Samaria in the seventeenth year of Jehoshaphat king of Judah, and he reigned two years over Israel', this is not there because God revealed it to the writer or to anyone else, but because it was public knowledge incorporated by the writer. Considerable elements of such material exist. What we are now saying is that this is not true only of historical data: the same applies also to some moral principles, some cosmological conceptions, and above all some ideas of God and of human nature. One easy way we might go, therefore, would be to say that the Bible is a mosaic, a mixture of revelatory elements with elements that were, in our phrase, anterior knowledge—of God, of the world, of humanity, of anything. If one asks the next question—namely, how do you distinguish between them?—the answer is, of course, you do not have to. For the elements that are anterior knowledge are taken up into the totality: revelation takes up into itself the anterior knowledge, and the Bible, as a witness to revelation, does the same. The canonical principle can thus help us, ironically, to understand natural theology as included within the final totality of scripture. But it should not be used as a principle to deny or overrule the generative sequence, under which material has really come from knowledge anterior to special revelation.

For those who like to have a 'Christological analogy', one may point out that such an analogy works for this view of scripture too.[33] Jesus 'after the flesh' takes up into incarnation not only the physical matter of Jewish humanity but also the inheritance of ideas, not all of which derive directly from canonical scripture, since they include all sorts of contemporary ideas, as well as ideas that are ancient but came into Israel from external contacts. All this matter is nevertheless united with divine being and passes through death into resurrection and new life. All this works just as well if natural theology is part of the matter involved, as if it is excluded. I do not urge this as a proof, since I think, with Markus Barth, that it is an illusion to suppose that a Christological analogy for scripture is necessary or even advantageous. But, for those who value it, I indicate that it can work this way as well.

More certainly, we can say, the dogmatic locus of the doctrine of scripture is that it should be part of the doctrine of the Church. It belongs there, along with the other resources that the Church uses and upon which it depends, like the doctrines of the nature of the Church, the ministry, the creeds, the sacraments and so on. This is so because, if we are to ask what the Bible 'properly' is, as distinct from 'transferred' terms like 'the Word of God', we would have to say, as I wrote long ago,[34] not revelation coming from God to humanity but the Church's (properly: Israel's and, later, the Church's) response to and interpretation of that revelation. That is what it directly and univocally is, and it is on these terms that we can approach it and enter into it exegetically. But its response and interpretation contain structures which derive from, and depend on, natural theology and other kinds of 'natural' knowledge.

Thus the terms like 'holy', 'inspired', and even 'infallible', often used of the scripture in traditional Protestantism, are viable and usable in so far as these terms have meanings analogous to those of the holiness, inspiration, infallibility, and so on of the Church as a

---

[33] For a good critique of the longing to establish a Christological analogy for views of scripture, see Markus Barth, *Conversation with the Bible* (New York: Holt, Rinehart & Winston, 1964), ch. 5, pp. 143–71. This work, which deserves to be better known, contains some strikingly fresh thoughts emerging from a position of a pretty extreme (Karl) Barthian type. M. Barth concludes (p. 170): 'It is therefore unlikely that the use of Christological analogy will solve the problem of scriptural authority. This analogy is but another yoke fabricated by those who want to impose the Bible upon its readers.'

[34] In my review of J. K. S. Reid, *The Authority of Scripture*, in *SJT* 11 (1958), 86–93: this review, which attracted some attention at the time, was one of my first attempts to evaluate the Barthian tradition about Bible and Christology in print.

whole.[35] The Bible has as much infallibility as the Church has (in Protestant terms, not too much). It is inspired in much the same way as the Church is inspired by the presence of the Spirit within it.[36]

The expression 'the Word of God' can certainly continue to be used, and rightly, of the Bible within the Church. In respect of its origins, its essence, its content, it must be seen as a metaphorical expression for the reasons I have given. Since we have seen that natural theology forms an element within scripture and provides important organizing structures within it, it is mistaken and confusing to insist on pinning the term 'revelation' upon the entirety of the Bible. The term 'Word of God' is used analogically of the *operation* of scripture within the community: that is, whatever its origin, whether in 'natural' theology or in revelatory events or otherwise, the material of the Bible operates in a mode which deserves to be described analogically as 'Word of God'.

---

[35] This point was well drawn to my attention in the reading of K. R. Trembath, *Evangelical Theories of Biblical Inspiration* (New York: Oxford University Press, 1987), which I reviewed for *JTS* 41 (1990), 322–4. According to him, the Bible belongs to 'the base', the foundational structure for belief, but the Church does not have the same character (his p. 117). To quote: 'the concept of church does not include the criterion of foundationality as does the concept of inspired Bible . . . the Bible is *norma normans*, while the church is *norma normata*.' Perhaps this is the foundational mistake of evangelicalism?

[36] It is perhaps a weakness of W. J. Abraham's treatment of the subject in his *The Divine Inspiration of Holy Scripture* (Oxford: Oxford University Press, 1981) that he takes as basic analogue for his proposal the (more secular) pattern of the inspiring teacher rather than the (on my terms more realistic and germane) pattern of the inspired and inspiring Church.

# 10

# Natural Theology and the Future of Biblical Theology

Let us begin by summarizing the results of our discussion so far. We have shown, I think, that principles akin to those of natural theology are present in the Bible, both in the New Testament and in the Old, and that the connection between them is enhanced and deepened when we take into account the transmission of ideas as between the two testaments and especially as illustrated by the so-called apocryphal literature. Even if the elements of natural theology are considered as a somewhat minor constituent within the Bible, the functions of these elements remain very essential. In particular, in certain relations they form the cement which links together various themes of scripture, and equally they form one of the channels through which themes are enabled to pass from the earlier stages of their formulation to the later, most importantly in the connection between Old and New Testaments. Thus we are in a position to say that theologies which in principle denied natural theology ran into a deep inner contradiction. Though they aspired to provide, through the rejection of natural theology, a much deeper and more consistent base for the deployment of biblical truth, in effect their own principle forced them away from the realities of the Bible.

Nor was the Bible the only consideration. Theological tradition was another. In so far as theologies which rejected natural theology also aspired to be a return to older, more traditional, theological patterns, they ran into the difficulty that natural theology had been a significant ingredient in most currents of traditional orthodoxy. This, however, has already been mentioned and will not be followed up further, since our concern here is with the Bible itself.

Now, as I have indicated, it might still be possible to maintain, on philosophical or on dogmatic grounds, that natural theology was a false track for Christianity to adopt. It could be said that, even if it was tried out within the Bible, more mature thought or analysis had shown that it was a wrong turning. It could be argued that people were no longer persuaded by it, or that, even if it had worked positively in the past, it now misled them into belief in a God quite different from that of traditional Christianity. But, if it had to be admitted that natural theology had nevertheless been present within the Bible, any such modern theology which rejected natural theology would have to stand rather aloof from the Bible and work explicitly in a very different way. Thus one of the most paradoxical consequences of our argument would be that, even if philosophical or dogmatic theology were to reject natural theology, biblical theology would have to accept it and integrate it into its own work, because natural theology is there in the Bible itself. The consideration of this problem will be the next part of our thinking.

The concept of 'biblical theology' has proved very difficult to define, and many people have found it simplest to deny that any such thing exists or can exist. I think, on the other hand, that it does exist and has some importance. But, rather than defining it in its totality, I will take one aspect, one of its limits, which may help us to see that part of its definition which is for our purpose most important. This is as follows: biblical theology, to be meaningful, must work within the meanings of the biblical culture. Only within that area can it have resources to work with, only there does it have criteria to assess assertions that are made. Only that condition makes it meaningful that there should be such a thing as 'biblical' theology as distinct from the totality of theology.

Now the position of biblical theology in this century has been much affected by the same question of natural theology which has been our subject here. Relations in this regard have been highly paradoxical. Few would doubt that the complete rejection of natural theology by Barth and others formed a strong stimulus to the growth of biblical theology. Natural theology being out of the way, it seemed as if any true theology would be based squarely on the Bible and on it alone. The entire Bible had an intrinsic community of thought, the harmony of which was destroyed as soon as ideas from without this community, of which natural theology was the supreme example, were admitted. Extra-biblical ideas and influences would all be seen as negative and distorting: the removal of them would enable the Bible to be clear and effective in its expression and direct in its relation to final theological affirmations. Greek thought, which had provided the terms for most classical natural theology, was the stock example of a distorting influence which could be and must be eliminated. Thus modern biblical theology to a large extent excluded the subject of natural theology from its purview. It spoke as if biblical theology and natural theology were mutually exclusive categories. In so doing it made itself something like a slave to the classic Barthian position on the matter, though scarcely to the final Barthian position as attained in the later years, the conscious-ness of which hardly penetrated into biblical theology at all. Thus even where biblical theologians ignored Barth, or disagreed with him, or took little account of him, they accepted a working atmo-sphere the outlines of which had been largely set by his side of the dialectical theology.

In this, however, there were many paradoxical aspects. Although, as I have said, Barth did much to stimulate biblical theology, it is not clear that he actually approved of it. He thought, of course, that biblical scholars should be 'more theological', a demand which is still being re-echoed in various quarters.[1] But even those biblical theologians who were most 'theological' were also fairly clear that they were not working as dogmaticians. They did not class themselves as such, and in this they were right. Their modes of demonstration lay still within the area of biblical studies. Barth himself, on the other hand, did not think that there was *any* legitimate mode of biblical study other than the dogmatic, and that meant in effect his own dog-matics. Thus a truly insightful Barthian approach might have been one that condemned the project of 'biblical theology' altogether, and voices of this kind have been raised from time to time.[2] In the central period of twentieth-century biblical theology, however, little atten-tion was given to this aspect: biblical theology was supposed to have its main contrast and counterpart in *historical* study of the Bible, and biblical theologians for the most part thought that 'theology' was on their side, and not against them, in what they were doing.

---

[1] Cf. recently John Barton, 'Should Old Testament Study be More Theological?', *Exp. T.* 100 (1989), 443–8.

[2] See my 'The Theological Case against Biblical Theology', in G. M. Tucker, D. L. Petersen, and R. R. Wilson (eds.), *Canon, Theology and Old Testament Inter-pretation* (Childs FS; Philadelphia: Fortress, 1988), 3–19. Cf. also Dietrich Ritschl, *The Logic of Theology* (London: SCM, 1986), 68 f. (German original, *Zur Logik der Theologie* (Munich: Kaiser, 1984), 98 ff.: 'Die Fiktion einer biblischen Theologie').

Thus, as mentioned above, the subject of natural theology, even the possibility of it, more or less disappeared from works of biblical theology. The first time I recollect the mention of it reappearing within any of the major works in the latter field is in the work of H. H. Schmid.[3] In contrast with many earlier trends of biblical theology, Schmid put forward a very interesting and original proposal, according to which *creation* was the main and comprehensive horizon, the history of religion and the common ground with other religions was positively valued, and the themes of *order* and *peace* were given centrality. Anyone who thought in this way, however, he soon found, fell under suspicion for 'intending a natural theology', and for many people this was enough to rule out any thinking along these lines. Hostility to natural theology, it thus turned out, acted as an obstacle which prevented the progress of ideas within the field of biblical theology itself.

In fact the enslavement of biblical theology to the Barth–Bultmann axis of the dialectical theology was disastrous to the subject. I agree with the Finnish scholar Heikki Räisänen in his recent book *Beyond New Testament Theology* when he writes: 'New Testament scholarship made a fatal mistake when, in the aftermath of the First World War, it turned its back on the liberals and the history-of-religions school and succumbed to the rhetorical-theological appeal of dialectical theology.' And, as he says, the further development of the subject depends on the abandonment of the attitudes inherited from that period.[4] In fact, I have no doubt that the long-term effect of Barthianism has been to create a wider gap between theology and the Bible than was there before. In the beginning it looked as if Barthian theology was striving towards an enormous appropriation of the Bible into the work of theological understanding. This stimulated work of all kinds among biblical scholars. But the value of that stimulus was negated in the long run through the contemptuous ignoring of the main tradition of biblical scholarship by Barth and his followers and by the impossibility of even talking with Barthians about the methods or criteria of de-

---

[3] H. H. Schmid, *Altorientalische Welt in der alttestamentlichen Theologie* (Zurich: Theologischer Verlag, 1974), 9.

[4] See H. Räisänen, *Beyond New Testament Theology* (London: SCM, 1990), xv; cf. 90, etc. As my quotation implies, the same is true of Old Testament scholarship: and one might add that it was, on the whole, more persuaded by the Barthian side of the dialectical theology than were New Testament studies, which were more influenced by the dominant figure of Bultmann.

cision. The countless pages of wearisome, inept, and futile exegesis in the *Church Dogmatics*, especially in the later volumes, were only a testimony to the fact that the Bible cannot be used theologically when the work of biblical scholarship is brushed aside. Barth offered nothing to that scholarship and in the end achieved nothing for it. Some of the most truly ridiculous and useless pieces of biblical interpretation in this century came from the Barthian tradition,[5] and it was precisely the false intellectual assurance that that theology offered that was the cause of their ludicrousness. The later years showed that the justification of Barthian theology depended upon philosophical considerations and arguments from the history of ideas, and not upon the Bible. Seen in the long term, Barthianism led away from biblical authority.

For this ironic situation our topic of natural theology provides one set of illustrations. For if, as we have argued, natural theology does have a place within the Bible, and indeed a fairly important place within it, this fact is bound to make a very considerable difference to the idea of biblical theology and to the modes by which one may operate within that sphere.

We thus come to something close to the diametrical opposite of what it has been the fashion to think. The biblical theologian has to take account of processes of natural theology. Even if he or she personally dislikes natural theology, if it is there in the material it has to be taken into account. It forms part of the essential linkage between one part of the Bible and another, and these linkages, which hold the Bible together, are just the matter with which biblical theology is supposed to be concerned. There may, on the other hand, be philosophical or dogmatic reasons, or reasons arising from the modern situation, why natural theology should be ruled out. If that is so, then the dogmatic theologian has to explain why this aspect of biblical thought should be rejected and what effect such a rejection will have on the idea of the authority of the Bible. To most people, however, it would seem odd if natural theology was accepted as part of the working machinery of the Bible and yet was condemned as anti-Christian by dogmatic theology.

From this several features of any future biblical theology must follow. First of all, the purpose of a biblical theology cannot be primarily to demonstrate the *distinctiveness* of the Bible. The

---

[5] Examples abound in my *The Semantics of Biblical Language* (London: Oxford University Press, 1961).

biblical scholar will have to accept openly the existence of non-distinctive elements, and to interpret them not merely as negative hindrances but also as positive and creative tendencies. Even from such an approach, it is very likely that the Bible will emerge as highly distinctive: but that conclusion is one that must be left to emerge of its own from the evidence, and not one that the scholar should feel compelled to demonstrate.

Secondly, the same will have to be said about contacts with other and environing religions. As we saw from the beginning, any transreligiosity, any degree of adoption within the Bible of concepts and styles that exist also within some other religion, brings us close to the thematics of natural theology. The earlier biblical theology of the twentieth century sought above all to produce something that was different from a *religionsgeschichtlich* perspective on the Bible. But experience has shown, and this has been agreed among many more recent practitioners of biblical theology, that there is no real chance of producing a convincing theology of either Old or New Testament which does not adopt and take within itself the perspective of the history of religions. The biblical evidence itself makes this directly necessary. Such a view, however, must have important indirect systematic consequences, to which attention will have to be drawn.

Needless to say, this implies also that biblical theology should abandon, not only in practice but as a matter of principle, the attempt to contrast Hebrew thought as the contours of revelation itself with Greek thought as the paradigm of autonomous human reason. Hebrew thought has many differences from Greek thought, but this fact does not make it symmorphous with revelation, and the thought-forms of the Hebrew Bible show many aspects of coincidence with other Semitic and ancient Near Eastern thought-forms, which aspects make that side of the Old Testament more comparable to the operations of natural theology. Conversely, great as the differences of Greek thought may be, the entry of substantial elements of Greek thought into the later strata of the Bible—especially some of the Apocryphal books and the New Testament epistles—is too evident to be left unrecognized. Biblical theology has to abandon the attempt to canonize one current of thought, more or less

---

[6] That this 'revelational' style of work ends up with a sort of ethnic, almost racial, principle is well perceived by H. C. C. Cavallin, *Life after Death* (Lund: Gleerup, 1974), where he points out (16), that much scholarship implied that Paul and other

ethnically[6] defined, as definitive for revelation. And even if we take the Hebrew thought forms for themselves, they are like the Greek, in that they also, if in a quite different way, bear the signs of intrinsic relationship to the processes of natural theology.

Or, to put all this in another and a succinct way, biblical theology cannot work in a purely and strictly canonical mode. It has to move across the boundaries of any strictly defined canon of scripture. The matter of the materials which lie within the canon is such that it cannot be properly understood unless the lines of connection with extra-canonical materials are considered. Or, conversely, a strictly canonical interpretation could not fail to produce distortions in the resultant biblical theology. Most obviously is this the case in considering the connections between the Old Testament and the New. This is not to say that the canon of scripture is without importance. To most of us, Daniel is 'Holy Scripture' but Enoch is not, the Wisdom of Solomon is somewhat marginal, the Pauline letters are 'Holy Scripture' but the Didache is not. Let it be so; 'Scripture' is what the Church has decided ought to be normally read in worship. But, for the *understanding* of the books within this canon, writings that lie outside may be of first-rate importance. Paul, as we have emphasized, is likely to be ill understood if the Wisdom of Solomon is ignored, and Daniel—perhaps even Genesis—cannot be properly explained if Enoch is not taken into consideration. Biblical theology, even when understood strictly as the theology of the *canonical* books, can be practised only when the theology of the non-canonical books is positively taken into account.[7] And, of course, when we consider that natural theology, which may have relations lying entirely outside the biblical tradition, has a part within the Bible, then the incorporation of the books that are 'biblical' but not canonical is a very much smaller step, since these books clearly belong to the same general type and style as the canonical books.

The relevance of all this becomes clear when we think of some of the deep problems which have beset biblical theology. Primary among these is the perception of the unity of the two Testaments. As early Christians can have thought in only one way about life after death 'simply because they were Jews'. In the reduction of modern revelational theology to this sort of ethnically defined approach, nature was taking a well-deserved vengeance on revelation.

---

[7] A 'canonical' *reading*, strictly restricted to the canonical books, may indeed be possible, but what it would produce is indeed a *reading* and not a *theology*.

against the separation of the text into many elements, supposed to have been the effect of historical criticism, biblical theology was to be synthetic in method and bring together the large bodies of text into one. And let us say that this was indeed in some measure achieved for the Old Testament and also for the New. But, it seemed, the more the biblical theology approach succeeded for these two great corpora or canons, the more difficult it was found to be to bring these two into one great body and enunciate the theology of the Bible as a whole. Now for this there are, no doubt, several reasons, but one of them lies within our subject-matter in these lectures: the elimination of natural theology from the reckoning was one of the factors which made more difficult the perception of the ways in which the two Testaments were interrelated. As we have illustrated in these lectures, the faith of ancient Israel articulated itself in various ways, but one of these was a sort of natural theology by which certain basic tenets and practices were explained, justified, and defended. This explanation, justification, and defence in turn became part of the 'biblical' basis of New Testament Christianity, without which important parts of it cannot be understood. Natural theology is thus part of the set of historically given linkages between the Hebrew Bible and the New Testament (or parts of it), and an approach which seeks to eliminate natural theology is very likely to run into difficulties for this reason. The rejection of natural theology, which at first sight appeared to guarantee the unity of the Bible, turned out in the end to obscure it.

Similar thoughts emerge when we consider the *hermeneutical* aspect. It was widely, though not universally, felt that biblical theology had a hermeneutical function. It would help to provide the path towards an understanding, not just of how it was in ancient times, which might be a matter of historical-critical interpretation, but of what this should mean for people in the modern situation. But once again it has not been clear that much was achieved along this line. And one reason for this weakness follows from our discussion. The rejection of natural theology meant that interpretation was strongly inclined to restrict its sources of guidance to the *internal* relations perceptible within the biblical text itself. Because much (or most) biblical theology saw itself as in principle hostile to natural theology, and therefore forced to interpret texts entirely on the basis of their *internal* networks of indications, which (supposedly) derived purely and directly from divine revelation,

hermeneutics were forced into an unnatural and ultimately sterile
position. The contradiction is obvious on the modern academic
scene. People say: a historical description is not enough, you must
go on to actualize this for the life of the Church, for the modern
situation. So you actualize it for the life of the Church, for the
modern situation, and what happens? Immediately the same people
say: But you cannot get this out of the text, the text does not actually
say what you are discovering in it. Well, of course it does not.
Interpretation for the modern situation can occur only when you
bring to the text other factors, other ideas, other knowledge of situations, which are expressly other than the internal content and internal relations of the text. But the bringing to the text of these
extra-textual factors is something close to the application of
methods belonging to natural theology, or at least may sometimes
be so.

This is not surprising, since we have seen that, from the beginning,
within the Bible itself, texts were being reinterpreted, not on the
grounds of their own terminology and their own assumptions, but
on the grounds of the question: how does this fit with reality as we
know it from other sources? Something of the apologetic axis was
already operative, and with it the critical function which was the
other end of that same axis. Biblical interpretation for the modern
world cannot be carried out without recognition of this
theologically critical function. Of this the Old Testament provides
one startlingly vivid example, namely the practice of the חרם
(ḥerem), the 'ban' or ritual destruction of the population of con-
quered Canaanite cities, a practice that is heavily emphasized in
several books and especially in Deuteronomy and Joshua, and this
we shall discuss in the next part of this chapter.[8]

This institution is, of course, as everyone knows, one of the
supreme cases in regard to which people feel a moral revulsion
against the Old Testament and its God. Can one believe in a God
who, it appears, not only permitted or used, but commanded and
insisted upon, what seems to be the genocide of a large population?
Conversely, those who insist on the revelatory character of all the

---

[8] I agree with Lohfink that 'ban' is a quite unsuitable rendering for this term: he
suggests *Vernichtungsweihe*, which follows the 'consecration to destruction' already
used by Ullendorff in his edition of the Moabite Stone (D. Winton Thomas, *Documents from Old Testament Times* (Edinburgh: Nelson, 1958), 196).

Bible and its complete authority are at pains to justify this practice, invoking the supposed wickedness of the Canaanites and/or
the long-term advantages of the divine plan of salvation which
could not have proceeded if Israel had not become sole occu-
pants of the land. It is a classic example in which, at least at
first sight, revelational theology seems to be at loggerheads with
natural theology or natural morality. And, traditionally, one
may say, even the revelational party, though they thought they
could (somehow) justify the institution, have mostly followed
the defensive policy of keeping quiet about it unless they were
pressed about it; in other words, even they hardly put it forward
as a shining example of the moral excellence of the Old
Testament.

The biblical theology movement, by contrast, succeeded in
making a very positive use of the חרם and indeed of the entire holy
war tradition, as it came to be called. Its centrality and positive
importance were emphasized in von Rad's little monograph *Der
heilige Krieg im alten Israel* (1951). This and other studies cast a great
deal of light on Israelite warfare in general and on the command to
destroy the Canaanites in particular. It was easy to show that the
background and motivation of these practices are very different from
what the general lay public, seeing the matter from outside, might
imagine. Thus, for example, it can be pointed out that consecration
to destruction is not a sanction for hatred and vengefulness. On the
contrary, it is something more like a ritual, a sort of sacrifice,
whereby the population of captured cities, including even the dom-
estic animals, are destroyed; notice in particular that, by the same
rule, indestructible assets, objects of gold and silver, are not plunder to be kept by anyone but are to be taken and donated as offerings
to the God of Israel. To the non-Hebraist it is not visible that the
root *h-r-m* belongs to the semantic field of 'sacred, holy', which
fact justifies our rendering as 'consecration to destruction' or the
like. It seems to indicate the negative side of being sacred, that is, the
aspect of *removal*, making inaccessible or unavailable for common
use, while the more familiar term *q-d-š* indicates positive qualities of
holiness. Thus a person could 'devote' to the Lord, using the same
Hebrew expression, an animal or a field, and that entity then could
not be recovered and put to normal use. As Brekelmans expresses it,
in moments of extreme crisis one dedicated to Yahweh enemies
and/or booty, in order to be sure of his help in battle; the fulfilment

of this vow was an utterance of gratitude to the God of Israel who had granted the victory.[9]

In other words, the whole thing was the negation of an ethic of mere plunder and exploitation. It was a kind of ritual sanctification,[10] in which the captured persons, animals, and objects were devoted to Yahweh, and while objects, being indestructible, were simply donated to the sanctuary, persons were donated to the deity in the same way in which sacrificial animals were donated, that is, through returning their life to God the giver of life. Many people would doubtless have preferred, for themselves, to keep people alive as slaves, for human beings were a valuable asset, as were oxen and sheep and other animals, and it was for this reason that there were always persons who broke the ban, keeping something or someone for themselves. Stolz uses the expression 'the *ḥ-r-m* taboo' in this connection: captured spoils were taboo to the Israelite victors. There were, however, differing theories of the extent of this taboo. Old Testament texts again and again return to the question whether and under what conditions it was proper to gain and keep any booty taken in the wars.[11]

Moreover, it has been argued that the holy war in full-dress form, as depicted in Deuteronomy and Joshua, may never have been carried out by Israel. In many cases compromises with the existing inhabitants of the land were reached, as the story of the Gibeonites (Josh. 9) exemplifies, and there is considerable evidence of this. As is well known, the first chapter of Judges depicts the defeated Canaanites as remaining in the land and subjected to forced labour. Thus the holy war institutions as depicted may have a theoretical aspect about them: they may sometimes be rules that were not put literally into practice but were used to inculcate other principles altogether, such as a resistance to Canaanite religious practices. Even if the whole tradition of the holy war was 'a fiction', this does not deal with the problem: the problem is not whether the narratives are fact or fiction, the problem is that, whether fact or fiction, the ritual destruction is *commended*. The total destruction of the Canaanite population is commanded in the texts, and accounts of its

---

[9] C. H. W. Brekelmans, *De Ḥerem in het Oude Testament* (Nijmegen: Centrale Drukkerij, 1959); see German summary on 185–90.

[10] See the classic passage Lev. 27[28f.], and cf. BDB's article, 355 f.

[11] See F. Stolz, *Jahwes und Israels Kriege* (Zurich: Theologischer Verlag, 1972), 136 f. The (obviously very explosive) topic of spoil and booty is explored from different viewpoints in numerous biblical passages, e.g. Num. 31, 1 Sam. 30, etc.

being carried out, as at the capture of Jericho, are very emphatically phrased. If it was a fiction, it seems it was a fiction of which people approved and one which parts of the Bible sought to inculcate as a good model. And, though there is a wide variety of biblical depictions of warfare, there appears to be no passage that explicitly states disapproval of the *h-r-m* or denies that it was commanded by God.

Moreover, we know from the Moabite inscription that the entire practice was not unique to Israel but, doubtless with variations, was common property with at least one neighbouring and closely related nation and was in fact carried out against Israel on certain occasions. Since the inscription (the one piece of extant Moabite literature) may well be unfamiliar to readers who are not specialists in Old Testament, it may be helpful to quote a portion of it:

I am Mesha ... king of Moab ... Omri had taken possession of the land of Medeba and he [or: Israel] dwelt in it his days and half the days of his son, forty years; but Kemosh dwelt in it in my days ... The men of Gad had long dwelt in the land of Ataroth, and the king of Israel had built Ataroth for himself. But I fought against the town and took it and I slew all the people of the town, a spectacle for Kemosh and Moab ... Kemosh said to me, 'Go, take Nebo against Israel'. And I went by night and fought against it from the break of dawn till noon; and I took it and slew all: seven thousand men, boys, women and [girls] and female slaves, for I had consecrated it to Ashtar-Kemosh. And I took from there the vessels of Yahweh and dragged them before Kemosh. [12]

The inscription is nothing new: it has been known since 1868. It dates from about 830 BC. Mesha and his revolt against Israel are mentioned also in the Bible (2 Kgs. 3). The language of Moab is extremely close to biblical Hebrew; the identical term *h-r-m* is used, in verb form (translated as 'consecrated' in the extract above).

This Moabite text is of great importance. On the one hand it supports, at least in some degree, the realistic character and historical credibility of some of the biblical narratives and laws. On the other hand it suggests that the practices and principles involved were inherited by Israel from a background shared with the Moabites. This again is striking, for we have noted other possible elements of common religious elements between the two peoples, and of course the Old Testament itself regarded them as related,

---

[12] Translation of E. Ullendorff, from Winton Thomas, *Documents*, 196–7, slightly modified. The word rendered as 'spectacle' is uncertain: it might be more a term for some sort of sacrifice.

Moab being descended from Lot, Abraham's nephew (Gen. 19³⁷).
Were the practices of war a heritage of a common natural religion?

On the other hand, the Hebrew practice of consecration to destruction can scarcely be explained or extenuated, as many writers seem to
imply, on the ground that they were only doing the same as was
universal in the contemporary culture. It seems clear that this was not
so. Brekelmans in an exhaustive discussion considered possible
parallels to the Hebrew *h-r-m* in the Hittite, Egyptian, and Mesopotamian cultures, and also in later contexts (Roman, Celtic, Gallic,
and Germanic), but found nothing: apart from the Moabite Stone, the
answer was negative.[13] Kang, who in general wants to show that there
is 'nothing unique about divine war in the Old Testament texts',[14]
writes that 'the idea of ban [= our *consecration to destruction*] is not
attested in the ancient Near Eastern context except in the Moabite
Stone and in the Bible', though he does go on to consider a suggestion
by Malamat which would find a parallel at Mari. In other words, the
Hebrew practices or theories, even if shared with the closely related
Moabites, are by no means common to the general environment: on
the contrary, they seem to be quite distinctive. Massacres of a general
kind were of course common but these are not the same thing as the
Hebrew practice, with its strict divine requirement and punishment
for failure to execute. In this respect, the positive evaluation of the
Hebrew practice fits with the customary approach of biblical
theology, which sought to stress that which was distinctive as against
the environment. But these same features mean that there can be no
moral extenuation on the grounds that Israel simply fitted in with
what was normal in the environment. And, seen from a general moral
point of view, this distinctiveness may prove to be no recommend-
ation, but only an embarrassment: in this particular case that which is
distinctive turns out to be the *most offensive* element in the general
subject of ancient warfare.

So, as a part of the total enterprise of biblical theology, we can
probably build a sort of theology of holy war, within which all
these commands and practices and their social spin-off in ethics and
rhetoric and in later religion can be brought together and make

[13] Brekelmans, *Herem*; cf. the summary in Sa-Moon Kang, *Divine War in the Old
Testament and in the Ancient Near East* (BZAW 177; Berlin: de Gruyter, 1989),
81 n. 43.

[14] The words are those of Sanderson in her bibliography to the translation of G.
von Rad, *Holy War in Ancient Israel* (Grand Rapids: Eerdmans, 1991), 147. See Kang,
*Divine War*, 80–4.

excellent sense. Seen this way, the whole thing looks quite different from the way in which the uninitiated Bible-reader sees it.

Nevertheless, this leaves the whole central issue in a new way unapproached and unilluminated: according to the Old Testament texts, this is not just something that happened, not only something that can be understood as a meaningful part of ancient anthropology, not just something that can be fruitfully used in theological paraenesis; it is something that God commanded and very strictly insisted upon. It is here that a critical ethical voice can be heard: this cannot be justified as the picture of a moral deity. How can it be reconciled with what we otherwise know and believe of God? Quite possibly, natural morality or natural theology cannot settle the question: but they do succeed in insisting that the question should at least be *raised*. By contrast, biblical theology, through its general, if not universal, ignoring of natural theology, has led to a position where the issue is not raised at all, and where it would seem wrong even to raise it at all. Thus, in most works of biblical theology, during the twentieth-century floruit of that subject, we look in vain for even a discussion of the matter. Apparently, no moral problem exists, or if it does exist biblical theology seems unable to say anything about it.

Now indeed recent years have seen a growth of serious discussion of the question. The (long-delayed) appearance of the English translation of von Rad's monograph, with introduction by Ben Ollenburger and helpful bibliography by Judith Sanderson, shows evidence of considerable concern about it. Some shift of ideas seems to have taken place. People can be found who will argue for a 'pacifist' interpretation of the war traditions of ancient Israel.[15] The traditions of Hebrew warfare are to be understood, we are told, 'as a limitation of militarism and nationalism'.[16] Such interpretations may have something to be said for them, but it is to be feared that they are also in part optimistic attempts to obscure the serious moral offence that the texts seem to present.[17]

[15] See for instance works by Barrett, Eller, and Lind in Sanderson's bibliography in von Rad, *Holy War*; Eller and Lind not seen by me.

[16] Sanderson, reporting views of J. H. Yoder, in von Rad, *Holy War*, 166.

[17] Thus I am surprised by the rather slight attention given to the *herem* in a number of these works. A more pacifist-looking interpretation of Hebrew warfare can indeed be gained if this practice is left out of the picture. But I cannot see that it is marginal, either to the texts themselves or to the ethical questions arising from them. The same applies, but in a different way, to Craigie's *The Problem of War in the Old Testament* (Grand Rapids: Eerdmans, 1978). This popular work is not pacifist, but

It is not our purpose here to evaluate this newer discussion. Its character, however, confirms what has been said. A substantial portion of this discussion emanates from particular groups like the Mennonites who combine a convinced pacifism with a profound belief in biblical authority.[18] It has not, so far, been typical of the main stream of thought in biblical theology. Moreover, a great deal of it comes from very recent times: say, since about 1980, a time in other words, during which the influence of the older biblical theology was declining and social and moral problems which had been neglected were coming to receive fresh attention. For the main stream of biblical theology in this century our evaluation still stands: 'holy war' was creative as a theme in biblical theology, and there was no moral problem to bother about. Concern about the morality of the *ḥerem* was a sign of theological 'liberalism' and threatened an outbreak of a 'Marcionite' attitude which would diminish the authority of the Old Testament.[19] Not all formulated it as simply as did George Ernest Wright with his 'Yahweh was no paci-

like many others it is rather apologetic in intention, and, far from being 'very sensitive', as Sanderson says in her annotation (von Rad, *Holy War*, 139), it seems to me to be extremely naïve and ethically crude. Thus on his p. 98 he writes, 'The Old Testament also provides a realistic view of warfare; the violence endemic in the state may result in warfare, and warfare by definition involves ruthlessness and killing.' But even realistic views of war do not 'by definition' require genocidal destruction.

[18] There is, indeed, a great gulf between the issue of war and pacifism on the one side, and the matter of extermination or genocide on the other. My purpose here is to deal strictly and only with the latter. Nevertheless, in theological discussion some overlap commonly takes place. The position here sketched for biblical theology, which tended to bypass the moral problem of extermination, had a certain parallelism with the influence of Karl Barth on matters of war and pacifism. Barth had in fact a rather sophisticated and nuanced approach to the pacifist position; Yoder correctly writes: 'Karl Barth is the only European theologian of his stature in modern times to have gone as far as he did toward the [pacifist] position he criticizes. He declares the pacifist case to be "almost overwhelming"' (John H. Yoder, *Karl Barth and the Problem of War* (Nashville: Abingdon, 1970), 51). But in the earlier reception of Barth this was little known, even by many who were his followers in other respects. The relevant volumes of *KD* had not been translated. He was appreciated rather as the 'hammer of the pacifists'. What was remembered was his blithe remark in an early essay, 'The Strange New World within the Bible', about 'how unceremoniously and constantly war is waged in the Bible' (*The Word of God and the Word of Man* (Boston: Pilgrim, 1928), 39), an expression which, in its context, seemed to make it clear that 'moralistic' qualms about war should be forgotten. The Scottish Barthianism of my earlier experience, in spite of some theoretical quibbles, was strongly pro-war, and it was commonly said: 'if a man is a pacifist, you know that there's something wrong with his theology.'

[19] For a critique of the arguments, common in the apogee of the biblical theology movement, which identified 'Marcionism' in this way, see my article 'The Old Testament and the New Crisis of Biblical Authority', *Interpretation* 25 (1971), 24–40.

fist, nor am I',[20] but this was the general impression.[21] Although there were many scholarly contributions that proposed revisions to von Rad's seminal monograph,[22] many of these were concerned only with the outlines or history of the phenomenon as taken strictly within the Old Testament context itself, and did nothing to revive discussion of the ethical questions involved. Only late in the century did serious renewal of discussion of the problem take place, and only contributions like those of Norbert Lohfink and Dwight van Winkle faced squarely the central problem of consecration to destruction itself.[23]

How did a system that rejected all natural theology cope with this question? There were various traditional justifications, such as the extreme wickedness of the Canaanites: but the degree of their wickedness is probably in large measure legendary, having been invented or exaggerated precisely in order to furnish extenuation for the mass destruction which the texts insist upon. There is no historical evidence outside the Old Testament which could support such an evaluation of Canaanite culture, except one possible aspect, which will be mentioned shortly. And even within the Old Testament, although the Canaanites are frequently referred to as abominable, much of this may rest upon the cultural estrangement which one people experiences in its perception of another, and the Old Testament actually provides little hard evidence of such exceptional evil-doing.[24] On the contrary, where it gives detailed pictures of contacts with Canaanites and other non-Hebrew peoples, these are often remarkably sympathetic and suggest no such intolerable levels of 'wickedness'. Certainly

[20] Reported by P. D. Hanson, 'War and Peace in the Hebrew Bible', *Interpretation*, 38 (1984), 342, as a response to the rise of the peace movement during the Vietnam war.

[21] Cf. recently for instance Christoph Barth, *God with Us: A Theological Introduction to the Old Testament* (Grand Rapids: Eerdmans, 1991), with its section headings 'The Canaanites were corrupt' (p. 171) and 'The Canaanites were to be exterminated' (p. 172). His discussion mentions certain qualifications, such as I have mentioned; but the effect of these qualifications is not to emphasize the moral question, but to keep it out of sight.

[22] For good recent surveys, see Ollenburger's introduction to the English translation of von Rad, *Holy War*, and G. H. Jones, 'The Concept of Holy War', in R. E. Clements (ed.), *The World of Ancient Israel* (Cambridge: Cambridge University Press, 1989), 299–321.

[23] N. Lohfink, 'Der "heilige Krieg" und der "Bann" in der Bibel', *Internationale katholische Zeitschrift: Communio*, 18/2 (Mar. 1989), 104–12; D. van Winkle, 'Canaanite Genocide and Amalekite Genocide and the God of Love' (1989 Winifred E. Weter Faculty Award Lecture, Seattle Pacific University). And Lohfink too seems to me to seek to soften the problem through apologetic suggestions on the one hand and through a scheme of progressive revelation on the other.

[24] By contrast, see the attractive recent treatment by Niels Peter Lemche in his *The Canaanites and Their Land* (Sheffield: JSOT, 1991).

various religious abuses identified in the period of the kings were regarded as being imitations of Canaanite abominations, but these were abuses committed by *Israelites*, and some of them may have arisen from indigenous Israelite motives and instincts which the Old Testament texts found it convenient to combat by suggesting that they were of Canaanite origin. Comparably, the notorious homosexuality of the people of Sodom is depicted in Genesis 19, but a very similar story is told of Israelite Benjaminites in Judges 19.

What comes nearest to a recognizable Canaanite abomination is the sacrifice of children in fire. The grim reality of this practice, and its extent, have been vividly shown by recent excavations at Carthage, where the Tophet or place of sacrifice and burial has been recovered.[25] Some evidence may suggest that child sacrifices were a deeply entrenched practice, sometimes reaching major dimensions. Greek sources reported something of this kind. According to Diodorus as many as 500 children were sacrificed in the time of crisis when Carthage seemed to face military disaster in 310 BC. They feared that their catastrophe was caused by the anger of 'Heracles' (= Canaanite Baal?) and also of 'Kronos' (El?): 'There was in their city a bronze image of Kronos, extending its hands, palms up and sloping toward the ground, so that each of the children when placed thereupon rolled down and fell into a sort of gaping pit filled with fire.'[26] Naturally, there may be an element of legend and imaginative exaggeration in this. Nevertheless, since the evidence may go back as far as 700 BC, it may be that it reflects conditions of the Phoenician homeland and is relevant for the world of the Old Testament.[27] Moreover, according to Diodorus' account, the entire intent of the Carthaginians was based on memories of earlier times. Having been colonized from Tyre, they had in the first times regularly sent back tithes and the like to the

[25] See Lawrence E. Stager, 'The Rite of Child Sacrifice at Carthage', in J. G. Pedley (ed.), *New Light on Ancient Carthage* (Ann Arbor, Mich.: University of Michigan Press, 1980), 1–11, along with illustrations in Aïcha ben Abed ben Khader and David Soren, *Carthage: A Mosaic of Ancient Tunisia* (New York: American Museum of Natural History, 1987), 150–4. I am grateful to my colleague Dr Barbara Tsakirgis for help in obtaining information in this regard.

[26] Diodorus Siculus, 20. 14. 1 ff.; Teubner text, v. 192 f. The English wording follows Stager, 'Rite of Child Sacrifice', 3.

[27] If it is felt that Carthage is too far distant in time and space from ancient Canaan, then my argument is not affected: it only means that the one piece of possibly hard extra-biblical evidence for Canaanite abominations is removed. However, Punic sacrificial documents or 'tariffs' use some technical terms very similar to those of the biblical sacrificial system of Leviticus, and this supports the idea that a relationship in sacrificial concepts existed.

Tyrian gods, but gradually, capitalistic motives overtaking them, they had given up the practice, thus slighting the deity. Overtaken by serious crisis, they returned to it. At first sight, therefore, child sacrifice looks like a good example of Canaanite 'iniquity'. Later several Hebrew kings are severely blamed where they have indulged in this or a related practice: thus Ahaz king of Judah (mid to late eighth century) is censured because he had 'made his son to pass through the fire,[28] according to the abominable practices of the nations whom the Lord drove out before the people of Israel' (2 Kgs. 16[3], and compare the cases of Manasseh, 2 Kgs. 21[6], and the Moabite king of 2 Kgs. 3[27]). It is interesting that the Carthaginians expected the royal and other aristocratic families to provide the children for sacrifice; but this requirement had been neglected, and wealthy families had been buying unwanted children and keeping them for the purpose. This is why the sacrifice of 310 BC was a particularly important occasion, since it involved the genuine children of these same families. This aspect again may fit with the biblical narratives on the subject. Certainly, the matter was of real importance in Israel, and the destruction of the Tophet was a major element in the religious reform of Josiah (2 Kgs. 23[10]).

The reality of Canaanite child sacrifice is therefore, very likely, an important fact. One should hesitate, however, before supposing that it provides a moral justification for the ritual destruction of the entire Canaanite population by Israel, and this for several reasons. First of all, as indicated above, in the narratives of early Hebrew contacts with the Canaanites, a quite sympathetic atmosphere is often evoked: for example in the story of Dinah and the Shechemites in Genesis 34, where the Canaanites (or 'Hittites' as they are called) are very willing to make amends and co-operate with Jacob's family, and the story looks unsympathetically on the violence done by Simeon and Levi. While vague mentions of the 'iniquity' of the Canaanites occur, no explicit picture of terrible evil-doing is produced, and nothing at all is said about the sacrifice of children. Moreover, in the narratives that mention particular destructions of cities, notably that of Jericho, nothing is said about child sacrifice or any other abominations. As far as that story indicates (Josh. 6–7), the people of Jericho are conse-

---

[28] It is conceivable—I will not say more—that the strange Hebrew expression 'make [a child] to pass through the fire' implies a sort of token sacrifice, in which the child was not in fact destroyed. But even such a token sacrifice would still count as an abominable practice to the biblical writers. I have not seen this discussed, however.

crated to destruction for only one reason, namely that they are people living in Jericho. Thirdly, the Old Testament tends to conceal the probable relations involved, because it gives the impression that the pre-Israelite inhabitants of the land (variously called Canaanites, Amorites, Hittites, and other names, as may be) were quite unrelated to the Israelites and deeply alien from them: thus, as is well known, the genealogical map of Genesis 9[24ff.] and 10 classifies Canaan as son of Ham and as thus belonging to a quite different portion of humanity from the Hebrews, who are children of Shem. In fact the Canaanites— or at least the ones among them who can be related through Phoenicia to Carthage and thus to the evidence of child sacrifice—were closely related to the Israelites, and their language was very similar indeed. And this means that such evidence as there is of child sacrifice may well go back to ancient religious drives and instincts which were inherited in common by Phoenicia, by Carthage, and by Israel.

Child sacrifice was forbidden by the laws in Israel, but it was forbidden because it needed to be forbidden. One of the ways to reinforce that prohibition was to represent the practice as foreign and an abomination. Moreover, if the sacrifice of children was an abomination, it is a peculiar way to overcome this by slaughtering wholesale the entire population, including those same children of whom it is felt to be iniquitous if their own parents sacrificed them. The sacrifice of children, though indeed a gruesome practice, thus provides no sort of explanation or justification for the requirement that the Canaanite population should be totally exterminated. And, apart from this particular practice, there is no serious evidence of extraordinary 'wickedness' within Canaanite culture.

In any case, wickedness, however serious, does not constitute a justification for what appears to be genocide. The fact is that these massacres were commanded, not because of the wickedness of the populace, but for a quite different reason. Wickedness, however great, provides no reason why, for instance, the cattle and other animals should be destroyed. Canaanite populations were to be exterminated because that was part of the rule of warfare accepted in the society and hallowed by the commendations and narrations of religious tradition, and because they were the people of the land which Israel was to settle in.[29] If God's people needed a land of their own to

---

[29] For example, the very central law of Deuteronomy 20 provides three categories: (1) if a city outside the land (given by God as an inheritance to Israel) accepts an offer of peace, it is to become subject to forced labour; (2) if a city outside the land resists

live in and work out their role in the world's salvation, why could the inhabitants of Jericho and other cities not have been offered the choice of emigration, which they might well have grasped as an alternative to total extermination? (In fact the terms גרש, 'expel, drive out', and הוריש, 'dispossess, take over possession from', are both used quite a lot, for example Exodus 23[31], and Judges 1 repeatedly, but neither do the narratives depict, nor the laws envisage, expulsion as an alternative to extermination.) Again, to maintain that biblical practices of warfare were 'time-bound'—another suggested theological explanation—seems to mean that, though genocidal massacre is wrong in the modern world, there was an earlier time when there was nothing wrong with it. All such arguments are pitifully weak apologetic. Moreover, if the Moabites practised the same form of destruction, did they also have a mission of world salvation to perform? Or does the Moabite evidence not point in the opposite direction and suggest that the whole institution in Israel was in fact a piece of natural religion, practised by Israel because it was shared with elements of the surrounding culture? Perhaps it was itself part of that same notorious wickedness of the Canaanites, taken over rather than suppressed?

The fact is that, on the face of it, the command of consecration to destruction is morally offensive and has to be faced as such. Although, within the ancient Hebrew literature and society itself, it is only one part of the wider context of warfare and goes along with the images of God as warrior and other aspects, it is the *herem* itself that is uniquely and outstandingly a problem for Christian theology and ethical understanding. As soon as we consider interpretation for Christianity and for the modern world, it is an exceptional case. Over questions of war and peace it is accepted that there is room for disagreement; it is often held that war can be necessary for the long-term maintenance of peace, and Christians who are impressed by the high degree of human sinfulness often think that pacifism is over-optimistic in its hopes. But over the deliberate destruction of entire populations by divine command there is no room for disagreement of this kind—not least when this century has seen horrifying examples of genocide at work. Moreover, the attitudes engendered by attempts to justify consecration to destruction spill over into wide areas of

attack, all males are to be killed, but women, small children, cattle, and all other goods are to be taken and enjoyed as spoil; (3) if it is a city within the land of the inheritance, including Hittites, Amorites, Canaanites, and so on, nothing that breathes is to be left alive.

religion: into the invention of a sort of racial 'wickedness' of which there is no real evidence, into the production of views that 'wickedness' justifies mass destruction, into non-discrimination between innocent and guilty, into the perception of a sort of racial guilt, and above all into the belief that religious commands override morality and that it is good for us that this should be so.

As Stewart Sutherland expresses it:[30]

When difficulties arise, there is a retreat to the self-indulgent intellectual comfort of talk of 'mystery' and 'inscrutability'. Less often, but more strikingly, the gauntlet to moral belief is thrown down, and we are reminded of our status as finite creatures who have to live with paradox in one form and another.

In fact, the usual thing, as I remember it from the Barthian period, was to wheel out the saying of Kierkegaard about the 'teleological suspension of the ethical': that is to say, there are occasions when, for an ultimate supreme goal, normal moral judgement may be suspended.[31] In view of an ultimate salvation which requires appropriate preparation, an immediate genocide, though unpleasant, may be necessary and therefore acceptable. Against this we may set Sutherland's principle, from the same page of his book: 'A religious belief which runs counter to our moral beliefs is to that extent unacceptable.'

Now I do not think that, in this last chapter, I can hope to provide even a first step towards an answer to this problem. All I indicate is that the problem is there. It is one that biblical theology is simply unlikely to take seriously, so long as it holds that considerations of natural theology are to be ignored. But I would say this: that we cannot hope to make progress without willingness to accept that the whole tradition of the matter of the Canaanites involves a picture of God which is seriously defective in relation to the reality of his nature, and this on the grounds which Sutherland sets out, which are, in a way, grounds of natural theology. But in any case, when we have done this, we find that the same judgements may follow on the ground of revelational theology too. Even a purely revelational theology cannot ignore the question, for such a theology has to consider how the practice of holy war fits with Jesus' teaching, with his own life, and

---

[30] In *God, Jesus and Belief* (Oxford: Blackwell, 1984), 16.
[31] Kierkegaard used this expression in his explanation of the sacrifice of Isaac by Abraham.

with the entire account of him that traditional Christian doctrine provides; and it is just on that ground that some of the recent discussion has been inspired. But the acceptance of natural theology as a legitimate conversation-partner is the course most likely to lead to a real discussion, while the denial of natural theology tends to be accompanied with a refusal to see any importance in the question at all, a simple confidence that, if God has commanded something, that fact must override and blanket out all other ethical considerations. Possibly a more sophisticated and comprehensive understanding of salvation through Christ can be worked out, which would in some way take into account the moral problem of the destruction of the Canaanites, and this on revelational grounds. But, unless attention is given to the verdict of natural theology, it is likely that no attempt at any such improved understanding will be made. And, in particular, any attempt at a meaningful interpretation for the present day is bound to take extra-biblical facts, values, and considerations into account. For the situation in the present-day Middle East sufficiently demonstrates the result that follows, when ancient ideologies of war, people, and land are allowed to survive and grow without adequate ethical evaluation.

Biblical theology, then, being based within the meanings of the biblical culture itself, must take within its concerns the natural theology or theologies of that culture; and to some extent it has in the past done this, but often without recognizing that it was doing so. In so far as it seeks to debouch into an interpretation of the Bible for modern times, it is there likely to be particularly handicapped if it disregards the currents of more modern natural theology. And, of course, it is perfectly proper that it should lead towards a critique of natural theology; but, in so far as it does so, it is bound also to look critically at the elements of natural theology which operate within the Bible itself. And, since these elements are by no means insignificant, any such critique of natural theology must carry with it a revision of our ideas of the character of scripture itself.

It is now time to conclude with some thoughts about the long-term importance of our theme. First, it concerns the central problem of theological scholarship, namely the unity of theology as an enterprise. As we have indicated, the insistence on rejection of natural theology had in the long run a completely unintended result: the violent separation between biblical studies as they are actually carried on and the ideas of theologians about the place and authority of the Bible. Secondly, it is an ecumenical question.[32] The question of understanding between Protestant and Catholic Christianity is in considerable measure a question of the place of natural theology. Natural theology of course deserves to be subjected to a critique, but such a critique must be something different from a dogmatic rejection. Thirdly, it is a question of the relation between Christian belief and the actual beliefs and principles of the societies in which people live. Since the Bible itself built its account of revelation, at least in part, upon beliefs and principles of its own people and those of their ancestors and neighbours, it should not be surprising if modern theology has to do the same in relation to the beliefs and principles of our own time.

[32] Cf. the quotation from Schillebeeckx already cited above.

# Bibliography

## 1. PREVIOUS GIFFORD LECTURE SERIES AND OTHER SIMILAR SERIES

BARTH, KARL, *The Knowledge of God and the Service of God According to the Teaching of the Reformation* (London: Hodder & Stoughton, 1938).

CLARK, STEPHEN R. L., *From Athens to Jerusalem: The Love of Wisdom and the Love of God* (Oxford: Clarendon Press, 1984).

——*Civil Peace and Sacred Order: Limits and Renewals I* (Oxford: Clarendon Press, 1989).

DAICHES, DAVID, *God and the Poets* (Oxford: Clarendon Press, 1984).

JAEGER, WERNER, *The Theology of the Early Greek Philosophers* (Oxford: Clarendon Press, 1947).

MITCHELL, BASIL L., *Morality: Religious and Secular* (Oxford: Clarendon Press, 1980).

PEACOCKE, A. R., *Creation and the World of Science* (Oxford: Clarendon Press, 1979).

RAVEN, CHARLES E., *Natural Religion and Christian Theology* (2 vols., Cambridge: Cambridge University Press, 1953).

## 2. REFERENCE WORKS

COGGINS, R. J., and HOULDEN, J. L. (eds.), *A Dictionary of Biblical Interpretation*, (London: SCM, 1990).

*Evangelisches Kirchen-Lexikon* (Göttingen: Vandenhoeck & Ruprecht, 1985–).

*Harper's Bible Dictionary* (San Francisco: Harper & Row, 1985).

*Hastings' Dictionary of the Bible*, 1-vol. edn., rev. F. C. Grant and H. H. Rowley (Edinburgh: T. & T. Clark, 1963).

*The Interpreter's Dictionary of the Bible* (Nashville: Abingdon, 4 vols., 1962, and Supplementary Vol., 1976).

MAYER, COMELIUS (ed.), *Augustinus-Lexikon* (Basle: Schwabe, 1986–).

## 3. GENERAL THEOLOGICAL DISCUSSIONS

ABRAHAM, W. J., *The Divine Inspiration of Holy Scripture* (Oxford: Oxford University Press, 1981).

AHLERS, R., *The Community of Freedom: Barth and Presuppositionless Theology* (New York: Lang, 1989).

BARR, JAMES, *Old and New in Interpretation* (London: SCM, 1966).

——*Fundamentalism* (2nd edn., London: SCM, 1981).

BARR, JAMES, *Escaping from Fundamentalism* (London: SCM 1984) = *Beyond Fundamentalism* (Philadelphia: Westminster, 1984).
—— 'The Theological Case against Biblical Theology', in G. M. Tucker, D. L. Petersen, and R. R. Wilson (eds.), *Canon, Theology and Old Testament Interpretation* (Childs FS; Philadelphia: Fortress, 1988), 3–19.
—— 'Biblical Scholarship and the Unity of the Church' (R. T Orr Lecture, Huron College, 1989).
—— 'Exegesis as a Theological Discipline Reconsidered: And the Shadow of the Jesus of History', in Donald G. Miller (ed.), *The Hermeneutical Quest: Essays in Honor of James Luther Mays* (Allison Park: Pickwick, 1986), 11–45.
—— '"Fundamentalism" and Evangelical Scholarship', *Anvil*, 8 (1991), 141–52.
—— *Holy Scripture: Canon, Authority, Criticism* (Oxford: Clarendon Press, 1983).
BARTH, KARL, *The Word of God and the Word of Man* (Boston: Pilgrim, 1928).
—— *Kirchliche Dogmatik* (14 vols., Zurich: Evangelischer Verlag, 1947–70); ET, *Church Dogmatics* (13 vols., Edinburgh: T. & T. Clark, 1956–70).
BARTH, MARKUS, *Conversation with the Bible* (New York: Holt, Rinehart & Winston, 1964).
BECK, HEINRICH, *Natürliche Theologie: Grundriß philosophischer Gotteserkenntnis* (Munich: Pustet, 1986).
BERKHOF, HENDRIK, and KRAUS, HANS-JOACHIM, *Karl Barths Lichterlehre* (Theologische Studien 123; Zurich, Theologischer Verlag, 1978).
BIRKNER, H.-J., 'Natürliche Theologie und Offenbarungstheologie: ein theologiegeschichtlicher Überblick', *NZST* 3 (1961), 279–95.
BOHLMANN, R. A., 'The Criteria of Biblical Canonicity in Sixteenth-Century Lutheran, Roman Catholic and Reformed Theology' (dissertation, Yale University, 1968).
BRÅKENHIELM, CARL REINHOLD, 'Is Metaphysics Theologically Possible?', *St. Th.* 43 (1989), 181–96.
BRUNNER, E., and BARTH, K., *Natural Theology*, with introd. by John Baillie (London: Bles, 1946).
BULTMANN, R., 'The Problem of "Natural Theology"', in R. Bultmann, *Faith and Understanding*, ed. R. W. Funk (New York: Harper & Row, 1969), 313–31.
CLEOBURY, F. H., *A Return to Natural Theology* (London: James Clarke, 1967).
COBB, JOHN B., *A Christian Natural Theology Based on the Thought of Alfred North Whitehead* (Philadelphia: Westminster, 1965).
COCHRANE, CHARLES NORRIS, *Christianity and Classical Culture: A Study of Thought and Action from Augustus to Augustine* (London: Oxford University Press, 1944).
DAECKE, S., 'Gott erkennen in der Natur', *Evangelische Kommentare*, 17 (1984), 181–4.
DALFERTH, INGOLF U., 'Karl Barth's Eschatological Realism', in S. W.

Sykes (ed.), *Karl Barth: Centenary Essays* (Cambridge: Cambridge University Press, 1989), 14–45.

DEMBOWSKI, HERMANN, 'Ansatz und Umriße einer Theologie der Natur', *Ev. Th.* 37 (1977), 33–49.

——'Natürliche Theologie—Theologie der Natur', *Ev. Th.* 45 (1985), 224–48.

DILLISTONE, F. W., *Charles Raven: Naturalist, Historian, Theologian* (London: Hodder & Stoughton, 1975).

FIDDES, PAUL, *The Creative Suffering of God* (Oxford: Clarendon Press, 1988).

——'The Status of Woman in the Thought of Karl Barth', in Janet M. Soskice (ed.), *After Eve* (London: Marshall Pickering, 1990), 138–55.

FISCHER, H., 'Natürliche Theologie im Wandel', *Z. Th. K.* 80 (1983), 85–102.

FORD, DAVID F., 'Barth's Interpretation of the Bible', in S. W. Sykes (ed.), *Karl Barth: Studies of His Theological Methods* (Oxford: Clarendon Press, 1979).

FRETHEIM, TERENCE E., *The Suffering of God: An Old Testament Perspective* (Philadelphia: Fortress, 1984).

——'The Repentance of God: A Key to Evaluating Old Testament God-Talk', *Horizons in Biblical Theology*, 10 (1988), 47–70.

——'Suffering God and Sovereign God in Exodus: A Collision of Images', *Horizons in Biblical Theology*, 11 (1989), 31–56.

FUHRMANN, PAUL T., 'Philosophical Elements in the Early Reformed Tradition', *Columbia Theological Seminary Quarterly*, 57 (1964), 46–61.

GESTRICH, CHRISTOF, *Neuzeitliches Denken und die Spaltung der dialektischen Theologie* (Beiträge zur historischen Theologie, 52; Tübingen: Mohr, 1977).

GILKEY, LANGDON, 'The Creationist Issue: A Theologian's View', in David Tracy and Nicholas Lash (eds.), *Cosmology and Theology, Concilium*, 166 (1983), 55–69.

HAMMOND, T. C., *Reasoning Faith: An Introduction to Christian Apologetics* (London: Inter-Varsity Fellowship, 1943).

HENDRY, GEORGE S., *The Theology of Nature* (Philadelphia: Westminster, 1980).

HENRIKSEN, JAN-OLAV, 'How is Theology about Nature Natural Theology?', *St. Th.* 43 (1989), 197–209.

HILDEBRANDT, FRANZ, *This is the Message: A Continental Reply to Charles Raven* (London: Lutterworth, 1944).

HUBER, W., PETZOLD, E., and SUNDERMAIER, T., *Implizite Axiome: Tiefenstrukturen des Denkens und Handels* (Dietrich Ritschl FS; Munich: Kaiser, 1990).

HÜBNER, JÜRGEN, 'Schöpfungsglaube und Theologie der Natur', *Ev. Th.* 37, (1977), 49–68.

JÜNGEL, EBERHARD, 'Das Dilemma der natürlichen Theologie und die Wahrheit ihres Problems', in A. Schwann (ed.), *Denken im Schatten des Nihilismus* (Weischedel FS; Darmstadt; Wissenschaftliche Buchgesellschaft, 1975), 419–40.

JÜNGEL, EBERHARD, *Entsprechungen* (Munich: Kaiser, 1980).

—— *Theological Essays*, tr. J. B. Webster (Edinburgh: T. & T. Clark, 1989).

KASPER, WALTER, *The God of Jesus Christ* (London: SCM, 1984).

KIRJAVAINEN, HEIKKI, 'Natural Theology in the Light of Logic, Semantics and Metaphysics', *St. Th.* 43 (1989), 171–9.

KRTKE, W., 'Karl Barth und das Anliegen der "natürlichen Theologie"', *Z. d. Z.* 30, (1976), 177–83.

LEHMANN, P. L., 'Karl Barth and the Future of Theology', *RS* 6 (1970), 105–20.

LINK, CHR., *Die Welt als Gleichnis* (Munich: Kaiser, 1976).

—— 'Das menschliche Gesicht der Offenbarung', *K. u. D.* 26 (1980), 264–76

LOUTH, ANDREW, 'Barth and the Problem of Natural Theology', *Downside Review*, 87 (1969), 268–77.

McFAGUE, SALLIE, *Models of God* (Philadelphia: Fortress, 1987).

McWILLIAMS, WARREN, *The Passion of God: Divine Suffering in Contemporary Protestant Theology* (Macon, Ga.: Mercer University Press, 1985).

MEYER-ABICH, K. M., 'Zum Begriff einer praktischen Theologie der Natur', *Ev. Th.* 37 (1977), 3–19.

MEYNELL, H., *Grace versus Nature* (London: Sheed & Ward, 1965).

MOWINCKEL, SIGMUND, *The Old Testament as Word of God* (New York: Abingdon, 1959).

NIEBUHR, RICHARD R., *Schleiermacher on Christ and Religion* (New York: Scribners, 1964).

NOVAK, DAVID, 'Before Revelation: The Rabbis, Paul, and Karl Barth', *Journal of Religion*, 71 (1991), 50–66.

O'NEILL, J. C., *The Bible's Authority* (Edinburgh: T. & T. Clark, 1991).

PAGE, RUTH, *Ambiguity and the Presence of God* (London: SCM, 1985).

PANNENBERG, WOLFHART, *Theology and the Philosophy of Science* (London: Darton, Longman & Todd, 1976).

—— 'Revelation in Early Christianity', in G. R. Evans (ed.), *Christian Authority* (Henry Chadwick FS; Oxford: Clarendon Press, 1988), 76–85.

PLANTINGA, ALVIN, 'The Reformed Objection to Natural Theology', *Proceedings of the American Catholic Philosophical Association*, 54 (1980), 49–73.

PORTER, S. E., 'Two Myths: Corporate Personality and Language/Mentality Determinism', *SJT* 43 (1991), 289–307.

RICHMOND, JAMES, *Ritschl: A Reappraisal* (London: Collins, 1978).

RITSCHL, DIETRICH, *The Logic of Theology* (London: SCM, 1986); German original, *Zur Logik der Theologie* (Munich: Kaiser, 1984).

ROBERTS, RICHARD H., 'The Reception of the Theology of Karl Barth in the Anglo-Saxon World: History, Typology and Prospect', in S. W. Sykes (ed.), *Karl Barth: Centenary Essays* (Cambridge: Cambridge University Press, 1989), 115–71.

SCHLICHTING, WOLFHART, *Biblische Denkform in der Dogmatik* (Zurich: Theologischer Verlag, 1971).

SCHOLZ, H., 'Wie ist eine evangelische Theologie als Wissenschaft möglich?', *Z. d. Z.* 9 (1931), 8–53; also in G. Sauter (ed.), *Theologie als Wissenschaft* (Munich: Kaiser, 1971), 221–64.

SPENCER, S. R., 'Is Natural Theology Biblical?', *Grace Theological Journal*, 9 (1988), 59–72.

SPERRY, WILLARD L., *Jesus then and now* (New York: Harper, 1949).

STOCK, KONRAD, 'Tillichs Frage nach der Partizipation von Mensch und Natur', *Ev. Th.* 37 (1977), 20–32.

SYKES, S. W. (ed.), *Karl Barth: Studies of His Theological Methods* (Oxford: Clarendon Press, 1979).

——(ed.), *Karl Barth: Centenary Essays* (Cambridge: Cambridge University Press, 1989).

SZEKERES, A., 'Karl Barth und die natürliche Theologie', *Ev. Th.* 24 (1964), 229–42.

THIEMANN, RONALD F., *Revelation and Theology* (Notre Dame, Ind.: University of Notre Dame Press, 1985).

TORRANCE, T. F., 'The Problem of Natural Theology in the Thought of Karl Barth', *RS* 6 (1970), 121–35.

——'Phusikos kai theologikos logos: St Paul and Athenagoras at Athens', *SJT* 41 (1988), 11–26.

TREMBATH, K. R., *Evangelical Theories of Biblical Inspiration* (New York: Oxford University Press, 1987).

WEBB, STEPHEN H., *Re-figuring Theology: The Rhetoric of Karl Barth* (Albany, NY: State University of New York Press, 1991).

WEBSTER, J. B., *Eberhard Jüngel: An Introduction to His Theology* (Cambridge: Cambridge University Press, 1986).

WERBICK, J., 'Der Streit um die "natürliche" Theologie: Prüfstein für eine ökumenische Theologie', *Catholica*, 37, (1983), 119–32.

WIND, H. C., 'The Metaphysics of Love: Theology, Myth and Metaphysics with Special Reference to Søren Kierkegaard', *St. Th.* 43 (1989), 211–25.

WISNEFSKE, NED, *Our Natural Knowledge of God* (New York: Lang, 1990).

WISSINK, J. B. M., *De inzet van de theologie, een onderzoek naar de motieven en de geldigheid van Karl Barths strijd tegen de natuurlijke theologie* (Amersfoort: de Horstink, 1983).

YODER, JOHN H., *Karl Barth and the Problem of War* (Nashville: Abingdon, 1970).

ZAHN-HARNACK, AGNES VON, *Adolf von Harnack* (Berlin: Bott, 1936).

## 4. THEISM AND PHILOSOPHY OF RELIGION

ABRAHAM, W. J., *An Introduction to the Philosophy of Religion* (Englewood Cliffs, NJ: Prentice-Hall, 1985).

——'Revelation Revisited' (forthcoming).

——and HOLTZER, STEVEN W., *The Rationality of Religious Belief* (Basil Mitchell FS; Oxford, Clarendon Press, 1987).

ALLEN, DIOGENES, *Philosophy for Understanding Theology* (Atlanta: John Knox, 1985).

BARNES, JONATHAN, *The Ontological Argument* (London: Macmillan, 1972).

BARTH, KARL, *Anselm: Fides quaerens intellectum* (London: SCM, 1960);

German original first pub. 1931; new edn., *Fides quaerens intellectum*, ed. E. Jüngel and I. U. Dalferth (Zurich: Theologischer Verlag, 1981).

JENNINGS, THEODORE W., *Beyond Theism: A Grammar of God-Language* (New York: Oxford University Press, 1982).

JÜNGEL, EBERHARD, *God as the Mystery of the World* (Edinburgh: T. & T. Clark, 1983).

KENNY, ANTHONY, *The God of the Philosophers* (Oxford: Clarendon Press, 1979).

MACKIE, J. L., *The Miracle of Theism* (Oxford: Clarendon Press, 1982).

SUTHERLAND, STEWART R., *God, Jesus and Belief: The Legacy of Theism* (Oxford: Blackwell, 1984).

SWINBURNE, RICHARD, *The Existence of God* (Oxford: Clarendon Press, 1979).

## 5. GENERAL OLD TESTAMENT

ALBREKTSON, BERTIL, *History and the Gods* (Lund: Gleerup, 1967).

BARR, JAMES, 'The Problem of Israelite Monotheism', *TGUOS* 17 (1957–8), 52–62.

—— 'The Old Testament and the New Crisis of Biblical Authority', *Interpretation*, 25 (1971), 24–40.

—— 'Anthropomorphism', 'Monotheism', and 'Polytheism' in *Harper's Bible Dictionary* (San Francisco: Harper & Row, 1985), 32, 652, and 806 f.

—— 'Biblical Chronology: Legend or Science?' (Ethel M. Wood Lecture; University of London, 1987).

—— 'Do we Perceive the Speech of the Heavens? A Question in Psalm 19', in *The Psalms and Other Studies on the Old Testament Presented to Joseph I. Hunt* (Nashotah, Wis.: Nashotah House Seminary, 1990), 11–17.

—— 'Mowinckel, the Old Testament, and the Question of Natural Theology' (the Second Mowinckel Lecture, Oslo, 1987), *St. Th.* 42 (1988), 21–38.

—— 'Biblical Exegesis and Natural Theology', *Svensk Kyrkotidning*, 7–8 (4195–6), 85th year (17, 24 Feb. 1989), 85–91, 101–7.

—— 'La Foi biblique et la théologie naturelle', in *Études théologiques et religieuses*, 64 (1989), 355–68.

BARTH, CHRISTOPH, *God with Us: A Theological Introduction to the Old Testament* (Grand Rapids: Eerdmans, 1991).

BARTON, JOHN, *Amos' Oracles against the Nations* (Cambridge: Cambridge University Press, 1980).

—— 'Old Testament Theology', in John Rogerson (ed.), *Beginning Old Testament Study* (London: SPCK, 1983), 90–112.

—— 'Should Old Testament Study be more Theological?' *Exp. T.* 100 (1989), 443–8.

DION, PAUL E., 'YHWH as Storm-God and Sun-God: The Double Legacy of Egypt and Canaan as Reflected in Psalm 104', *ZATW* 103 (1991), 43–71.

GESE, HARTMUT, *Zur biblischen Theologie* (Munich: Kaiser, 1977).

GIBSON, J. C. L., 'The Theology of the Ugaritic Baal Cycle', *Orientalia*, 53 (1984), 202–19.

—— 'Language about God in the Old Testament', *Cosmos*, 5 (1989), Glenys Davies (ed.), *Polytheistic Systems*, 43–50.

HAYMAN, PETER, 'Monotheism: A Misused Word in Jewish Studies', *JJS* 42 (1991), 1–15.

HUGHES, JEREMY, *Secrets of the Times: Myth and History in Biblical Chronology* (JSOT Supplement Series 66; Sheffield: Academic Press, 1990).

LABUSCHAGNE, C. J., *The Incomparability of Yahweh in the Old Testament* (Leiden: Brill, 1966).

LANG, BERNHARD, *Monotheism and the Prophetic Minority* (Sheffield: Almond, 1983).

LEMCHE, NIELS PETER, *The Canaanites and Their Land* (Sheffield: JSOT, 1991).

LEVENSON, JON D., 'The Sources of Torah: Psalm 119 and the Modes of Revelation in Second Temple Judaism', in P. D. Miller, Jr., Paul D. Hanson, and S. Dean McBride (eds.), *Ancient Israelite Religion* (Philadelphia: Fortress, 1987), 559–74.

—— *Creation and the Persistence of Evil: The Jewish Drama of Divine Omnipotence* (San Francisco: Harper & Row, 1988).

OTZEN, BENEDIKT, 'The Old Testament Wisdom Literature and Dualistic Thinking in Late Judaism', *VTS* 28 (1974), 146–57.

PATRICK, DALE, *The Rendering of God in the Old Testament* (Philadelphia: Fortress, 1981).

RAD, GERHARD VON, 'Natur- und Welterkenntnis im Alten Testament', in *Gottes Wirken in Israel* (Neukirchen-Vluyn: Neukirchener Verlag, 1974).

ROGERSON, J. W. (ed.), *Beginning Old Testament Study* (London: SPCK, 1983).

SCHMID, H. H., *Altorientalische Welt in der alttestamentlichen Theologie* (Zurich: Theologischer Verlag, 1974).

THOMAS, D. WINTON, *Documents from Old Testament Times* (Edinburgh: Nelson, 1958).

TUCKER, G. M., PETERSEN, D. L., and WILSON, R. R. (eds.), *Canon, Theology and Old Testament Interpretation* (Childs FS; Philadelphia: Fortress, 1988).

## 6. LAW AND NATURAL LAW

BARR, JAMES, 'Biblical Law and the Question of Natural Theology', in T. Veijola (ed.), *The Law in the Bible and in Its Environment* (Publications of the Finnish Exegetical Society 51; Helsinki, Finnish Exegetical Society, 1990), 1–22.

BARTON, JOHN, 'Natural Law and Poetic Justice in the Old Testament', *JTS* 30 (1979), 1–14.

FINNIS, JOHN, *Natural Law and Natural Rights* (Oxford: Clarendon Press, 1980).

GEHMAN, H. S., 'Natural Law and the Old Testament', in J. M. Myers, O. Reimherr, and H. N. Bream (eds.), *Biblical Studies in Memory of H. C. Alleman* (Locust Valley, NY: Augustin, 1960) 109–22.

HART, H. L. A., *The Concept of Law* (Oxford: Clarendon Press, 1961).

HORST, F., 'Naturrecht und Altes Testament', *Ev. Th.* 10 (1950–1), 253–73 = H. W. Wolff (ed.), *Gottes Recht* (1961), 235–59.

## 7. WISDOM LITERATURE

BLENKINSOPP, JOSEPH, *Wisdom and Law in the Old Testament* (Oxford: Oxford University Press, 1983).

COLLINS, JOHN J., 'The Biblical Precedent for Natural Theology', *JAAR* 45/1, Supplement (Mar. 1977), B: 35–67.

CRENSHAW, JAMES L., *Old Testament Wisdom: An Introduction* (Atlanta: John Knox, 1981).

MCKANE, WILLIAM, *Prophets and Wise Men* (London: SCM, 1965).

PREUβ, HORST DIETRICH, 'Erwägungen zum theologischen Ort alttestamentlicher Weisheitsliteratur', *Ev. Th.* 30 (1970), 393–417.

——'Alttestamentliche Weisheit in christlicher Theologie?' *Bibliotheca Ephemeridum Theologicarum Lovaniensium*, 33 (1974), 165–81.

RAD, G. VON, *Wisdom in Israel* (London: SCM, 1970).

ROGERSON, J. W., 'The Old Testament View of Nature: Some Preliminary Questions', in A. S. van der Woude (ed.), *Instruction and Interpretation* (Leiden: Brill, 1977), 67–84.

THOMAS, J. HEYWOOD, 'Philosophy and the Critical Study of Wisdom Literature', *Heythrop Journal*, 20 (1979), 290–4.

## 8. THE OLD TESTAMENT AND WARFARE

BARRETT, LOIS, *The Way God Fights: War and Peace in the Old Testament* (Scottdale, Pa.: Herald, 1987).

BEN ABED BEN KHADER, AÏCHA, and SOREN, DAVID, *Carthage: A Mosaic of Ancient Tunisia* (New York: American Museum of Natural History, 1987).

BREKELMANS, C. H. W., *De Herem in het Oude Testament* (Nijmegen: Centrale Drukkerij, 1959).

CRAIGIE, PETER C., *The Problem of War in the Old Testament* (Grand Rapids: Eerdmans, 1978).

ELLER, VERNARD, *War and Peace from Genesis to Revelation* (Scottdale, Pa.: Herald, 1987).

HANSON, PAUL D., 'War and Peace in the Hebrew Bible', *Interpretation*, 38 (1984), 341–62.

HOBBS, T. R., *A Time for War: A Study of Warfare in the Old Testament* (Wilmington, Del.: Glazier, 1989).

JONES, G. H., 'The Concept of Holy War', in R. E. Clements (ed.), *The*

*World of Ancient Israel* (Cambridge: Cambridge University Press, 1989), 299–321.

KANG, SA-MOON, *Divine War in the Old Testament and in the Ancient Near East* (BZAW 177; Berlin: de Gruyter, 1989).

LIND, MILLARD C., *Yahweh is a Warrior: The Theology of Warfare in Ancient Israel* (Scottdale, Pa.: Herald, 1980).

LOHFINK, NORBERT, 'Der "heilige Krieg" und der "Bann" in der Bibel', *Internationale katholische Zeitschrift: Communio*, 18/2 (Mar. 1989), 104–12; English summary in *Theology Digest*, 38/2 (Summer 1991), 109–14.

RAD, GERHARD VON, *Der heilige Krieg im alten Israel* (Göttingen: Vandenhoeck & Ruprecht, 1951); ET, *Holy War in Ancient Israel* (Grand Rapids: Eerdmans, 1991), with introd. by Ben C. Ollenburger and bibliography by Judith E. Sanderson.

STAGER, LAWRENCE E., 'The Rite of Child Sacrifice at Carthage', in J. G. Pedley (ed.), *New Light on Ancient Carthage* (Ann Arbor, Mich.: University of Michigan Press, 1980), 1–11.

STOLZ, FRITZ, *Jahwes und Israels Kriege: Kriegstheorien und Kriegserfahrungen im Glauben des alten Israel* (Zurich: Theologischer Verlag, 1972).

WINKLE, DWIGHT VAN, 'Canaanite Genocide and Amalekite Genocide and the God of Love' (1989 Winifred E. Weter Faculty Award Lecture, Seattle Pacific University).

## 9. THE IMAGE OF GOD

BARR, JAMES, 'The Image of God in Genesis: Some Linguistic and Historical Considerations', *Old Testament Studies* (Papers read at the Tenth Meeting of Die OT Werkgemeenskap in Suid-Afrika, Pretoria, 1967), 5–13.

——'The Image of God in the Book of Genesis: A Study of Terminology', *BJRL* 51 (1968–9), 11–26.

BIRD, PHYLLIS A., '"Male and Female he Created them": Genesis 1: 27b in the Context of the Priestly Account of Creation', *HTR* 74 (1981), 129–59.

BRUNNER, EMIL, *Der Mensch im Widerspruch* (3rd edn., Zurich: Zwingli, 1941).

CAIRNS, DAVID, *The Image of God in Man* (London: SCM, 1953).

CLINES, D. J. A., 'The Image of God in Man', *Tyndale Bulletin*, 19 (1968), 53–103.

FIDDES, PAUL, 'The Status of Woman in the Thought of Karl Barth', in J. M. Soskice (ed.), *After Eve* (London: Collins/Marshall Pickering, 1990), 138–55.

JERVELL, JACOB, *Imago Dei: Genesis 1, 26f. im Spätjudentum, in der Gnosis und in den paulinischen Briefen* (Göttingen: Vandenhoeck & Ruprecht, 1960).

JÓNSSON, GUNNLAUGUR A., *The Image of God: Genesis 1: 26–28 in a Century of Old Testament Research* (Lund: Almqvist & Wiksell, 1988).

SAWYER, J. F. A., 'The Meaning of אלהים בצלם in Genesis i–ix', *JTS* 25 (1974), 418–26.

SCHMIDT, WERNER H., *The Faith of the Old Testament* (Oxford: Blackwell, 1983).

STAMM, J. J., 'Die Imago-Lehre von Karl Barth und die alttestamentliche Wissenschaft', in *Antwort* (Karl Barth FS; Zurich: Evangelischer Verlag, 1956), 84–98.

## 10. RABBINICS AND HELLENISTIC JUDAISM

CHADWICK, HENRY, 'Philo and the Beginnings of Christian Thought', in A. H. Armstrong (ed.), *Cambridge History of Later Greek and Medieval Philosophy* (Cambridge: Cambridge University Press, 1967), 137–57.

HAYMAN, PETER, 'Monotheism: A Misused Word in Jewish Studies', *JJS* 42 (1991), 1–15.

MEYER, R., *Hellenistisches in der rabbinischen Anthropologie* (BWANT 4th Series, 22; Stuttgart: Kohlhammer, 1937).

NEUSNER, JACOB, 'Physics in an Odd Idiom: The Stoic Theory of Mixtures in the Applied Reason of the Mishnah', *BSOAS* 52 (1989) 419–29.

NOVAK, DAVID, *The Image of the Non-Jew in Judaism* (New York: Mellen, 1983).

WASSERSTEIN, ABRAHAM, 'Die Hellenisierung des Frühjudentums: Die Rabbinen und die griechische Philosophie', in W. Schluchter (ed.), *Max Webers Sicht des antiken Christentums* (Frankfurt: Suhrkamp, 1985), 281–316.

## 11. APOCRYPHAL BOOKS, INTERTESTAMENTAL PERIOD, AND GREEK CULTURE

BERGER, KLAUS, *Die Weisheitsschrift aus der Kairoer Geniza* (Tübingen: Francke, 1989).

BOSWELL, JOHN, *Christianity, Social Tolerance, and Homosexuality* (Chicago: University of Chicago Press, 1980).

COLLINS, JOHN J., *Between Athens and Jerusalem: Jewish Identity in the Hellenistic Diaspora* (New York: Crossroad, 1986).

DOVER, K. J., *Greek Homosexuality* (London: Duckworth, 1978).

HADAS, MOSES, *Aristeas to Philocrates (Letter of Aristeas)* (New York: Harper, 1951).

——*Hellenistic Culture: Fusion and Diffusion* (London: Oxford University Press, 1959).

HENGEL, MARTIN, *Judaism and Hellenism* (2 vols., London: SCM, 1974).

PRICE, A. W., *Love and Friendship in Plato and Aristotle* (Oxford: Clarendon Press, 1989).

REESE, JAMES M., *Hellenistic Influence on the Book of Wisdom and its Consequences* (Analecta Biblica 41, Rome: Biblical Institute Press, 1970).

SKEHAN, PATRICK W., and DI LELLA, ALEXANDER A., *The Wisdom of Ben Sira* (Anchor Bible 39; New York: Doubleday, 1987).

WINSTON, DAVID, *The Wisdom of Solomon* (Anchor Bible 43; New York: Doubleday, 1979).

## 12. NEW TESTAMENT

BARR, JAMES, 'Words for Love in Biblical Greek', in L. D. Hurst and N. T. Wright (eds.), *The Glory of Christ in the New Testament* (G. B. Caird Memorial Volume; Oxford: Clarendon Press, 1987), 3–18.

BARRETT, C. K., *A Commentary on the Epistle to the Romans* (New York: Harper, 1957).

BARTH, KARL, *The Epistle to the Romans*, ET, E. C. Hoskyns (London: Oxford University Press, 1933).

BORNKAMM, G., 'Gesetz und Natur: Röm 2, 14–16', in *Studien zu Antike und Urchristentum*, ii (Munich: Kaiser, 1959), 93 ff.

BRUCE, F. F., *The Acts of the Apostles* (London: Tyndale Press, 1951).

CAIRD, GEORGE B., 'Paul's Theology', in *Hastings' Dictionary of the Bible*, rev. F. C. Grant and H. H. Rowley (Edinburgh: T. & T. Clark, 1963), 736–42.

CAVALLIN, H. C. C., *Life after Death: Paul's Argument for the Resurrection of the Dead in 1 Corinthians 15*. Part 1: *An Enquiry into the Jewish Background* (Lund: Gleerup, 1974).

COLLINS, JOHN, 'New Testament Cosmology', in David Tracy and Nicholas Lash (eds.), *Cosmology and Theology, Concilium*, 166 (1983), 3–7.

CONZELMANN, H., 'The Address of Paul on the Areopagus', in L. Keck and J. Louis Martyn (eds.), *Studies in Luke-Acts* (London: SPCK, 1968), 217–30.

—— *Die Apostelgeschichte* (HBNT 7; Tübingen: Mohr, 1963).

—— *Acts* (Hermeneia; Philadelphia: Fortress, 1987).

CRANFIELD, C. B., *Romans* (ICC; Edinburgh: T. & T. Clark, 1975).

DONFRIED, KARL P. (ed.), *The Romans Debate* (Minneapolis: Augsburg, 1977).

DUPONT, J., 'Le Salut des Gentils et la signification théologique du Livre des Actes', *NTS* 6 (1959–60), 132–55.

ELLIOTT, NEIL, *The Rhetoric of Romans* (Sheffield: JSOT Press, 1990).

KÄSEMANN, ERNST, *An die Römer* (4th edn., Tübingen: Mohr, 1980).

KECK, L., and MARTYN, J. LOUIS (eds.), *Studies in Luke-Acts* (London: SPCK, 1968).

KLEIN, GÜNTER, 'Paul's Purpose in Writing the Epistle to the Romans', in Karl P. Donfried (ed.), *The Romans Debate* (Minneapolis: Augsburg, 1977), 32–49.

O'NEILL, J. C., *The Theology of Acts in Its Historical Setting* (London: SPCK, 1970).

RÄISÄNEN, HEIKKI, *The Torah and Christ* (Publications of the Finnish Exegetical Society 45; Helsinki: Finnish Exegetical Society, 1986).

—— *Beyond New Testament Theology* (London: SCM, 1990).

REICKE, B., 'Natürliche Theologie bei Paulus', *SEÅ* 22–3 (1957–8), 154–67.

SANDERS, E. P., *Paul, the Law, and the Jewish People* (Philadelphia: Fortress, 1983).

SCHMITHALS, WALTER, *Der Römerbrief* (Gütersloh: Gerd Mohn, 1988).

SYREENI, KARI, 'Matthew, Luke and the Law', in T. Veijola (ed.), *The Law in the Bible and in Its Environment* (Publications of the Finnish Exegetical Society 51; Helsinki: Finnish Exegetical Society, 1990), 126–55.

VIELHAUER, PHILIPP, 'On the "Paulinism" of Acts', in L. E. Keck and J. Louis Martyn (eds.), *Studies in Luke-Acts* (London: SPCK, 1968), 33–50; German, 'Zum "Paulinismus" der Apostelgeschichte', *Ev. Th.* 10 (1950–1), 1–15.

WESTERMANN, CLAUS, *The Parables of Jesus in the Light of the Old Testament* (Minneapolis: Fortress, 1990).

ZIESLER, JOHN, *Pauline Christianity* (Oxford: Oxford University Press, 1983).

## 13. HISTORY OF DOCTRINE

BARTH, PETER, 'Das Problem der natürlichen Theologie bei Calvin', *Th. Ex. H.* 18 (1935), 1–60.

BOUWSMA, WILLIAM J., *John Calvin* (New York: Oxford University Press, 1988).

DOWEY, EDWARD A., *The Knowledge of God in Calvin's Theology* (New York: Columbia University Press, 1952).

LEITH, JOHN H., *John Calvin's Doctrine of the Christian Life* (Louisville, Ky.: Westminster/John Knox, 1989).

RICHMOND, JAMES, *Ritschl: A Reappraisal* (London: Collins, 1978).

TORRANCE, THOMAS F., *Calvin's Doctrine of Man* (London: Lutterworth, 1949).

WALLACE-HADRILL, D. S., *The Greek Patristic View of Nature* (Manchester: Manchester University Press, 1968).

WEIR, D. A., *The Origins of the Federal Theology in Sixteenth-Century Reformation Thought* (Oxford: Clarendon Press, 1990).

## 14. GERMAN CHURCH

BARANOWSKI, SHELLEY, *The Confessing Church, Conservative Elites, and the Nazi State* (Lewiston/Queenston: Mellen, 1986).

CONWAY, J. S., *The Nazi Persecution of the Churches* (London: Weidenfeld & Nicolson, 1968).

—— 'The German Church Struggle: Its Making and Meaning', in Hubert G. Locke (ed.), *The Church Confronts the Nazis: Barmen then and now* (Toronto: Mellen, 1984), 93–143.

ERICKSEN, ROBERT P., *Theologians under Hitler* (New Haven, Conn.: Yale, 1985).

KERSHAW, IAN, *Popular Opinion and Political Dissent in the Third Reich: Bavaria 1933–45* (Oxford: Clarendon Press, 1983).

NOWAK, KURT, 'Deutsche Christen', *Evangelisches Kirchenlexicon*, I (1986), cols. 825–7.

SCHOLDER, KLAUS, *The Churches and the Third Reich* (2 vols., Philadelphia: Fortress, 1988–).

WRIGHT, JONATHAN R. C., 'The German Protestant Church and the Nazi Party in the Period of the Seizure of Power 1932–3', *Studies in Church History*, 14 (Oxford, 1977), 393–418.

## 15. LINGUISTIC AND LITERARY ASPECTS

BARR, JAMES, *The Semantics of Biblical Language* (London: Oxford University Press, 1961).
—— *Biblical Words for Time* (2nd edn; London: SCM 1969).
—— '"Determination" and the Definite Article in Biblical Hebrew', *JSS* 34 (1989), 307–35.
BASSON, A. H., and O'CONNOR, D. J., 'Language and Philosophy: Some Suggestions for an Empirical Approach', *Philosophy*, 22 (1947), 49–65.
CAIRD, GEORGE B., *The Language and Imagery of the Bible* (London: Duckworth, 1980).
CLARKE, BOWMAN L., *Language and Natural Theology* (Janua Linguarum, Series Minor, 47; The Hague: Mouton, 1966).
ERICKSON, RICHARD J., *James Barr and the Beginnings of Biblical Semantics* (Notre Dame, Ind.: Anthroscience Minigraph Series, Foundations Press, 1984).
PRICKETT, STEPHEN, *Words and the Word: Language, Poetics and Biblical Interpretation* (Cambridge: Cambridge University Press, 1986).
SOSKICE, JANET M., *Metaphor and Religious Language* (Oxford: Clarendon Press, 1985).

## 16. RELATIONS WITH SCIENCE

BARR, J., 'Man and Nature: The Ecological Controversy and the Old Testament; *BJRL* 55 (1972–3), 9–32, repr. in D. Spring and E. Spring (eds.), *Ecology and Religion in History* (New York: Harper Torchbooks, 1974), 48–75.
FOSTER, M. B., 'The Christian Doctrine of Creation and the Rise of Modern Natural Science', *Mind*, 43 (1934), 446–68.
—— 'Christian Theology and Modern Science of Nature I and II', *Mind*, 44 (1935), 439–66; 45 (1936), 1–27.
O'NEIL, W. M., *Early Astronomy from Babylonia to Copernicus* (Sydney: Sydney University Press, 1986).
OPPENHEIM, A. LEO, 'Man and Nature in Mesopotamian Civilization', in *Dictionary of Scientific Biography*, xv (New York: Scribners, 1970–80), 634–66.
SODEN, W. VON, 'Leistung und Grenze sumerischer und babylonischer Wissenschaft', published together with Landsberger's 'Die Eigenbegrifflichkeit der babylonischen Welt' (Darmstadt: Wissenschaftliche Buchgesellschaft, 1965).

# General Index

Abed ben Khader, A. b. 215 n.
abortion 149
Abraham, W. J. 132 n., 198 n.
Adam 58 ff., 122 f., 156 ff., 166
Addison, J. 86
Akhenaten 84
Albrektson, B. 143 n.
Althaus, P. 114
Ambrose 157 n.
animals 62, 64, 66, 69 f., 85, 156, 171 ff.
Anselm 129 ff.
anterior knowledge 1 f., 123, 184, 187, 189, 196
anthropomorphism 139 ff., 146, 158, 169, 187
Antiochus 52
apologetics 4 f., 28, 107, 109, 118 ff., 127, 131, 175 f., 207, 213 n., 214 n., 218
Aquinas, Thomas 13, 158
Areopagus speech 20–38, 45, 104 n., 135
   compared with Romans 51 f., 69 ff.
Aristeas, letter of 47 n., 67 n., 70 n.
Aristotle 45, 52 n., 86 n., 149 n.
Armstrong, A. H. 76 n.
astronomy 68, 88 n., 109, 177
Athanasius 157 n.
atheism 42 n., 110, 117, 128, 131, 133, 153 f.
Auerbach, E. 129
'Aufruf der 93' 115
Augustine 45 n., 129 n., 157

Baillie, J. 6, 173
Barmen Declaration 11, 124
Barnes, J. 130 n.
Barrett, C. K. 41 ff.
Barrett, L. 212 n.
Barth, C. 214 n.
Barth, K. *passim*
   and Areopagus speech 197
   and biblical scholarship 117 ff., 167, 185, 202 f.
   and canon 78 ff.
   Christian approach to Old Testament 122 ff.
   conflict with Brunner 3, 6, 11 f., 60, 102, 109 n., 133 f., 161 ff., 172 f.
   'context', use of 79, 88 f.
   and exegesis 20, 26, 38, 50, 78 f., 103, 136, 202 f.
   Gifford Lectures 6 ff., 12, 14, 104, 113, 131
   and image of God 156–73
   and 'Lights' 188 f.
   and National Socialism 10 ff., 111 ff.
   natural theology: dependence on? 128 ff.
   and view of scripture 103 f., 195 ff.
Barth, M. 197
Barth, P. 109 n., 162 n.
'Barthian captivity' 105, 108
Barton, J. 54 n., 94, 201 n.
Basson, A. H. 185 n.
Beck, H. 3 n.
Berkhof, H. 23 n., 86 n., 87 n., 106 n., 188 f.
biblical theology 17, 71, 76, 119 ff., 128, 139, 199 ff.
Biblical Theology Movement 15, 121, 131
biblicism 119
Bird, P. 160, 163
Birkner, H. J. 17 n., 60 n.
Bohlmann, R. A. 80
Boman, Th. 185
Bonhoeffer, D. 159 f.
Bornkamm, G. 56 f.
Boswell, J. 51 n., 52 n.
Bouwsma, W. J. 88 n., 109
Brekelmans, C. H. W. 208 f., 211
Brockington, L. H. 75 n.
Bruce, F. F. 27
Brunner, E. 3, 6, 10 f., 12 ff., 17 ff., 20 n., 60, 102, 114, 135 n., 158 n., 161 ff., 172 f.
Buber, M. 140 n.
Bultmann, R. 12, 47 n., 113 n.

Caird, G. B. 17 n., 70 n., 187 n.
Cairns, D. 156 n., 157 n.
Calvin, J. 8 f., 20, 42 n., 88 n., 100, 105, 107, 109 ff., 153 ff., 188 ff.
Calvinism 7, 9, 106, 113, 117, 123, 190
Canaanites 207 ff.
canon 68, 77 ff., 196 f., 205 ff.
Carthage 215 ff.
Cavallin, H. C. C. 204 n.
Chadwick, H. 60 n., 76, 195 n.
child sacrifice 63, 215 ff.
Christology 13, 193 f., 196
    Christological analogy (for scripture) 196 f.
Cicero 75, 109
Clements, R. E. 214 n.
Cleobury, F. H. 18
Cobb, J. 18
Coggins, R. J. 17 n.
Collins, J. J. 91 f.
conscience 40, 45, 51, 71
consecration to destruction 207 ff.
context 78 f., 88 f.
contraception 126
Conzelmann, H. 25 n., 135 f.
covenant 94, 168, 183 f.
Craigie, P. C. 212 n.
Cranfield, C. B. 41 ff.
creation 5, 34, 37, 39, 41 ff., 48, 65, 68, 72 f., 75, 77, 81 ff., 86 n., 133, 147 ff., 154, 169, 172, 175 ff., 180, 202
Cullmann, O. 143

Damaris 22, 30
DC, *see* German Christians
death 60 ff.
definite article 185 f.
Dembowski, H. 151 n.
depravity 15, 66, 179
Deutero-Isaiah 63, 65 f., 146
Deutschmann, J. 60 n.
devil 61
dialectical theology 12, 14 n., 19, 60 n., 121, 150, 161, 196, 201 f.
Dillistone, F. W. 14 n.
Diodorus 215
Dion, P. 84
Dionysius the Areopagite 22, 30
Dover, K. J. 52 n.
Dowey, E. A. 108 f.
Driver, G. R. 87 n.

ecology 18, 83, 149, 159, 180
ecumenicity 50, 80, 221
Eleazar 51
Eliot, G. 129 n.
Eller, V. 212 n.
Enoch, Book of 177
Epicurean(ism) 21, 28, 32, 35, 93
Ericksen, R. P. 114 n.
Erickson, R. J. 182 n., 185 n.
eternity 139, 143, 152
euhemerism 67
evangelical(ism) 9, 106 ff., 116
Evans, G. R. 195 n.
Eve 59 f., 62, 166, 187
existentialism 117, 121, 140
expansiveness (of exegesis) 50, 134 ff.

failure theory (of Paul at Athens) 28 ff.
Fall of man 47, 59 ff., 161 f.
fascism 116
feminism 160
Fichtner, J. 61 n.
Fiddes, P. 163 n.
Ford, D. 26 n., 129
Foster, M. B. 176 n.
Frei, H. 129
fundamentalism 106 n., 152 n., 153
Funk, R. W. 47 n., 113 n.

Gardner, H. 129
Gärtner, B. 31, 55, 72 n.
German Christians (DC) 10, 111 ff., 124
Gese, H. 79 f.
Gestrich, C. 112 n., 113 n., 124 n., 125 n., 128 n.
Gibson, J. C. L. 145 n.
Gifford, Lord 1, 7, 9 ff.
Gifford Lectures 1, 6, 8, 12, 14, 17 n., 104, 131
Gleason, H. J. 185
Gogarten, F. 14 n., 114 n.
Graham, W. W. 95
Grant, F. C. 17 n.
Greek philosophy 15, 27, 32 f., 57, 65, 73 ff., 93, 119 f.
Greek thought 15 f., 32 f., 56 f., 71, 74, 76, 92, 119 ff., 186, 201, 204 f.
Grønbech, V. 120
Gunkel, H. 87, 158
Guthkelch, A. C. 86 n.

Haas, P. 182 n.
Hadas, M. 67 n.
Hammond, T. C. 107
Hammurabi 97
Hanhart, R. 60 n.
Hannah 62
Hanson, P. D. 214
Harnack, A. 14 n., 106
Hayman, P. 61 n., 144 n.
Hebblethwaite, B. L. 126
Hegel, G. W. F. 117, 131
Hendry, G. S. 83 n.
Hengel, M. 94
Henriksen, J.-O. 83 n.
Heraclitus 129
*herem* 207 ff.
hermeneutics 206 f.
Herrmann, W. 106
Hirsch, E. 114
historical criticism 103, 206
historical Jesus 118, 194
historical study 5, 201
Hodge, C. 106
Homer 139 f., 144
homosexuality 51 f., 54, 64, 66, 69,
    148, 215
Houlden, J. L. 17 n.
Howard, W. F. 29 n.
Hughes, J. 176 n.
Humbert, P. 158
Hunt, J. I. 87 n.
Hurst, L. D. 70 n.

idolatry 21, 33 ff., 53, 63 ff., 70, 72 f.,
    89, 95, 148, 151 f., 169 ff., 194
image of God 156 ff.
immortality 61 f., 74 f.
interculturality 88, 92 f., 176
interpretation 141, 150 ff.
interreligiosity 84, 88, 92 f., 176, 187,
    204
Irenaeus 157
Islam 5, 25, 154
Isocrates 167

Japan 17 n.
Jerome 80, 143, 192
Jervell, J. 165 n.
Jesus Christ 19, 29, 56, 122, 130
    as image of God? 164 f.
    teaching in parables 16, 188 ff.
Jethro 98 ff.
Jones, G. H. 214 n.

Jónsson, G. 156 n., 157 n., 158, 159 n.,
    167 n., 169 n.
Josephus 52
Judaism 5, 34, 42, 59, 65, 70 f., 80, 92,
    100 f., 146 f.
Jülicher, A. 117 n.
Jüngel, E. 18, 110 n., 140 n., 158,
    188 n., 190 n.
Justin Martyr 27

Kang, S.-M. 211
Käsemann, H. 46 ff., 53, 69, 77
Kasper, W. 128 n.
Keck, L. E. 25 n.
Keller, A. 12 n.
Kenites 145 f.
Kenny, A. 143 n.
Kershaw, I. 12 n.
Kierkegaard, S. 219
Köhler, L. 60 n., 119 n., 158
Kraus, H.-J. 23 n., 86 n., 106 n.,
    188 n.

La Fontaine, J. 175
Landsberger, B. 175 n.
law, biblical 8, 33, 40, 44 f., 48 f.,
    52 f., 55, 65, 77, 87 ff., 94–101,
    146, 190 n., 217 n.
Lehmann, P. 17 n., 161
Leith, J. 108, 162 n.
Lemche, N. P. 214 n.
Lemcio, E. 24 n.
Levenson, J. D. 89 f., 180
Lind, M. C. 212 n.
Link, C. 10 n., 18, 46, 50 n., 56 f.,
    60 n., 83 n., 92, 101, 121, 168, 189
list science 175 f.
Lohfink, N. 207 n., 214
Louth, A. 127
Luther, M. 8 f., 20, 101, 158
Lystra 28 ff., 36 f., 83 n., 84

McFague, S. 191
McKane, W. 90
Mackie, J. L. 130 n.
Macmurray, J. 140 n.
Maimonides 91, 146 f.
Malamat, A. 211
Marcionism 213
Martyn, J. L. 25 n.
Mayer, C. 129 n.
Mealand, D. L. 75 n.
medicine 126, 149 f., 177 ff.

Melanchthon 101 n.
metaphor 187
Meynell, H. 16 n.
Miller, D. G. 118 n.
miracles 4, 152
Moabites 207 n., 210 ff., 218
modern Protestantism 7, 9, 19, 105 ff.
monotheism 144 ff., 169, 176
Moulton, J. H. 29 n.

National Socialism 10 ff., 111 ff.
natural law 101
'natural man' 91 n., 125 f.
natural religion 5 f., 146, 218
natural theology *passim*
   concept of 1–6
   dependence on religion? 132, 138 ff.
   Hebraic basis of 36, 55 ff.
'nature' and divine law 40, 51 ff., 69,
   76 f.
   as theological criterion 51 ff., 76 f.,
   126, 149 f.
Niebuhr, R. R. 105, 108 f.
Novak, D. 64 n.
Nowak, K. 112 n.

obscurantism 126 f.
O'Connor, D. J. 185 n.
Ollenburger, B. 212
omnipotence 139 f.
omniscience 139 ff.
O'Neil, W. M. 177 n.
O'Neill, J. C. 27 n., 128 n.
Oppenheim, A. L. 175 n.
orders (*Ordnungen*) 112, 173, 202
Orelli, K. von 119 n.
original sin 59

pacifism 213 f., 218
Page, R. 126 n.
Pannenberg, W. 195 n.
pantheism 25, 53
parable 16, 31, 82 n., 92 n., 174, 188 ff.
parousia 143 f.
Patrick, D. 85 n.
Paul 15, 17 n., 20–59, 64 ff., 77, 84,
   103, 121 ff., 133, 138, 165, 167,
   193
Peacocke, A. R. 14 n., 21 n.
Pedersen, J. 120
Pedley, J. G. 215 n.
Petersen, D. L. 201 n.
Philo 47, 53, 65, 75 ff., 146 f., 164

philosophy of religion 3
Plantinga, A. 2
Plato 51, 52 n., 75, 131
poetic justice 95
point of contact 6, 29 n., 46, 161,
   172 f.
polytheism 64, 69
population control 126, 149
Porter, S. E. 186 n.
predestination 109, 111
Preuß, H. D. 91 n., 93 n.
Price, A. W. 52 n.
Prickett, S. 129 n.
proofs of God 2 f., 103, 113, 138
propaganda 115 f., 182
Protestant(ism) 15, 17, 35 n., 41, 43,
   50, 68, 103, 105 ff., 112 ff., 132 n.,
   154, 221
Pusey, E. B. 118 n.

Qoheleth 63, 93 ff.

Rad, G. von 92, 159, 190, 208, 212 ff.
Rahlfs, A. 61 n.
Räisänen, H. 117 n., 202
Rankin, O. S. 90 f.
Raven, C. E. 14 ff., 59 n., 82, 179,
   191 ff.
realistic narrative 128 f.
reason 2 ff., 41, 43, 45 f., 86, 95, 106 f.,
   118, 126 n., 138, 174
Reese, J. M. 61 n.
Reformers, Reformation 7 ff., 42,
   103 ff., 136
Reicke, B. 45 f.
Reid, J. K. S. 197 n.
Reiner, E. 175 n.
*Religionsgeschichte* 202, 204
revealed natural law 90
revelation *passim*
rhetoric 38, 55, 115 f., 182
Richmond, J. 106 n.
Ritschl, A. 106
Ritschl, D. 140 f., 201 n.
Roberts, R. H. 16 n., 17 n.
Rogerson, J. 54 n.
Roman Catholic(ism) 7, 11 f., 18 f.,
   35 n., 50 n., 78, 112 f., 154, 221
Romans, Letter to the 10, 39–57,
   64 ff., 104 n., 138
   comparison with Acts 51 ff., 69 ff.
Rowley, H. H. 17 n.

sacrifice of children 63 f., 215 ff.
Sanders, E. P. 49 n.
Sanderson, J. E. 211 n., 212 n., 213 n.
Sawyer, J. F. A. 169 n.
Schillebeeckx, E. 50 n., 221
Schleiermacher, F. D. E. 13, 105
Schlichting, W. 140 n.
Schmid, H. H. 202
Schmidt, W. H. 169 n.
Schmithals, W. 48 ff., 54, 148 n.
Scholder, C. 12 n.
science 4 f., 16, 126, 146, 174 ff.,
    180 ff., 191 f.
Scots Confession 7
scripture, doctrine of 19, 103 f., 195 ff.
Seneca 110
sickness 177 ff.
socialism 133
Soden, W. von 175 n.
Soren, D. 215 n.
Soskice, J. M. 163 n., 187
Sparks, H. F. D. 75 n.
Spencer, S. R. 83 n., 108 n.
Sperry, W. L. 14
Stager, L. E. 215 n.
Stamm, J. J. 159 n., 167 n.
Stendahl, K. 120
Stoic(ism) 21, 28, 32, 35 f., 45, 49, 56,
    76, 93, 110, 189
Stolz, F. 209 n.
Sutherland, S. R. 219
Sykes, S. W. 12 n., 16 n., 17 n., 19 n.,
    26 n.
Syreeni, K. 49 n.
Szekeres, A. 13 n.

temple 22, 33 f., 53
TeSelle, E. 129 n.
theism 3 f., 18, 138 ff.
theology of nature 18, 83
theriomorphism 70
Thiemann, R. F. 181 n.
Thomas, D. W. 207 n., 210 n.

Thurneysen, E. 14 n.
Torrance, T. F. 13 n., 23 n., 108,
    125 n., 132 n., 181 n.
Trembath, K. R. 198 n.
Trinity, Trinitarian 50, 141, 159 f.,
    162 f.
Tsakirgis, B. 215 n.
Tucker, G. M. 201 n.

Ugaritic 145 n.
Ullendorff, E. 207 n., 210 n.
Unknown God 22, 37 f.

Veijola, T. 49 n.
Vielhauer, P. 25 n.
Vischer, W. 159 n.

Webb, S. 116 n.
Webster, J. B. 140 n., 188, 190 n.
Westermann, C. 168, 187, 193 n.
Westminster Confession 7
Wilson, R. R. 201
Winkle, D. van 214
Wisdom literature 90 ff.
Wisdom of Solomon 58–80, 91, 133,
    138
Wisnefske, N. 18, 79
Wolff, C. 110 n.
Word of God 8, 19 ff., 89, 103, 113,
    195 ff.
Wright, G. E. 213 f.
Wright, J. R. C. 112 n.
Wright, N. T. 70 n.

Xenophanes 146

Yoder, J. H. 212 n., 213 n.

Zadokite document 22 n.
Zahn-Harnack, A. von 14 n.
Zelophehad 99 f.
Zeus 24, 28
Ziesler, J. 27

# Index of Biblical References

In the Old Testament, the order of books follows that of the Hebrew Bible.

**Genesis**

| | |
|---|---|
| 1 | 81, 84, 134, 158, 167, 171, 180 |
| 1–2.4a | 168 |
| 1.26 | 159 n., 162 n. |
| 1.26 f. | 156, 166 f. |
| 2–3 | 165 |
| 2.4b ff. | 168 |
| 4.26 | 122 |
| 5 | 163 |
| 5.1 | 156 |
| 5.3 | 158 |
| 9 | 163 |
| 9.6 | 156, 162 |
| 9.24 f. | 217 |
| 10 | 217 |
| 19 | 215 |
| 19.20 | 143 |
| 19.37 | 211 |
| 21.27 | 184 |
| 21.32 | 184 |
| 34 | 216 |

**Exodus**

| | |
|---|---|
| 15.25 | 179 |
| 18 | 98 |
| 20 | 65 |
| 21.1 ff. | 97 |
| 21–23 | 97 |
| 21.28–32 | 97 |
| 23.31 | 218 |

**Leviticus**

| | |
|---|---|
| 18.22 | 51 f. |
| 20.13 | 51 f. |
| 27.28 f. | 209 n. |

**Numbers**

| | |
|---|---|
| 25 | 146 |
| 27.1 ff. | 99 |
| 31 | 209 n. |
| 36 | 99 |

**Deuteronomy**

| | |
|---|---|
| 20 | 217 n. |

**Joshua**

| | |
|---|---|
| 6–7 | 216 |
| 9 | 209 |
| 9.6 f. | 184 |
| 9.15 | 184 |

**Judges**

| | |
|---|---|
| 1 | 218 |
| 4.11 | 145 |
| 19 | 215 |

**1 Samuel**

| | |
|---|---|
| 2.6 | 62 |
| 15.29 | 142 |
| 30 | 209 n. |

**1 Kings**

| | |
|---|---|
| 4.32 f. | 175 |
| 5.12 | 184 |
| 8.13 | 33 f. |
| 11.33 | 183 |
| 22.51 | 196 |

**2 Kings**

| | |
|---|---|
| 3 | 210 |
| 3.27 | 216 |
| 16.3 | 216 |
| 21.6 | 216 |
| 23.10 | 216 |

**Isaiah**

| | |
|---|---|
| 1.18 | 95 |
| 5.8 f. | 95 |
| 43.8 ff. | 95 |
| 43.27 | 59 |
| 44.9 ff. | 35 |

**Jeremiah**

| | |
|---|---|
| 34.8 ff. | 94 |

**Ezekiel**

| | |
|---|---|
| 26 | 142 |
| 29.17 ff. | 142 |

**Psalms**

| | |
|---|---|
| 8 | 158, 171 |
| 8.6 f. | 157 |
| 14.1 | 153 |
| 17.33 (LXX) | 186 |
| 18.33 (MT) | 186 |
| 19 | 81, 85 ff., 189 n. |
| 19.3 f. | 87 |
| 50.8 ff. | 24 |
| 73.22 | 172 |
| 92.7 | 172 |
| 104 | 81 ff. |
| 104.29 | 62 |
| 104.30 | 84 |
| 119 | 89 f. |
| 119.1 f. | 89 |
| 119.89 ff. | 89 f. |
| 132.5 | 34 |

**Proverbs**

| | |
|---|---|
| 1.8 | 88 |
| 6.20 | 88 |
| 12.1 | 172 |
| 20.27 | 107 |
| 26.1 ff. | 175 |
| 30.2 | 172 |
| 30.24 ff. | 175 |

**Qoheleth**

| | |
|---|---|
| 1.13 f. | 93 |

**Wisdom**

| | |
|---|---|
| 1.4 | 72 |
| 1.13 | 62 |
| 2.23 | 61, 74, 171 |
| 3.1 ff. | 74 |
| 3.4 | 74 |
| 4.1 | 74 |
| 4.12 | 72 |
| 4.16 | 72 |
| 4.18 f. | 74 f. |
| 7.1 ff. | 72 |
| 7.17 ff. | 68, 177 |
| 7.24 | 72 |
| 7.25 | 68 |
| 8.2 | 70 |
| 8.13 | 74 |
| 8.17 | 74 |
| 8.15 | 74 |
| 8.16 | 72 |
| 12.1 | 68, 75 |
| 13–15 | 63 |
| 13.1 ff. | 66 |
| 13.5 | 47 n., 67 f. |

| | |
|---|---|
| 13.6 | 70 |
| 13.8 | 68 |
| 13.10 ff. | 35 |
| 13.17 ff. | 67 |
| 14.12 | 63, 67 |
| 14.23 ff. | 63 f. |
| 14.26 | 69 |
| 15.3 | 74 |
| 15.18 | 64 |
| 16 | 68 |

**Ben Sira**

| | |
|---|---|
| 17.3 ff. | 172 |
| 30.14 ff. | 178 |
| 30.18 f. | 63 n. |
| 38.1 ff. | 178 |
| 44.5 | 87 n. |

**4 Maccabees**

| | |
|---|---|
| 5.8 | 52 |
| 5.25 | 52 |
| 14.5 | 74 |
| 16.13 | 74 |

**1 Enoch**

| | |
|---|---|
| 69.11 | 62 |

**Syriac Baruch**

| | |
|---|---|
| 54.17 f. | 75 n. |

**Matthew**

| | |
|---|---|
| 24.34 | 143 |

**John**

| | |
|---|---|
| 3.16 | 192 n. |

**Acts**

| | |
|---|---|
| 14.8 ff. | 36 |
| 14.15 ff. | 47 n. |
| 14.17 | 84 |
| 14.21 | 37 |
| 17 | 20 ff., 70 |
| 17.4 | 30 |
| 17.16 ff. | 21 |
| 17.18 | 23, 30 |
| 17.22 | 47 n. |
| 17.23 | 22 f. |
| 17.25 | 28 |
| 17.28 | 28 |

**Romans**

| | |
|---|---|
| 1 | 47, 148 n. |
| 1–2 | 50, 54 |
| 1.18 ff. | 39, 46 |
| 1.18–3.30 | 48 f. |

| | |
|---|---|
| 1.19 f. | 57 |
| 1.20 | 67 |
| 1.20 f. | 10, 41 f. |
| 1.20 ff. | 66 |
| 1.21 f. | 72 |
| 1.23 | 70, 172 |
| 2 | 47 |
| 2.1 | 39 f., 42 |
| 2.9 | 40 |
| 2.14 | 40, 44 |
| 2.14–16 | 57 n. |
| 3.1 | 44 |
| 5.12 ff. | 59 n. |
| 7.21 ff. | 45 n. |
| 8.29 | 164 |

1 Corinthians

| | |
|---|---|
| 1.21 ff. | 29, 45 |
| 2.1 f. | 29 |
| 9.9 | 172 |
| 11.7 | 156 n., 165 |
| 15.12 f. | 59 n. |
| 15.45 ff. | 59 n. |
| 15.49 | 164 |

2 Corinthians

| | |
|---|---|
| 3.18 | 164 |
| 4.4 | 164 |

Galatians

| | |
|---|---|
| 3.16 | 167 |

Colossians

| | |
|---|---|
| 1.15 | 164 |
| 3.10 | 164 |

1 Timothy

| | |
|---|---|
| 2.13 f. | 59 n. |

Hebrews

| | |
|---|---|
| 10.1 | 164 |

James

| | |
|---|---|
| 2.17 | 142 |

2 Peter

| | |
|---|---|
| 2.12 | 172 |
| 3.3 ff. | 144 |

Jude

| | |
|---|---|
| 10 | 172 |